AS & A Level
BUSINESS
through diagrams

Andrew Gillespie

OXFORD
UNIVERSITY PRESS

OXFORD

UNIVERSITY PRESS

Great Clarendon Street, Oxford OX2 6DP

Oxford University Press is a department of the
University of Oxford. It furthers the University's objective
of excellence in research, scholarship, and education by
publishing worldwide in

Oxford New York

Auckland   Cape Town   Dar es Salaam   Hong Kong   Karachi
Kuala Lumpur   Madrid   Melbourne   Mexico City   Nairobi
New Delhi   Shanghai   Taipei   Toronto

With offices in

Argentina   Austria   Brazil   Chile   Czech Republic   France   Greece
Guatemala   Hungary   Italy   Japan   Poland   Portugal   Singapore
South Korea   Switzerland   Thailand   Turkey   Ukraine   Vietnam

Oxford is a registered trade mark of Oxford University Press
in the UK and in certain other countries

British Library Cataloguing in Publication Data

Data available

ISBN 978-0-19-915068-7

10 9 8 7

Typesetting, design and illustration by Hardlines, Long Hanbourgh, Oxon

Printed in Great Britain by Bell & Bain Ltd, Glasgow

CONTENTS

AS AND A LEVEL BUSINESS STUDIES
AS Level Business Studies   4
Revising for AS Level   5
A Level Business Studies   7
Examination skills   9
General revision tips   13
Answering Business Studies questions   13

AN INTRODUCTION TO BUSINESS
Organisations   15
Business formats 1   16
Business formats 2 (Companies)   18
Business formats 3   21
Small firms   22
Growth   23
Economies and diseconomies of scale   24
The business environment   25

MARKETING
Marketing   26
Market analysis, marketing objectives, marketing
    strategy and marketing planning   28
Market research   32
Market research and customer buying   34
Segmentation   35
Product life cycle   36
Product portfolio analysis   38
Price   39
Product   40
Distribution   42
Promotion   43
Elasticity of demand   45

FINANCE
Sources of finance   47
Accounting   48
Balance sheet 1   49
Balance sheet 2   50
Working capital (net current assets)   53
Profit and loss statement   54
Ratios   56
Break-even analysis   61
Costing   63
Budgeting   65
Cash flow   67
Investment appraisal   68

HUMAN RESOURCE MANAGEMENT
Human resource management (HRM)   70
Management structure and organisation   72
Recruitment and selection   75
Employment   76
Communication   79
Motivation in theory   81
Motivation in practice   83
Leadership   86

Employee participation and involvement   88
Teams   89
Trade unions   90
Employment law   92

PRODUCTION
Operations management   95
Operations management and technology   97
Location   98
Stocks   100
Quality   101
Lean production   103

EXTERNAL ENVIRONMENT
Market conditions (including labour markets)   105
Political environment   108
Legal environment   110
Economic environment   111
Interest rates and exchange rates   113
Inflation   115
Unemployment   116
International trade   117
Europe   118
Social environment and technology   120
Social responsibility   121
Information technology   124
Change   125

**OWNERSHIP, MANAGEMENT OBJECTIVES
   AND CULTURE**
Starting up   126
Change in ownership   128
Mission and objectives   130
Corporate culture   131
Management process   132

INFORMATION, DATA AND DECISION MAKING
Information management   133
Decision making   134
Decision making and decision trees   135
Strategy   137
Presenting and analysing data   138
Forecasting   140
Operations research   141

CURRENT BUSINESS ISSUES
Reshaping   145
Successful organisations   146
What the gurus say   147

REVISION HELP
Key points to remember   149
Revision exercises   150
Revision charts   153

INDEX   157

AS Level Business Studies

The AS Level is an examination intended for students who have completed the first year of Business Studies in the sixth form. It is assessed by three exams, called units.

AQA AS level

• Unit 1 Marketing and finance
60 marks (+ 3 marks for quality of language)
1 hour 15 minutes   *[30% of total AS exam]*

This paper consists of two data questions. The questions will be based on real firms or business scenarios. One question will be primarily on marketing and one will be primarily on finance. The paper will test the lower level skills (Knowledge and Application) more than the higher level skills (Analysis and Evaluation).

Breakdown in terms of skills assessed

Skills	Percentage of marks on this paper
Knowledge and understanding	33.3%
Application	33.3%
Analysis	23.3%
Evaluation	10%

• Unit 2 People and operations
60 marks (+ 3 marks for quality of language)
1 hour 15 minutes   *[30% of total AS exam]*

This paper will consist of two data questions. The questions will be based on real firms or business scenarios. One question will be primarily on people and one will be primarily on operations. The paper will test the lower level skills (Knowledge and Application) more than the higher level skills (Analysis and Evaluation).

Skills	Percentage of marks on this paper
Knowledge and understanding	33.3%
Application	33.3%
Analysis	23.3%
Evaluation	10%

• Unit 3 External influences and objectives and strategy
80 marks (+ 4 marks for quality of language)
1 hour 30 minutes   *[40% of total AS exam]*

This paper will be a case study covering external influences and objectives and strategy. The paper assesses all the different skills equally as shown below:

Skills	Percentage of marks on this paper
Knowledge and understanding	25%
Application	25%
Analysis	25%
Evaluation	25%

OCR AS Level

Unit 2871 Businesses, their objectives and environment
60 marks
1 hour 15 minutes   *[30% of total AS exam]*
This paper consists of two compulsory questions, each directly related to an unseen case study.
The specification includes: the nature of business, classification of business, objectives, objectives and strategic planning, external influences, other influences.

Unit 2872 Business decisions
60 marks
1 hour 15 minutes   *[30% of total AS exam]*
This paper consists of two compulsory questions based on unseen data response material. It assumes teaching of the material in unit 2871.
This unit builds on the material covered in unit 2871. It also includes marketing, accounting and finance, people in organisations and operations management.

Unit 2873 Business behaviour
80 marks
1 hour 30 minutes   *[40% of total AS exam]*
This question paper consists of four compulsory questions each directly related to a *pre-issued* case study.
This unit builds on the material covered in unit 2871. It also includes marketing, accounting and finance, people in organisations and operations management.

Edexcel AS Level

Unit 1 Business structure, objectives and external influences
1 hour 15 minutes   *[30% of total AS exam]*
Students have to answer structured questions. All questions are compulsory.

Unit 2 Marketing and production
1 hour 30 minutes   *[40% of total AS exam]*
Students answer an unseen case study. All questions are compulsory.

Unit 3 Financial management
1 hour 15 minutes   *[30% of total AS exam]*
Students answer structured questions. All questions are compulsory.

Welsh Board (WJEC) AS Level

Unit 1 Objectives and the business environment
1 hour 30 minutes   *[40% of the AS level]*
Short answer questions and stimulus response questions.

Unit 2 Marketing, accounting and finance
1 hour 15 minutes   *[30% of the AS level]*
Two compulsory stimulus response questions one of which will assess marketing and one which will assess accounting and finance.

Unit 3 People in operations and operations management
1 hour 15 minutes   *[30% of the AS level]*
Two compulsory stimulus questions. One will assess people and one will assess operations management.

Revising for AS level

This book covers A Level Business Studies, which includes AS level and A2 level. Obviously if you are preparing for the AS level you will not need to know all of the material which is included. These checklists will help you focus your revision for AS level. Find the exam board that you are studying and cover the topics and pages listed.

AQA AS Level

Marketing

Specification area	Relevant pages
10.1 Market analysis	26, 27, 28, 32–35
10.2 Marketing strategy	29, 30, 36–38
10.3 Marketing planning	31, 39–46

Accounting and finance

Specification area	Relevant pages
10.4 Classification of costs, profit, contribution and break even analysis	61, 62, 63
10.5 Company accounts	47, 53, 67
10.6 Budgeting	65, 66
10.7 Cost centres and profit centres	64

People

Specification area	Relevant pages
11.1 Management structure and organisation	72–74
11.2 Motivation	81–87
11.3 Human resource management	70, 71, 75

Operations management

Specification area	Relevant pages
11.4 Productive efficiency	24, 95–96
11.5 Controlling operations	100, 101, 102
11.6 Lean production	103–104

External influences

Specification area	Relevant pages
12.1 Economic opportunities and constraints	105, 111, 113–116
12.2 Governmental opportunities and constraints	108–110, 112
12.3 Social and other opportunities and constraints	120–122

Objectives and strategy

Specification area	Relevant pages
12.4 Starting a small firm	15, 16, 17–20, 25, 126–127
12.5 Business objectives	130
12.6 SWOT analysis	137

OCR AS Level

Module 2871 Businesses, their objectives and environment

Specification area	Relevant pages
The nature of business	15, 146
Classification of business	15, 16–21
Objectives	126–127
Objectives and strategic planning	130, 137
External and other influences	25, 105, 108–123

Module 2872 Business decisions and 2873 Business behaviour

Specification area	Relevant pages
Marketing	26–27
The market, its definition and structure	26–27
Market research and analysis	32–35
Market planning	28–31, 36–38, 39–46
Accounting and finance	47–48
Budgets	65–66
Cash flow	53, 67
Costs	61–62, 63
Investment decisions	68–69
Final accounts	49, 52, 54, 55
People in organisations	70
Human resource planning	71, 75–77
Motivation and leadership	81–87
Management structure and design	72–74
Operations management	96–97
Operational efficiency	24, 95, 103–104
Organising production	96
Quality	101–102
Stock control	100

Revising for AS level continued

Edexcel AS Level
Unit 1: The structure of business

Specification area	Relevant pages
1. Business structure, objectives and external influences	16–21, 25
2. Business objectives and stakeholders	126–127, 130, 137, 146
3. Economic influences	111–119, 105–106
4. Legal, political, social influences	108–110, 120–123
5. Internal organisation	72–74
6. Communication in business	79–80
7. Motivation in business	81–85, 86–87

Unit 2: Marketing and production

Specification area	Relevant pages
1. Nature and role of marketing	26–27, 28–31, 36–38
2. Market research	32–35
3. Product	40, 36–38
4. Pricing, promotion and place	39, 41–46
5. Operational efficiency	24, 95–97, 100, 103–104
6. Quality	

Unit 3: Financial management

Specification area	Relevant pages
1. Financial accounts	47, 49–50, 52, 53, 54, 55, 56–60
2. Budgeting	65–66, 67
3. Classification and analysis of costs	61–62, 63

WJEC AS Level
Objectives and the business environment

Specification area	Relevant pages
Public and private sectors	15
Goods and services	15
Sectors	15
Types of business organisations	16–21, 146
Business objectives and planning	126–127, 130, 137
Organisational structure	72–74
Impact on business of external influences	25, 105, 108–123

Marketing accounting and finance

Specification area	Relevant pages
Nature and role of marketing	26–27, 28–31
Market research	32–35
Marketing plan	36–38
Forecasting	140
International marketing	26–27
Sources of finance	47
Budgeting and cash flow	53, 65–66
Balance sheets and profit and loss accounts	49, 52, 54, 55
Classification of costs and breakeven analysis	61–62, 63

People in organisations and operations management

Specification area	Relevant pages
Human resources management and planning	70, 71, 75–77
Motivation	81–85, 86–87
Employer/ee relationships	88–91, 92–94
Organisation and management structures	72–74
Operational efficiency	24, 95–97, 100, 103–104
Quality	101–102
Technology	120
Business location	98–99

A Level Business Studies

The A Level is an examination intended for students who have completed two years of study in Business Studies.

What does the A Level consist of?

A Level Business Studies consists of six different exams (called units). Three of these exams make up the AS Level and three are at a higher level (known as A2). When all six are completed you have completed the A Level course. One of the exams may be coursework.

> 3 AS units + 3 A2 units = A level

AS and A2 units

The AS units focus on the lower level skills more than the higher level skills (see pages 9–12). Knowledge and understanding and application account for about 60% of the marks at AS level. Analysis and evaluation account for about 40%.

In the A2 exams the emphasis is reversed: about 60% of the marks are for the higher level skills and 40% for the lower level skills. This means that the A2 units are much more challenging than the AS units; they are designed for students who have studied Business Studies for two years, not one year. The A2 units also contain subject content which is not covered in the AS units.

AQA A2 units

- **Unit 4 The decision making paper**

80 marks (+ 4 marks for quality of language)
1 hour 30 minutes   *15% of A Level marks*

This is a case study paper. It will consist of four questions. One will focus on marketing, one on finance, one on people and one on operations. Each question will have 20 marks. One of these questions will be largely numerical. Decisions have to be made on the basis of quantifiable and qualitative data. Questions will be based on the integrating themes of external influences and objectives and strategy and good answers may, therefore, draw on all areas of the specification.

- **Unit 5**

80 marks (+ 4 marks for quality of language)
1 hour 30 minutes   *15% of A Level marks*

either
Coursework (Note: the specification includes a great deal of advice on possible titles and approaches for coursework)
or
The numerical report plus essay
1 hour 30 minutes

This exam has two parts. Section A asks students to write a business report based on the data presented to them. The focus is on interpreting the data (this will not involve many calculations) and drawing conclusions based on this. Candidates must recommend a course of action based on their analysis.
For Section B candidates must write one essay (from a choice of four).

- **Unit 6 The synoptic case study**

80 marks (+ 4 marks for quality of language)
1 hour 30 minutes   *20% of A Level marks*

The case study assesses candidates' understanding of all the different elements of the course (and the relationships between them). It uses integrating themes from external influences and objectives and strategy. Numerical and graphical data may be present but the only numerical question could be decision trees. The case will be based on a wide range of business contexts – small or large and primary, secondary and tertiary sectors.

AQA A Level units
Percentage of Advanced Level (%)

Unit	Level	Content	Application	Analysis	Evaluation	TOTAL
1	AS	5	5	3.5	1.5	15
2	AS	5	5	3.5	1.5	15
3	AS	5	5	5	5	20
4	A2	3	4	5	3	15
5	A2	3	3	3	6	15
6	A2	4	3	5	8	20
TOTAL		25	25	25	25	100

Edexcel A2 units

Unit 4 Analysis and decision making

1 hour 15 minutes   *15% of A Level marks*
Students answer structured questions.

Unit 5

                                       15% of A Level marks
Coursework assignment: students choose one title out of two given by the Board. Approximately 3000 words.
or
business planning: an unseen case study.
1 hour 30 minutes

Unit 6 Corporate strategy
1 hour 30 minutes   *20% of A Level marks*

Students answer questions on a pre-seen case study.

Edexcel A Level units
Percentage of Advanced Level (%)

Unit	Level	Content	Application	Analysis	Evaluation	TOTAL
1	AS	4.5	4.5	3	3	15
2	AS	6	6	4	4	20
3	AS	3.75	3.75	3.75	3.75	15
4	A2	3	3	4.5	4.5	15
5	A2	3.75	3.75	3.75	3.75	15
6	A2	5	5	5	5	20
TOTAL		25	25	25	25	100

A Level Business Studies continued

OCR A2 units

One from:

2874	**Further marketing**	*1 hour 30 minutes*
2875	**Further accounting and finance**	*1 hour 30 minutes*
2876	**Further people in organisations**	*1 hour 30 minutes*
2877	**Further operations management**	*1 hour 30 minutes*

These papers are based on unseen case studies and have 60 marks each. Each paper is 15% of the A Level marks.

2878	**Business project**	

or

2879	**Business thematic enquiry**	*1 hour 30 minutes*

This paper is an unseen case study but the report focuses on a pre-issued theme. Candidates are expected to combine their knowledge, gained from local study, with evidence provided by the case study when writing a report. This paper has 90 marks and represents 15% of the A Level marks.

2880	**Business strategy**	*2 hours*

This is a compulsory unit which is synoptic (i.e. brings together all the themes within the specification). The paper has three questions designed to assess students' understanding of the connections between the different elements of the subject and the ability to provide integrated responses. The questions are based on a pre-issued case study. This paper has 80 marks and represents 20% of the A level marks.

OCR A Level units

Percentage of Advanced Level (%)

Unit	Level	Content	Application	Analysis	Evaluation	TOTAL
2871	AS	4.5	4	3.5	3	15
2872	AS	4.5	4	3.5	3	15
2873	AS	6	5.25	4.75	4	20
2874–2877	A2	3	3.5	4	4.5	5
2878 *or* 2879	A2	3	3.5	4	4.5	15
2880	A2	4	4.75	5.25	6	20
	TOTAL	25	25	25	25	100

WJEC A2 units

Unit 4
15% of the A level
1 hour 15 minutes

Two questions are set on each area of the specification (objectives and business environment; marketing; accounting and finance; people in organisations; operations management). Student must answer two questions, but not more than one from any section. Each question will have several parts to it, e.g. 1a, 1b, 1c, etc.

Unit 5
15% of the A level
1 hour 30 minutes

Either
A written paper involving one stimulus response question to assess the AS and A2 specification content
or
Coursework: an investigative study

Unit 6
20% of the A level
1 hour 45 minutes

Questions based on a case study to assess AS and A2 specification content.

WJEC A Level units

Percentage of Advanced Level (%)

Unit	Level	Content	Application	Analysis	Evaluation	TOTAL
1	AS marks	15	13	12	10	50
2	AS marks	12	10	10	8	40
3	AS marks	12	10	10	8	40
	TOTAL AS MARKS	39	33	32	26	130
	AS %	**30**	**25**	**25**	**20**	**100**
4	A2 marks	8	8	12	12	40
5	A2 marks	10	10	15	15	50
6	A2 marks	10	10	15	15	50
	TOTAL A2 MARKS	28	28	42	42	140
	A2 %	**20**	**20**	**30**	**30**	**100**
	A Level %	**25**	**22.5**	**27.5**	**25**	**100**

Examination skills

The skills you will need

The AS and A2 exams test four different skills:

- Knowledge and understanding
- Application
- Analysis
- Evaluation

Knowledge and understanding (Content)

This is the ability to show that you understand the relevant concepts. You have to be able to identify relevant points when answering a question and show that you know what different terms and business ideas mean.

Application

You have to show that you can apply your ideas to the context of the given business situation. Wherever possible you need to relate your answers to the actual business in the data question or in the case study.

Analysis

Analysis occurs when you develop your ideas. For example, you show why an idea is significant, why it matters, what its consequences are.

Evaluation

Evaluation occurs when you show judgement. You show when an idea is more or less important; you discuss what makes it more or less significant.

Knowledge and understanding (Content)	Application	Analysis	Evaluation
Identify relevant factors	Place these factors in context; refer to the scenario; relate to the type of business and its particular situation; relate to the type of product or service	Develop the ideas; show why they matter; why they are significant	Weigh up the different ideas; show why they matter; show why they are more or less important in different situations
		"X is relevant BECAUSE... and THEREFORE..."	"It depends on X BECAUSE..." "X is the most important factor of this situation BECAUSE..." "X is the most likely cause/consequence BECAUSE..."

Knowledge and understanding and application are called **lower level skills**; analysis and evaluation are called **higher level skills** because they are more demanding. To achieve the higher grades you need to be able to demonstrate the higher level skills.

In terms of the exam as a whole, the lower level skills account for about 60% of the marks at AS Level; the higher level skills account for about 40%. However, the breakdown will vary from one unit to another (see pages 5–6).

At A2 the lower level skills account for about 40% of the marks; the higher level skills account for about 60%.

The marking approach

The marking approach for most examination boards uses a level of response approach for individual skills. This means that a particular question will focus on particular skills (i.e. content, application, analysis and evaluation); each skill will have a given number of marks available and within this total there will be different levels of response (e.g. limited application versus good application). To do well you must obviously demonstrate the skills required by the question and you must show each of these at a high level.

For example, in the mark scheme below there are 9 marks overall. A candidate demonstrating limited content, application and analysis may get Content 1 mark, Application 2 marks, Analysis 1 mark = 4/9.

A candidate showing high quality content, application and analysis would get 2 + 4 + 3 = 9/9. Notice that apart from content marks it is the quality of the given skills which matters, not how many points you make. If you show good quality application or analysis, for example, you can get full marks for these skills. A common mistake students make is to spend too long listing lots of different points, rather than taking a few ideas and developing them in depth. The quality of your argument matters much more than the quantity, so make sure you really develop your arguments.

Content (2 marks)		Application (4 marks)		Analysis (3 marks)	
Level 2	2 marks Two or more relevant factors identified	Level 2	4–3 marks Good application to the given context/ scenario	Level 2	3–2 marks Good analysis
Level 1	1 mark One relevant factor identified	Level 1	2–1 marks Limited application to the given context/scenario	Level 1	1 mark Limited analysis
Level 0	0 marks No relevant factors identified	Level 0	0 marks No application to the context/scenario	Level 0	0 marks No relevant analysis

Examination skills continued

Higher level skills: analysis

Analysis involves:

- developing your points
- showing why these points are significant; why they matter

To do this it helps to:

1. use business theory
2. use business terminology

---

1. Examples of business theory

- **Price elasticity of demand:** whenever you suggest a price change you should consider the effect on sales by discussing the price elasticity of demand. If demand is price elastic the percentage change in quantity demanded is greater than the percentage change in price.

- **Investment appraisal:** whenever you suggest a firm expands or invests in, for example, an advertising campaign, a new factory, new premises, consider issues such as the payback period, the average rate of return and the net present value.

- **Return on capital employed:** whenever you consider a particular course of action you should consider the expected rate of return on capital employed. If this is too low relative to the risk involved you should not proceed.

- **Opportunity costs:** whenever you are considering a decision you should look at the opportunity cost. What else could you be doing? What are you giving up by choosing this course of action?

- **Motivation:** whenever you are discussing the impact of a particular policy on people you can refer to their motivation and to motivational theorists. Consider the work of Maslow, Mayo, Herzberg and Taylor for example, and bring it into your analysis of people issues wherever you can.

- **Capacity:** a very important issue in business. Firms cannot produce more unless they have the capacity. Increasing capacity can take time e.g. to acquire the funds to purchase new equipment and premises. At the same time having too much capacity can be very expensive because of high fixed costs. A firm will, therefore, try to consider the long term match between supply and demand.

- **Objectives:** you can only assess whether a particular plan is effective or not when you know what the firm is trying to achieve.

- **Context:** you need to think about why things have happened in the context of the firm. For example, if a firm's stock levels are increasing is this a good or a bad thing? This depends on whether the firm is deliberately stocking up (e.g. for the Christmas rush) or whether stocks are increasing because sales are very low.

A high rate of return on capital employed may be quite impressive in a boom and extremely impressive in a recession.

---

2. Examples of business terminology

This simply means that you should use terms precisely and that you should try to use business terms rather than more general colloquial ones.

For example, many candidates fail to distinguish between:

- unit costs and costs (if you produce more units, costs will rise although unit costs may fall due to economies of scale)

- output and productivity (if you produce the same output with fewer employees, productivity has risen)

- profits and profitability (profitability relates profits to e.g. sales or capital employed; a firm may increase profits but the profit per sale may actually have fallen)

Developing your points

To analyse effectively you need to develop your arguments. Whenever you make a point explain why it is relevant and then explain why it matters and why it is significant. To gain analysis marks you need to develop a chain of argument: "*X may lead to Y BECAUSE of Z and THEREFORE Q*". "*An increase in Z may result in M due to L and CONSEQUENTLY…*".
Follow through the argument you are making to show why it matters in the context of the question.

Look at the following statements and notice how they fail to develop the argument enough for analysis:

- a motivated workforce may be more productive (*Why? And so what? What is the importance of this?*)

- a lower price may increase sales (*By how much? What does it depend on? And so what?*)

- Budgets are financial targets and can be used to control costs (*So? Why does this matter? What is the significance of this?*)

Higher level skills: evaluation

To evaluate effectively you need to consider the arguments you have put forward in your answer and weigh these up. You must show judgement in your conclusion and show that you have considered which factors out of all the ones you have mentioned are more or less important.

Things to consider might be :

- **The short run versus the long run** Short run reactions may differ from long run ones. For example, in the short run a firm may cut the price or cut back on some of its advertising; this may boost short run sales but damage the long run brand. In the short run a firm may cut back on investment, training and new product development. Again this might damage the long run success of the firm.

  Alternatively a firm may enter a market with a low price to gain market share. This might mean low profits in the short run; in the long run this may lead to more power and economies of scale.

  Investment in training, new product development, research and development and new technology are all likely to reduce short term profits but may boost long term profits.

- **The ability of the management** The ability of a firm to anticipate change and to react effectively depends on the skill of the managers. Note that large firms are not necessarily better managed than small ones.

- **Financial resources** e.g. the liquidity position of the firm, its gearing, its return on capital. These will all affect its ability to finance projects, to sustain losses and to attract investors.

- **The nature of the product and sales mix** What does the firm produce? (e.g. are the products income or price elastic?) What is the product range? (e.g. is the firm dependent on a single product or does it have several? In this case, what is the nature of its portfolio?) Where does it sell? (e.g. how dependent is it on the UK market?)

- **The extent and duration of the change** e.g. how much have interest rates increased or decreased?

- **The flexibility and efficiency of the operations process** e.g. how quickly can a firm react to changes in the market? What are the unit costs?

- **The culture of the organisation** i.e. is it bureaucratic or innovative? Does it encourage employees to use their initiative or does it expect employees to seek advice from their superiors if the situation is uncertain?

Weighing up the arguments

Evaluation involves weighing up the arguments. Evaluation can often centre on the phrase "It depends". This certainly highlights the fact that there is no given answer – your answer depends on the context of the firm. However do not just say "It depends" without explaining what it depends on and why – support your argument.

Always look for references in the question which you can refer to in your evaluation. Is it a small firm or large? Is it profitable or not? Is the change unexpected or not? Has the change been rapid or not? These can all be considered in your answer.

Evaluation also includes an appreciation of what is realistic. Many answers fall down because they fail to take account of what is realistic or likely: firms cannot in general suddenly increase their capacity; managers are unlikely to lay off half of their workforce suddenly; a promotional campaign may take weeks or months to plan.

Evaluation can occur when students consider what might be done in the short run compared to the long run. For example firms may reduce overtime in the short term and only lay off people when they are certain demand has fallen permanently. In the short term a firm may try and work its existing resources harder; in the long term it may acquire more assets and increase the scale of production.

Evaluation can also show through when a student judges what is appropriate in the circumstances, i.e. given the background and culture of the firm and management.

Essentially evaluation is the realisation that there is no one answer to most Business Studies questions. The best solution to any problem, the impact of any action, the best reaction to changed circumstances will depend on a range of factors: What are the aims of the firm? What are its strengths and weaknesses? What are the market conditions? How long has it got to react? And so on…

Evaluative answers recognise the need for discussion and debate.

Types of evaluation question

- **Discuss the factors which a firm may consider when …**
  To answer this you might outline two or three factors and then decide which one is most important and why. *"For this firm X is likely to the most important BECAUSE…" "For this type of decision at this time Y is likely to be the most significant BECAUSE…"*

> [FACTOR ONE]
>
> [FACTOR TWO]
>
> [FACTOR THREE]
>
> } Develop these and then discuss which one is most important (explain why this is the case)

- **Discuss whether a firm should...**
  To answer this type of question you should outline the case for, the case against and then come to a conclusion about whether the firm should or should not follow the course of action.

  "In this situation/at this time/this type of firm should/should not do this BECAUSE…"

  You need to outline two sides of an argument and then decide which is the most significant or most likely and explain why.

> [THE CASE FOR]   [THE CASE AGAINST]

Weigh up the two sides.
Which side is more important? Why/When?

Examination skills continued

Words to watch out for in the examination

- "Assess the possible **IMPLICATIONS** of X..."
  To answer this you must consider the consequences of X, i.e. in what ways could it affect the firm?

- "Discuss the **ADVERSE** consequences of X ..."
  This means that you need to discuss the unfavourable or negative results of X.

- **DISCUSS**: to answer a question that begins with "Discuss" you need to analyse your arguments and weigh them up.

- **EVALUATE**: this means that you have to weigh up your points and show judgement.

- **ASSUMPTIONS:** Some calculation questions ask you to state your assumptions. It is tempting simply to describe what you have just calculated; but in fact you have to state what you have had to assume to work out the calculations. For example you may have assumed that all the items produced were sold, or that a shop was open for 50 weeks a year, or that the depreciation policy of a firm uses the straight line policy

Stem words

ANALYSIS	EVALUATION
At AS level the stem words used which require you to analyse are typically: * **ANALYSE** * **EXAMINE** * **EXPLAIN WHY**	At AS level the stem words used which require you to evaluate are typically: * **EVALUATE** * **DISCUSS** * **TO WHAT EXTENT.....?**
	At A level: as above but others may include * **ASSESS** * **CONSIDER**

General advice for examination answers

- Remember that to do well in Business Studies you have to take a few ideas, apply them, analyse them and weigh them up. It is not about making long lists of ideas – you may get some content marks for this but you are not likely to get much more unless you develop your ideas.

- Pure theory is not as good as theory applied to the business situation. If you are simply writing out the work of motivational theorists you've probably missed the point. It is more likely that you will be asked to relate the work of theorists to the way managers in a particular firm are dealing with their staff. Make use of your theory by applying it.

- Real-life business examples can be useful to highlight particular points (e.g. the power of pressure groups, social responsibility, effective product launches, niche marketing) but be careful of being too descriptive. If you are simply writing out a business story you are unlikely to be gaining many marks.

- Read the question. I know this is obvious but too many people lose marks because they are not answering the question set; they either misread it or reinterpret it so it is the question they think the examiners should have asked, not the one they did ask. Read each question a couple of time before answering and for big mark questions keep referring back to it.

- Watch your language, e.g. avoid "will" and "must" and use instead terms such as "could", "might" or "may". If you say something "will" happen you are almost challenging the examiner to try and think of a situation where it will not! You are being too definite: very little will definitely happen – there are usually many different possibilities.

  If you say something "may" happen you are recognising that there could be alternatives and this makes a much better impression. For example "An increase in unit costs will lead to an increase in price" is wrong – you do not know this will happen. "An increase in unit costs may lead to an increase in price" is much better: it recognises it may lead to this but it may not. If you go through your answer and change "will" to "might " or "could" or "may" the quality of your answer will increase significantly (this is definite!).

General revision tips

- Get started early – the earlier you start the more time you have to get it right. Many of us delay starting our revision because once we start it means we've admitted that the exams are not too far away! Do try and begin well in advance because it gives you the time to learn in a planned and controlled manner rather than having to rush everything.

- Don't panic! Even if you have left your revision until quite late there is still time to improve. It's easy to get more and more worried by exams and this can actually get in the way of your studying. Whatever time you have left, whether it is three months or three days, it can make a difference to your grade if used properly. Don't give up – keep at it!

- Plan your revision. Don't just rush in and revise the first thing you can think of. Sit back and think what you need to do and how much time you have. What is your priority? What could you spend time on most usefully?

- Think about your study environment. Try and find somewhere you can concentrate properly (whether at home, at school or college, or in the library). To maximise the effectiveness of your study you need somewhere you can focus without too many distractions.

- Plan the exam. Make sure you know the format of each exam exactly. How long does it last? How many sections are there? What types of questions have been asked before? Once you are in the exam room write down the times when you need to have completed each question/section.

- Don't work for too long or too late. You cannot concentrate for hours on end so take regular breaks. These can be short but you do need to stop around every forty minutes or so to review what you have done, and to refresh your mind ready for the next stage. Be wary of studying late into the night (particularly before an exam) – it tends to reduce your effectiveness. You will not remember things as well and will not be as fresh in the exam itself, which is likely to impair your performance.

- Get hold of the specification (syllabus), past papers and examiners' reports. Your revision needs to be structured and focused. The best place to start is the specification – this will set out exactly what you need to know. Your revision should always be based around the specification.

You also need to look at past papers or example papers to get a feel for the way questions are asked and what has been assessed in the past. Past exam papers come with mark schemes which show what the examiners were looking for. Clearly these are very useful to look at to understand more about what the examiners are looking for.

You should also try to read the Chief Examiner's report. After each exam the Chief Examiner writes a review of how students coped with the questions; this report gives you a very valuable insight into what the examiners thought was good and bad practice.

Your teacher should have these resources; if you have any problems getting them it is possible to buy them from the exam boards; you might also check out the exam boards' web sites.

Answering Business Studies questions

Answering data questions

- **Make sure you read the question carefully.** Too many candidates lose marks because they have not answered the question set. For example, they discuss the benefits of a particular plan to "employers" not "employees"; or they talk about the problems of lean production generally rather than referring more particularly to the problems of *introducing* lean production.

  Take the time to make sure you are answering the exact question set.

- **Look at the stem word.** Make sure you know what you have to do to answer the question properly. Do you simply need to define the term? Do you need to explain or analyse or evaluate? Obviously if the question asks you to evaluate but you only explain your points, you are not answering the question set.

  You need to practise adjusting your answer to the question. For example, how would your answer differ for the following questions?

  "What is meant by market research?"
  "Explain two possible benefits to a firm of undertaking market research"
  "Analyse the possible benefits to a firm of using market research"
  "To what extent can market research benefit a firm?"

  These are all slightly different questions and require a different approach to reflect the different stem words.

- **Show you understand the concept.** It is often useful to define a term or concept (particularly for the big mark questions) to show you have a clear understanding of the concept. However, try to do this quickly; don't spend too long defining things if this means you are not getting on with directly answering the question.

- **Relate your answer to the given situation.** Try to refer to the given scenario in your answer (to gain the application marks). Is the market growing or shrinking? (And why does this matter?) Is the firm profitable or not? Has the firm got a range of products or is it a single product business? Is it highly geared? Liquid? Is it selling products which sell in large volumes and are sold through wholesalers and retailers, or are products sold direct to the final user?

  Good answers relate to the given context.

- **Watch your timing.** Make sure that you do not spend too long on the questions which appear relatively straightforward and forget, ignore or avoid the ones which appear more difficult. It is very important that you complete the whole paper if you are to do yourself justice.

  Make sure you have a clear idea of how long to spend on each question before you enter the exam room.

Answering Business Studies questions continued

- **Use business terminology and concepts**. Look over the work you have written recently. To what extent is it using business terminology and ideas?
  Compare the sentence "A firm could lower prices and sell more." with "As part of a penetration pricing policy a firm could lower the price to gain greater market share. The success of this would depend on the price elasticity of demand."

The basic idea is the same in both cases but the second answer uses relevant terms and concepts.
Similarly, compare these answers:
"Delegation gives people more work to do and makes them try harder"
"Delegation can meet employees' higher level needs (Maslow) which may lead to greater motivation and higher levels of productivity."
Once again the second answer is more technical and makes better use of business theory.

Answering case studies

All of the above comments are true for case study questions as well as data questions. However for case studies it is particularly important to place things in context: what would this firm do at this time in this situation? Your answers should be very specific and apply general business ideas to a particular scenario.
Case study answers will also tend to be more evaluative. You need to explore different courses of action which the firm could take and justify why you would choose one rather than the other. Make sure that when you evaluate you defend your answers. Simply saying "It depends on the type of firm, the market, the competition, the external environment and the firm's objectives" is not evaluation – it is simply a list.
To evaluate you need to say "It depends on the type of firm BECAUSE…, the firm's objectives BECAUSE…, and so on. In other words, come to a conclusion and explain why you think this it is appropriate.

Numerical reports

The AQA numerical report presents you with a range of numerical information. Your job is to make sense of this information and make a recommendation based upon it. You need to structure your answer so it has clear sections and comes to a conclusion (e.g the case for, the case against, arguments for the investment, arguments against the investment, recommendation, see below)

Things to do

- **Do** read the question carefully: this will set out the structure you will need to use (i.e. the headings you need for your report).

- **Do** use a report format i.e. clear headings, numbered points, title, date and headings saying who the report is to and who it is from (see below).

- **Do** analyse the data.

- **Do** look for the underlying theme. For example, should the business close the factory or not? Should it launch the product or not?
  Come to a conclusion based on the arguments developed in your answer.

Things not to do

- **Do not** over-use your calculator; most of the significant calculations should have been done already. The aim of this paper is to make you analyse the information provided rather than have to undertake lots of calculations.

- **Do not** write in essay or letter form.

Example of numerical report

To: Mr Watts, Managing Director
From: Miss Perkins, Market Researcher
Date: 26/05/01

New Product "Bambini"

1. Arguments for launching the new product
1.1 ....
1.2 ....
1.3 ....

2. Arguments for not launching the new product
2.1 ....
2.2 ....
2.3 ....

3. Recommendations

Writing essays

The key to good essay writing in business studies is to:

- **Read the question very carefully.** There will be information in the question you can pick up on in your evaluation, e.g. it may be a "small" firm, a "declining" market, a "sudden" change. All of these can be explored in your answer.

- **Take a few ideas and deal with them in depth.** You do not need lots of ideas; it is much better to develop your analysis of a few.

- **Evaluate.** There will be no fixed answer to a business studies essay question. The answer will depend on a range of factors – the nature of the business, the nature of the market and the nature of the change. You must consider which of these factors are important and why.

Organisations

An **organisation** is a collection of people which exists to achieve collective goals and in which behaviour is controlled.

Organisations can be categorised by:

- size — based on e.g. turnover, assets, number of employees, market capitalisation

- sector — private sector – owned by private individuals
  public sector – owned by the Government

- activity — primary – directly related to natural resources e.g. fishing, farming, mining
  secondary – processing of materials e.g. manufacturing
  tertiary – services e.g. banking, insurance, tourism, education

- legal form — e.g. whether it is a company with a legal identity separate from its owners and with limited liability or a sole trader with unlimited liability

Business functions

These are the sections within a business such as:
- marketing
- finance
- production (often called operations)
- human resource management (HRM)

Key business terms

Producer	provides or makes a good or service
Market	involves buyers and sellers
Customer	person who buys the product
Consumer	person who uses the goods or services (e.g. you might buy someone a present; you are the customer, they are the consumer)
Business objectives	the targets set by managers

External influences

These are factors outside the firm which can affect its success, e.g.
- competitors
- economic factors
- the legal environment
- the social environment
- pressure groups
- new technology

Goods and services

A **good** is a physical product such as a car.

A **service** is intangible, e.g. teaching, financial advice.

All organisations transform inputs into outputs:

Adding value

INPUTS
e.g.
people,
raw materials,
money,
land

→

TRANSFORMATION PROCESS
e.g.
extracting, manufacturing,
assembling, refining,
adding, designing,
mixing, combining

→

OUTPUTS
e.g.
finished
goods
and
services

The aim of organisations is to generate outputs which have a greater value than the inputs used, i.e. to add value.

Business organisations generally value inputs and outputs in monetary terms; therefore the aim is usually to generate a revenue which is greater than the costs, i.e. to make a profit.

Value added: the difference between the value of the outputs and the value of the bought-in inputs.
This is used to :
- reward employees (e.g. wages and salaries)
- reward owners (e.g. dividends)
- invest (retained profit)
- pay tax

Competitive advantage: an aspect of the firm's behaviour or performance which gives it a competitive edge over its competitors. For example, it may be a lower cost producer, or have a unique selling proposition (USP), such as being the only company to deliver to your door the next day.

Business formats 1

People set up a business because:
- they want to work for themselves (independence)
- they have been made redundant from their last job
- they cannot find another job
- they want to achieve something for themselves (self actualisation)
- it is a natural progression from a hobby or interest

An entrepreneur is someone who:
- combines resources
- identifies opportunities
- takes risks
- makes decisions

Famous UK entrepreneurs include Richard Branson (Virgin), James Dyson (Dyson cleaners) and Trevor Bayliss (clockwork radios)

To achieve the finance to set up a business, individuals often require a business plan.

Business plan: a report showing plans of the business; often used to attract finance from investors. Businesses which put time and effort into their business plans, thinking about the competition and the financial consequences of their proposals, are more likely to be successful than those which do not.

The main elements of business plan include:

- **A description of the business**
  What does it make? What service does it provide?

- **A statement of its aims**
  What are the aims of the business in the short and long term?

- **A marketing plan**
  e.g. Who needs the product/service? Why?
  What makes the business different, i.e. what is its unique selling proposition (USP)?
  Who is the competition?
  What will the price be?

- **A list of key personnel**
  Details of who is setting up the business (background, experience)

- **A projected profit and loss** showing revenue and costs

- **A projected balance sheet** showing assets

- **A projected cash flow statement** showing cash inflows and outflows

- **Details of the finance required**
  What will it be used for?
  What is the expected rate of return for investors?

Sole trader

An individual who owns the business, e.g. a window cleaner, local shopkeeper, or hairdresser

Advantages
- can make decisions quickly
- keeps all the rewards
- easy to set up
- privacy of business affairs
- can be motivating (self actualisation)

Disadvantages
- limited sources of finance (e.g. own funds)
- unlimited liability, i.e. can lose personal assets
- often has limited managerial skills
- no one to share workload with
- no one to share ideas with

Partnership

Two or more people trading together 'carrying on business with a view to profit' (1890 Partnership Act).

A maximum of 20 partners is allowed, except for partnerships in the professions such as law and accountancy.

Advantages
- share resources/ideas
- can cover for each other, e.g. during holidays
- more sources of finance than sole trader
- partners can specialise, e.g. one may specialise in company law, another may focus on criminal law

Disadvantages
- usually unlimited liability
- limited sources of finance
- profits must be shared between partners
- slower decision making than sole trader

Deed of partnership: a legal document which forms a contract between the partners. It covers issues such as the division of profits, the dissolution (closure) of the partnership; the rights of each partner; the rules for taking on new partners.

Sleeping partner: invests in partnership but does not take part in day-to-day business; has limited liability. At least one partner must have unlimited liability.

Co-operative

A democratic organisation where all members have one vote. It's possible to have shareholders in a co-operative, but the shareholders have one vote each rather than one vote per share. This means no one member can easily dominate.

There are several types of co-operative, e.g.
- **Worker co-operative:** organisation owned by employees. Employees should be motivated but can have problems managing themselves.
- **Retail co-operative** set up to benefit consumers, e.g. the CO-OP. Surpluses are distributed via lower prices.

Public sector organisations

Owned or directed by the Government.

Examples include the BBC, the Bank of England, the armed services, and local authority services such as schools, parks, museums and libraries. Revenue often comes from the taxpayer as well as customers. Likely to have social objectives; not just be profit oriented.

Non profit organisations,

e.g. charities such as Oxfam, sports clubs, pressure groups or societies. Profit is not the overriding objective for such organisations.

Types of organisation

PUBLIC SECTOR organisation owned by the government

PRIVATE SECTOR Organisation owned by private individuals e.g. sole traders and companies

Business formats 2 (Companies)

Companies
- A company has a separate legal identity from its owners.
- A company owns assets, and it can sue and be sued.
- A company is owned by shareholders. Shareholders have limited liability, i.e. they can lose the money they have invested in the business but not their personal assets.

Why is limited liability so important?
It means investors know the maximum extent of their losses. Without this sense of security investors would be less likely to invest and firms would struggle to raise the finance they need.

Forming a company
The owners must complete:

memorandum of association	**articles of association**
includes:	internal rules of company
name of company	e.g. powers of directors, rights of shareholders, types of share
company objectives	
location of registered office	

+

These are sent to the Registrar of Companies who sends back a Certificate of incorporation

Private company (Ltd)	**Public company (plc)**
- must have 'Ltd' after its name	- must have plc after its name
- restrictions can be placed on sale of shares	- can be quoted on Stock Exchange
- not allowed listing on Stock Exchange	- minimum £50,000 authorised share capital
- not allowed to advertise its shares	- shareholders have right to sell their shares to whoever they want
- usually smaller than plcs (although some are large e.g. Littlewoods)	- usually larger than Ltds

v

'Flotation': process of becoming a plc
To become a plc, i.e. to float, a company must:

Ltd → plc

- produce a prospectus giving details about the company, e.g. its activities and accounts
- meet the requirements of the Company Acts and the Stock Exchange

Problems of a flotation
- cost (e.g. of lawyers, accountants, stockbrokers)
- may not be able to sell shares at desired price
- loss of control
- new owners may have different objectives

Shareholders
elect
Directors
who oversee
Managers

Shareholders and control
Directors – elected by shareholders; oversee managers to ensure they are working in the interests of the shareholders; the directors are the 'watchdogs' of the shareholders; the directors are responsible for the overall strategy of the company, subject to approval by the shareholders; their conditions of appointment and powers are stated in articles of association. Non executive directors are part-timers who have no day-to-day involvement (no executive powers) in the organisation.

Company Secretary – company official with responsibility for maintaining a register of shareholders, notifying shareholders of annual general meeting, and preparing the company's annual returns.

Cadbury Committee – goverment body that reported on the role of directors. It recommended more non-executive directors to keep an independent eye on the business. Public limited companies must state the extent to which they comply with the Cadbury Codes of Best Practice in their annual report.

Corporate governance – issue of who really controls companies, e.g. do the institutional investors exercise too much power? How do shareholders ensure that managers act on their behalf? Do the directors act in the shareholders' best interests?

All companies: must produce a set of accounts for each shareholder; a copy of the accounts is kept at Companies House. The annual report and accounts must include: a balance sheet, profit and loss, a cash flow statement, a directors' report, and an auditor's report. The annual report of a plc is more detailed than a Ltd's.

Some firms have become a plc and then returned to being a Ltd e.g. Andrew Lloyd Webber's Really Useful Group, and Richard Branson with Virgin.

Advantages of being a plc compared to a Ltd

- access to more share finance (can sell shares to the general public)

- greater status (perceived as bigger and more successful than Ltds)

- higher public profile (likely to get more media coverage)

- can use shares to make takeover bid (paper offer)

But

- have to disclose more information in accounts

- more vulnerable to takeover (cannot restrict who shareholders sell their shares to)

- may come under pressure to change objectives from new investors

Is being a plc better than being a Ltd?

Depends on:
- objectives – do the owners want to keep control?

- need for finance – to what extent does the firm need to sell more shares?

- ability to sell shares – what is the likely demand for the firm's shares?

- degree of government regulation

- ability/willingness to pay costs of preparing and implementing flotation and of extra administration costs e.g. producing a fuller set of accounts

- willingness to reveal more information in annual reports

Reasons to remain a private limited company

A company may wish to remain private if it:

- does not need additional finance through share issue

- does not want to sell shares to others

- does not want to meet all the regulations governing plcs

What is the value of a company?

Market capitalisation: market value of company. This equals

the market price of shares × number of shares

Book value: value of company as stated in its accounts.

The market value of a company is often greater than the book value. This may be because:

- some assets may not be listed in the accounts e.g. brands

- some assets may be listed at their original cost rather than their present value e.g. property

Divorce between ownership and control

As firms grow there will often be a divorce between ownership and control. The owners (shareholders) do not actually manage the business on a day-to-day basis. Managers control the business but do not own it.

This can cause problems because the objectives of the two groups may clash e.g. the owners may want higher dividends but the managers may want to retain the funds for investment. The managers may take a long term view; the owners may focus on short term gains.

Also there have been criticisms that some managers and directors have paid themselves too much (so called 'fat cats') and have not always acted in the best interests of the owners. The issue of corporate governance i.e. how the behaviour of managers is regulated, has become an important one in recent years. Suggestions have included having more non-executive directors on the Board of Directors (i.e. directors who do not have a job within the firm and so may be more independent).

Business formats 2 (Companies) continued

Different types of shares

Ordinary shareholders
- have one vote per share
- can attend annual general meeting (AGM)
- are sent company accounts
- receive a dividend if one is paid
- can vote on directors

Preference shares
- have no vote
- receive a fixed dividend
- are paid in preference to ordinary shares but after loan repayments

Types of share capital
Authorised: maximum value of shares which company can issue; listed in the articles of association.

Issued: amount of shares actually issued. The issued share capital cannot be greater than the authorised.

Called up share capital: face value of all the shares paid for by shareholders.

Owning other companies
Holding company: controls other companies but is not involved in their day-to-day running.

Subsidiary: Company B is a subsidiary of A if company A has more than 50% of the shares in B or has a controlling interest.

Associate company: Company B is an associate company of A if company A has between 20 and 50% of the shares of B.

Stock Exchange
Market for shares; mainly second hand shares are traded i.e. shares which have already been issued by companies.
FTSE – Financial Times Stock Exchange
An index of the share prices of the top 100 companies listed in the Financial Times. Its base is 1000.

Share price:
The price of a share is determined by:
- the number of issued shares
- the expected dividends
- stockbrokers' and analysts' reports
- the rates of return available elsewhere
- the present and expected profitability of the company

Reasons to buy shares
- to get a vote and influence company policy
- to receive dividends
- to benefit if the share price increases (which means you can sell them and make a profit)

Ownership of shares in the UK
The main shareholders in the UK are financial institutions, such as pension funds, not individuals.

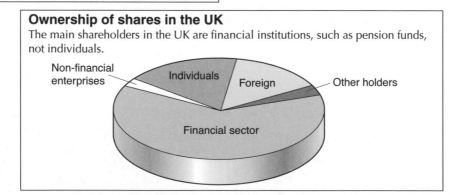

Paying dividends
Dividends are paid out of profits. The directors propose the dividend which must be approved by the shareholders.
The amount of dividend paid depends on:
- the firm's profits
- the pressure from shareholders for higher returns
- the need to keep funds for investment
- the share price; if this is falling the directors might suggest more is paid out to boost the price

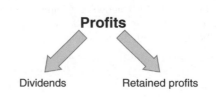

Profits

Dividends   Retained profits

Business formats 3

Franchises
A franchisor sells the right to use/sell a product or service to a franchisee in return for a fixed fee and/or percentage of the turnover, for example: McDonald's, Unigate Dairies, Hertz, Kall Kwik

Why buy a franchise?

- existing, established product; already known, therefore cheaper market research and promotional costs
- may receive help and training from franchisor
- can share marketing costs, research findings, new product development costs
- lower start up costs

Why sell a franchise?

- quicker growth; can cover a geographic area more quickly
- provides funds
- managers more motivated as they own the franchise

Multinationals
Firms with production bases in more than one country; they may have locations around the world but have their headquarters in one country, e.g. BP, Shell

Reasons for becoming multinational:
- to make use of resources abroad e.g. raw materials
- to be closer to overseas markets
- to avoid legislation in their own country which may prevent firms getting too big
- to gain tax advantages or grants from overseas governments
- weakens domestic unions by spreading bases around the world

Why should a government welcome a multinational to its country?

- provides jobs
- pays taxes
- provides skills and management techniques
- provides goods and services
- reduces levels of imports

Why might a government be suspicious of a multinational locating in its country?

- may not share skills or knowledge
- may not invest in country
- may not train locals
- may pressurise government

A government's reaction to a multinational should depend on: which multinational it is and the extent to which it will be or can be regulated.

Problems for multinationals
- difficulties controlling bases which are geographically distant
- communication problems
- problems maintaining common direction/common objectives
- pressure groups often accuse multinationals of exploiting local economies
- often face high level of media attention

Entrepreneurial culture
The UK is often criticised for not encouraging enough entrepreneurs compared to, say, the USA. Part of the problem is the culture; in the USA failure is more acceptable so people are more willing to try. In the UK if you fail once it is very difficult to get finance or support to start again.

Joint ventures/ strategic alliances
Companies work together on specific projects. They can share costs and profits, e.g. Ford and Mazda produce cars together.

Closure of a business
1986 Insolvency Act: covers the options open to a company which is insolvent. An insolvent company may seek a voluntary agreement under which the company and its creditors agree to a scheme of reduced or delayed payments.

If this is not possible, a firm may ask for a bankruptcy court to appoint an 'administrator' to try to reorganise the company. If successful, the administrator returns the company to its management. If unsuccessful, the next stage is receivership – assets are sold to pay off secured creditors. If the company still cannot be saved, it may be 'wound up' – assets sold and proceeds distributed amongst its creditors.

If an individual is insolvent this is called 'bankruptcy'.

Why do firms fail?
- poor planning
- cashflow problems
- overtrading
- increased competition
- decline of market
- failure to react to market trends

Small firms

Small firms

The definition of a 'small' firm varies. In the UK the Department of Trade has the following definitions:

- 'micro' – employs up to nine people
- 'small' – employs ten to ninety-nine people
- 'medium' – employs one hundred to four hundred and ninety-nine people

Other official definitions of 'small' use a turnover of less than £1m or £500,000 as well as fewer than 200 or 500 employees.

The 1971 Bolton Committee concluded that small firms had three main characteristics:

- a relatively small share of the market
- managed by owners and part owners in a personalised way without a formal management structure
- not part of a larger organisation (e.g. not owned by another larger company)

Statistics

- small and medium-sized businesses account for about two thirds of private sector employment
- small companies account for nearly one quarter of gross domestic product

- well over 90% of UK businesses have a turnover of less than £1m
- nearly 80% of UK business have a turnover of less than £100,000

How do small firms survive?

- offer personal service
- serve niche markets
- have greater flexibility
- innovative

Why do governments like small firms?

- innovative
- create jobs
- fill niches
- provide competition for larger firms
- sell abroad, increasing exports

- Loan Guarantee Scheme – government guarantees a proportion of a small firm's loan in return for a fee. Provides small firms with more opportunity to borrow.

- Business Links – provide a range of business support services to local small and medium size enterprises. Include information and advice services, personal business advisors and access to specialist courses.

- Small Business Service – provides help from start up to a wide range of businesses to micro to high growth firms and those employing up to 250 employees. Also provides help for those wishing to become self employed, including venture capital provision.

Government help

- Alternative Investment Market – provides market for shares of smaller firms without as many regulations and expenses as a full listing on the Stock Exchange.

- Business Start Up Scheme – provides financial help for unemployed individuals setting up new businesses (previously the Enterprise Allowance).

- Small Firms Merit Award for Research and Technology (SMART) – financial support for development of new technology with commercial potential for firms with fewer than 50 employees.

- Tax allowances – small firms may pay a reduced rate of corporation tax.

- Less government interference – various schemes have been introduced to reduce government regulations and bureaucracy for small firms, e.g. the accounts small companies have to file are simpler than for larger companies.

Growth

The size of a firm can be measured by e.g. assets, employees, turnover.

A firm may be large using one indicator but small using another, e.g. the National Health Service has a large number of employees but a low turnover.

Types of growth

Internal
- firm expands without involving other businesses
- 'organic' growth involves expanding by selling more of existing products
- often slower

External
- can be via acquisition/take-over or merger
- quicker than internal growth

Why grow?
- economies of scale e.g. managerial, technical, purchasing, financial
- personal ambition
- market power
- to increase the status of the firm
- larger firms are less likely to be taken over

Financing growth
- borrowing e.g. loans/debentures (but consider gearing and interest cover)
- issue shares (but consider loss of control)
- internal finance (but consider impact on working capital and liquidity)

Growth and cashflow
Growth can place strains on cashflow as:
- firms invest in more stocks
- firms expand into new premises
- firms invest in new equipment

In order to expand firms must prepare and increase capacity; this costs money and it is likely to take time before the goods are sold and the cash is received from sales. Meanwhile it can cause cashflow problems; this is called 'overtrading'.

Managing growth
To control a business as it grows a firm may consider:
- using management by objectives
- using an appraisal system
- setting budgets
- improving internal communication systems
- developing formal organisational structure e.g. a functional structure
- producing job descriptions

Problems of growth
- cashflow problems – overtrading
- diseconomies of scale – control, communication and coordination problems
- personal issues, e.g. having to learn how to manage other people rather than doing everything yourself
- risk of loss of direction and control, i.e. different departments, business units, managers set their own objectives

From boss to manager
- In small firms the boss can be very hands on; he or she can be involved with most major issues. People tend to ask the boss what to do. This can be a very centralised organisation with a power culture.
- As firms grow bosses have to manage people (i.e. rather than doing everything themself they focus on 'getting things done through others'). Some individuals may not be able to or want to delegate and so struggle with the changed role. Also they may lack the skills to manage a bigger business.

Turning the business from national to international
Consider:
- new laws
- new market conditions
- new distribution channels
- exchange rate risk
- possible protectionism (e.g. tariffs and quotas)

Overseas markets
Should the firm enter the overseas market by:
- exporting
- undertaking a venture with an overseas firm
- setting up a production base overseas

Consider:
- knowledge of the market
- risk
- possible gains of operating in more than one geographical market (e.g. may spread risk)

Changing from a private limited to public limited company
Consider:
- cost of flotation (e.g. cost of brokers, merchant banks, lawyers, producing prospectus)
- likely demand for shares
- likely price of shares
- willingness of existing owners to lose control
- possible objectives clash e.g. will existing owners disagree with new owners over the direction of the business?
- need for additional finance; uses of additional finance
- value of plc status

Retrenchment
Firm decides to withdraw from certain products or markets to focus on key operations.

Economies and diseconomies of scale

Unit cost
This is the average cost or cost per unit. To calculate it use the equation

$$\frac{\text{Total cost}}{\text{Quantity}}$$

e.g. if total costs are £10,000, output is 2000 units, unit cost is £5.
Economies of scale occur when a firm expands and unit costs fall. Total costs will still be increasing.

Economies of scale
Cost advantage of producing on a larger scale. As output increases, cost per unit falls.

Firms may be able to lower price

Firms may benefit from higher profit margins

Significance of economies of scale

Will influence the size of a firm

Will influence market structure i.e. how many firms operate in a market e.g. Is it competitive or not?

Diseconomies of scale
If firm gets too big the cost per unit may increase. This may be due to problems with:

- communicating
- coordinating
- controlling
- motivating, as individuals get 'lost in the crowd'.

Economies of scale

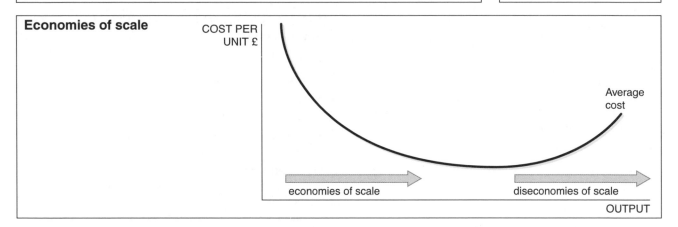

COST PER UNIT £

Average cost

economies of scale   diseconomies of scale

OUTPUT

Causes of economies and diseconomies of scale
Economies and diseconomies of scale may occur due to:
- internal growth, e.g. a firm increases its output levels
- external growth, e.g. horizontal integration: one firm acquires another firm in the same industry

Benefits of economies of scale
A firm can:
- keep its prices the same and benefit from higher profit margins.
- reduce its prices due to the lower unit cost and still maintain profit margins.

Preventing diseconomies of scale
Firms can try to avoid diseconomies of scale by
- introducing effective control mechanisms, e.g. appraisals, management by objectives, budgeting, works councils
- improving communications, e.g. more use of IT, introducing greater employee participation (e.g. works councils)
- adopting a motivating style of management, e.g. delegating, teamwork
- maintaining small business units within the overall organisation so employees can still identify with their part of the organisation
- developing a strong unifying organisational culture

Types of economy of scale
- Technological (or technical): as a firm expands it can use different processes which increase scale and reduce unit cost, e.g. mass production *v* job production.
- Managerial: as a firm grows it can employ specialists in particular business areas; better decision making in these areas can reduce unit cost.
- Bulk purchasing: e.g. of materials and media space. A big buyer is more important to suppliers and is usually able to negotiate a lower cost per unit.

The business environment

Organisations are continually reacting to changes in the environments in which they operate. To make effective decisions organisations must constantly scan their environment to identify change and prepare for it.

- **Macroenvironment:** factors beyond the immediate control of the firm.

  This includes **PEST** factors: **P**olitical, **E**conomic, **S**ocial, **T**echnological

  Can also be categorised as **SLEEPT**: **S**ocial, **L**egal, **E**conomic, **E**nvironmental, **P**olitical, and **T**echnological factors

- **Microenvironment:** factors in the immediate environment of the firm. e.g. suppliers, workforce, investors, customers, distributors. Organisations can influence micro factors more easily than macro factors.

- **Internal environment:** the functions of the organisation e.g. marketing, production, finance, and human resource management

Macroenvironment

Includes factors such as:

- **Political/Legal** – changes in the law and political environment can affect both costs and demand (e.g taxes)

- **Economic** – changes in interest rates, exchange rates, inflation, unemployment will all impact on a firm's competitiveness and success

- **Social** – social trends will affect the workforce and the customer e.g. willingness to work under certain conditions, desire for certain types of products

- **Technological** – environment will affect the firm's production process (how things are done) and product (what is actually produced)

Microenvironment

A firm's behaviour will be affected by other organisations in its immediate environment. For example:

- the availability and terms of suppliers will affect costs and quality

- the co-operation of the local community will affect its recruitment and planning (e.g. expansion)

- the nature of distributors and retailers will affect the price of the product, where and how it is sold, the ability to get to market

- the competition within the market will affect profitability

Proactive v reactive firms

Proactive firms try to anticipate change in their external environment; they monitor their environment e.g. by using market research to help them predict change. This means that they can plan and be prepared (e.g. contingency planning).

Reactive firms wait until change has happened and then have to decide what to do. They are taken by surprise and tend to move from one crisis to another. As a result decision making is rushed and tends to be less effective.

Functions of a business

- *Marketing*: concerned with e.g. identifying market opportunities, developing new products, distributing them, promoting and selling them.

- *Production*: concerned with e.g. research and development, production methods, stock control, quality control, and production levels.

- *Finance*: concerned with e.g raising finance, measuring and controlling financial inflows and outflows, maintaining financial records, financial planning.

- *Human Resource Management* concerned with e.g. identifying human resource requirements, the recruitment and selection of employees, training, developing, assessing, promoting and transferring people.

These functions are interrelated. For example, an increase in sales may require more employees (human resource management), more production, modifications to products (production function), or a new advertising campaign (marketing) and funds for initial promotional expenditure (finance)

Marketing

Marketing Identifying, anticipating and meeting customer needs and wants in a mutually beneficial process. It must be beneficial for both sides; it involves meeting the organisation's objectives as well as the customers'.

Market and product orientation

Market orientation
The organisation focuses on customer needs and wants. The starting point of its planning is what customers want.

CUSTOMER ⟶ ORGANISATION

'The purpose of a business is to get and keep a customer'. Theodore Levitt

Product orientation
The organisation focuses on what it wants to do and hopes customers will buy.

ORGANISATION ⟶ CUSTOMER

Product orientation can be successful if there is limited competition (e.g. a monopoly or protected market), but nowadays firms generally need to be more market oriented. For example, in the 1980s British Airways paid too much attention to their planes and not enough to their customers; they were too product oriented.

Market myopia: marketing short sightedness; organisations which fail to appreciate changes in their markets. In the 1970s US car companies kept producing large cars despite a major increase in the price of petrol. As a result they lost market share to Japanese producers because consumers wanted smaller, fuel efficient cars.

Why is market orientation becoming more important?
Greater competition, shorter life-cycles, more demanding consumers, markets more fragmented, competitors have a clearer idea of customer needs, customers are more informed and choice is easier, markets are more open.

Asset led marketing: marketing based on the strengths of the firm rather than simply what the customer wants. The planning starts with examining the firm's assets (e.g. its staff, its location or its distribution network) as well as customer wants.

Marketing mix: the tools of marketing
The best known elements of the marketing mix are the four P's:

Price	What does it cost the consumer? Are there easy payment terms? Are there discounts?
Product	What does it do? What does it look like?
Promotion	How does the consumer find out about it? What are they told?
Place (Distribution)	How does it get to the consumer? Direct from the manufacturer or via intermediaries?

However, it is possible to include others:

People	What are the staff like? Are they well trained? Co-operative?
Process	Is the buying process easy, e.g. can customers pay by credit card? How many forms are there to fill in? Can the goods be bought by phone?

Marketing mix

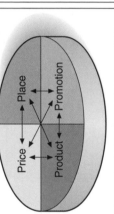

The combination of factors which influence a customer's decision to buy a good or service.

An integrated mix
All of the elements of the marketing mix must complement each other e.g. a high price is often associated with exclusive distribution, a strong brand, a speciality product such as Rolex; a lower price may be complemented by widespread distribution, mass market appeal, a more standardised product and wide promotion.
Effective marketing involves all the elements of the mix working together to provide customer satisfaction.

Value:
The value of a product is the combination of benefits it provides in relation to its price.
- Good value occurs when the benefits are high in relation to the price.
- Poor value occurs when the benefits are low in relation to the price.
- An expensive product can be good value provided the benefits are high.
- A cheap product can be poor value if the benefits are low.
- Firms must aim to provide superior value compared to the competition.

Niche market – a small part of the market which major producers are not concerned with, e.g. Privilege offers car insurance for high risk categories such as high performance cars and young drivers; High and Mighty stores focus on tall men.

Mass market – market with a large volume or value of sales, e.g. soap powders.

Marketing and other business functions
Marketing is linked to all the other functions of a business.
- Marketing helps production determine what to produce, when to produce it and what it must cost.
- Marketing generates the revenue for the firm to make a profit.
- Marketing will influence the numbers and skills of employees required.

At the same time marketing activities are influenced by the other functions.
- The capacity of the firm will influence the amount the firm aims to sell.
- The skills of the employees may influence what is offered to the market.
- The financial position of the firm may influence the price.

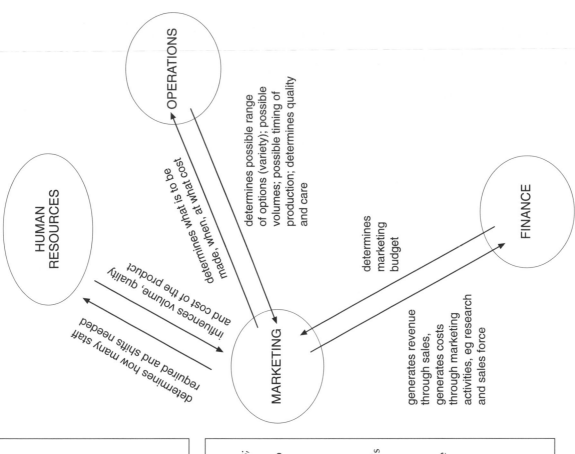

determines possible range of options (variety); possible volumes; possible timing of production; determines quality and care

determines what is to be made, when, at what cost

influences volume, quality and cost of the product

determines how many staff required and shifts needed

determines marketing budget

generates revenue through sales, generates costs through marketing activities, eg research and sales force

OPERATIONS

HUMAN RESOURCES

MARKETING

FINANCE

Markets

Market size – may be measured by the number of units sold or the value of sales.

Market share – a firm or product's market share is its percentage of all the sales in the market. It can be measured as a percentage of the number of units sold or of the value of sales, e.g. if market sales are £50,000 and a firm's sales are £10,000 then the firm has a 20% market share.

The benefits of greater market share

- may mean more sales (and so economies of scale; higher profit margins)

- more power in the market e.g. over suppliers and distributors

- may mean greater brand awareness enabling brand extension

Note: a bigger market share does not necessarily mean more sales; it depends on what the market as a whole is doing (e.g. if your share of a declining market is increasing, sales could actually be falling).

Marketing overseas

Have to consider:

- political differences

- cultural differences

- transport costs (if transporting goods there)

- economic differences

- legal differences

Entering overseas markets

Can enter through:

- export i.e. produce domestically and transport overseas; this reduces risk of operating overseas

- franchise or licence i.e. enable a firm based overseas to produce your product in return for a fee; this lets firms which know the market produce and market the products

- joint ventures – set up in partnership with a local firm; this enables you to benefit from their expertise

- direct investment i.e. set up for yourself overseas. This is the most risky choice since you may be entering a market with which you are unfamiliar.

Why market overseas?

- domestic market saturated (e.g. in maturity phase of the life cycle)

- to spread risks

- domestic market has become increasingly competitive

- to exploit market opportunities

Market analysis, marketing objectives, marketing strategy and marketing planning

Marketing model sets marketing objectives; undertakes an audit of the firm's present position; and develops and implements plans to achieve its objectives, i.e. it considers: Where is the firm now? Where does it want to be? How can it get there? and then, Has it got there?

When undertaking the marketing process a firm will:

Set corporate objectives	e.g. profitability, growth
Gather information	using market research
Assess existing situation	This is known as undertaking a **market analysis** or a marketing audit Using e.g. product portfolio analysis, product positioning, product life cycle, and market segmentation firms, produce a SWOT analysis (Strengths, Weaknesses, Opportunities, and Threats)
Set marketing objectives	e.g. market share, revenue
Select marketing strategy	e.g. using Ansoff matrix
Implement marketing plan	using marketing tactics, i.e. marketing mix
Review	using marketing research

Market analysis

An examination of market conditions such as market size, market share, market growth and segmentation.

Market size: can be measured in terms of volume (how many units are sold) or value (the expenditure in this market i.e. the number of pounds spent on the goods or services).

Market share: the percentage of sales of one brand (or firm) compared to the total market; e.g. a 20% share means the brand accounts for 20% of all sales in the market.

Market growth: the rate at which the size of the market is increasing; e.g. a 5% annual growth rate means that sales are increasing by 5% a year.

Market growth

In a shrinking market firms are likely to compete more aggressively because overall sales are falling. Prices and profit margins may need to be cut to try and gain market share.

In a declining market, market share may increase even if sales do not. A bigger share of a declining market may not mean more sales overall.

Value of market analysis

- identifies the existing state of the market

- estimates future trends within the market

- an essential part of the marketing process – only if you know where you are now can you decide how to get to where you want to be.

Sales

Declining sales may lead to:

- undercapacity

- a need to rationalise

- a need to change marketing mix

Increasing sales may require

- more capacity

- more employees

- a change in the marketing mix

Positioning
How a product is perceived by a consumer relative to its competitors, e.g. stronger, faster

Positioning map
Illustrates the position of products relative to each other, e.g. one consumer's perception of the chocolate market may be:

Positioning map

Low price

Kit Kat

Rolos

Creme Egg

Dairy Milk

Light chocolate

Toblerone   Mars Bar

Turkish Delight   **Rich chocolate**

Bounty

Maltesers

Fry's Chocolate Cream

Aero

For example, an Aero is perceived by this customer as a light chocolate and fairly expensive.

High price

Munchies

Re-positioning
occurs when a firm tries to change customers' perception of a product.

Marketing objectives
These are quantifiable marketing targets such as:
- to increase market share by 10% over the next two years
- to increase brand awareness by 5% this year
- to increase sales of brand X by 25% over three years

The marketing objectives must be derived from the firm's corporate objectives.

Marketing strategy: the strategy is the long term plan to achieve the marketing objectives

Types of marketing strategy
1 market penetration, market development, new product development, diversification (see Ansoff Matrix)
2 niche v mass
3 differentiation v cost leadership

Successful marketing strategy:
- matches the right products to the right markets
- builds on strengths
- defends against weaknesses
- exploits opportunities
- protects against threats
- achieves the marketing objectives

Ansoff Matrix
Marketing strategies can be examined using the **Ansoff Matrix.**

| | | PRODUCT | |
		Existing	New
MARKET	Existing	Market Penetration	New Product Development
	New	Market Development	Diversification

Market analysis, marketing objectives, marketing strategy and marketing planning continued

The Ansoff matrix sets out four marketing strategies.

1 Market penetration

Attempt to gain a greater share of an existing market, e.g. by changing price or increasing promotion. Involves changing elements of the marketing mix such as the price and promotion to increase sales.

3 Market development

Launching existing product into new markets, e.g. sell overseas or target new segment.

- Entering overseas markets. Consider e.g. the political stability, legal differences, economic factors, social and cultural factors.
  Methods of entering overseas markets: export, use agent, franchise or license, joint venture, direct investment.

- Moving into new segment, e.g. Dr Martens moved from workwear to fashion wear.

2 New product development

Developing a new product for an existing market

Stages

Idea generation	generate ideas 'internally' (e.g. from employees or research and development department) or 'externally' (e.g. from patent office, external inventors, universities, competitors, consumers)
Analyse	assess feasibility (also called 'screening')
Development	produce mock ups or prototypes
Product testing	test for safety and quality
Test marketing	test sales in selected outlets
Launch	sell nationally or 'roll out' (gradually introducing in one region then another)

4 Diversification

Enter new market with new product. A high risk element due to unfamiliarity; but spreads risk – less vulnerable to changes in one market, e.g. Michelin tyres, maps and guidebooks.

Niche *v* mass marketing strategies

Why choose a niche marketing strategy?
- may fit with limited resources e.g. production capability
- avoids head on clash with major firms
- may fit with USP
- returns may be relatively high

Why choose a mass marketing strategy?
- fits with resources e.g. flow production
- may be higher returns
- exploit brand name
- to benefit from economies of scale
- less vulnerable to changes in demand by one or two customers

Problems of mass market strategy
- need high levels of investment in production facilities and if demand changes the firm is committed to high fixed costs

Differentiation *v* cost leadership

Differentiation: occurs when a firm attempts to provide more benefits than the competition so it can justify higher prices e.g. Ferrari

Cost leadership: firms attempt to produce similar products to the competition but at a lower cost so they can sell at lower prices e.g. Aldi retail stores

Problems occur if firms fail to adopt these strategies effectively, e.g. they charge higher prices but do not provide extra benefits so they do not provide customers with good value for money. Or they charge less but their goods are of a much lower standard and so are poor value for money.

Product differentiation

Within a mass market such as soaps, washing powders and newspapers, firms will try to differentiate their products to gain market share.

Marketing strategy

The choice of strategy depends on
- resources e.g. financial, marketing and human resources
- findings of SWOT analysis e.g. the firm's strengths; potential threats in the market
- market conditions, e.g. emerging segments
- external factors, e.g. competitors' actions
- marketing objectives, e.g. short term *v* long term profitability

Marketing plan

A marketing plan will set out:
- what a firm wants to achieve in marketing terms (marketing objectives)
- how much it intends to spend on marketing (marketing budget)
- how it intends to fulfil its objectives (marketing strategy)
- its tactics (the marketing mix)

Marketing plan and other functions

Marketing plan will influence:
- what is produced, how much is produced and when it is produced (operations management)
- the numbers and skills of employees required (human resources)
- the design, costs and selling price (finance)

Long run marketing actions
- building brands
- developing new products
- establishing new distribution channels
- building a sales team

Short term marketing actions
- promotional offer
- price cut

Marketing budget

Sets financial targets for marketing activities, e.g. sales and spending targets.
e.g. A marketing expenditure budget will be set to control and monitor spending in this area.

> The marketing expenditure budget may depend on:
> - present resources – How much do we have?
> - objectives – How much do we need to achieve our objectives?
> - sources of finance – How much can we raise?
> - competitors – What are they spending?

Typically firms set the expenditure budget as a percentage of this year's projected sales, as a percentage of last year's sales, or to try to match competitors' budgets.

If sales are declining, a firm might reduce its expenditure budget due to lack of finance, even though this may be the time to increase the budget to boost sales.

The value of marketing planning

- ensures continual evaluation of objectives and strategies
- should ensure efficient use of resources
- helps establish criteria for success; this can motivate and make it easier to monitor progress
- improves decision making
- involves people in discussion and should increase their commitment
- involves a process of analysis; this should ensure the organisation is better prepared for change
- coordinates activities
- should avoid wasteful or conflicting activities
- should involve rational decision making based on quantifiable data

Marketing objectives, strategy and marketing mix

The marketing mix must be designed to help achieve the objectives, e.g. an attempt to move from a niche to a mass market may require lower prices, wider distribution and greater promotion. A decision to move a product up market may require higher prices and more limited distribution.

Marketing tactics: short term decisions to implement the marketing strategy e.g. deciding on the marketing mix

Market research

Market research

Gathering, recording, analysing, and presenting information relevant to the marketing process. Part of marketing planning.

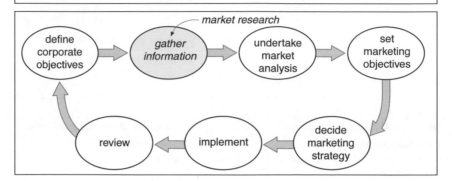

Market research is used to:

- identify opportunities and threats, e.g. how is the market changing?
- analyse alternative courses of action, e.g. would a price change be more effective than more advertising?
- review progress, e.g. monitor sales after a promotional campaign

When undertaking research a firm will:

- identify a problem
- decide a method of gathering data, e.g. field or desk research; postal survey or face to face
- gather the data
- analyse the data
- present its findings

Primary and secondary research

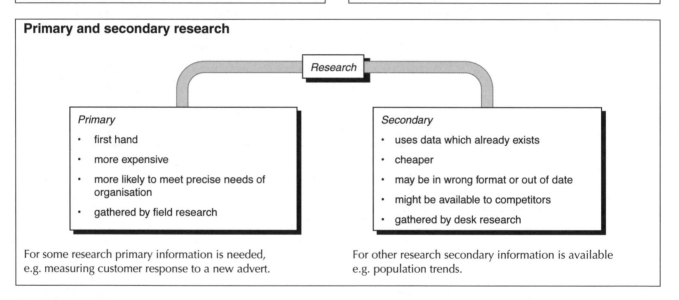

For some research primary information is needed, e.g. measuring customer response to a new advert.

For other research secondary information is available e.g. population trends.

Qualitative research

In-depth research into people's attitudes and their motives for buying a product. Usually undertaken in small groups (called focus groups) or in-depth interviews. The number interviewed is likely to be small and so not statistically reliable.

Sources of secondary data

- Internal data e.g. sales records, production records, including 'backdata' – previous records held by the firm, such as past sales figures
- Government e.g. Social Trends, Census, Annual Abstract of Statistics, Monthly Digest of Statistics (data on e.g. output and balance of payments)
- Independent Forecasting Groups e.g. Henley Centre
- Newspapers e.g. Financial Times
- Trade associations and trade magazines e.g. Campaign (for the advertising industry)

Marketing research gathers and analyses information to help the firm's marketing

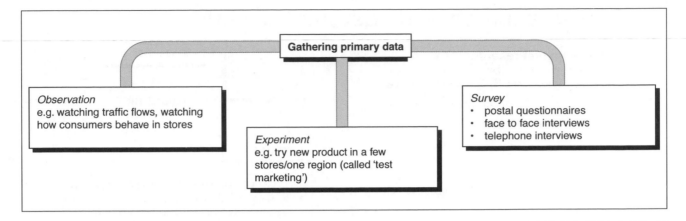

Gathering primary data

Observation
e.g. watching traffic flows, watching how consumers behave in stores

Experiment
e.g. try new product in a few stores/one region (called 'test marketing')

Survey
- postal questionnaires
- face to face interviews
- telephone interviews

Internal *v* external data
Internal data is information gathered within the firm itself, e.g. from its own sales records.
External data is information gathered from outside the firm, e.g. from customers, from competitors, from market research agencies.

Sampling terms
- **Population** – the total number of items or people the researcher is interested in.
- **Census** – a survey of the total population. Not usually feasible due to time and expense.
- **Sample** – a small group which is thought to represent the market as a whole.

Samples
To save time and money, researchers may take a sample rather than testing/questioning every member of the population. Sampling is subject to error because the sample may not be representative. Using statistical techniques, the results are expressed in terms of probability and the confidence with which they can be used. For example, when estimating future sales, researchers may produce a 95% confidence interval of £120m to £130m. This means that 95% of the time sales will be between these two values; the firm can be 95% confident that sales will be between £120 and £130m.

The confidence level will depend on:
- the size of the sample – the bigger the sample the more confident researchers can be about the results
- the range – if researchers estimate 79–80% of the population prefer Brand A this is a very specific prediction and so they may not be that confident; if they predict between 78 and 82% of the population will prefer brand A this is a wider range and so the researchers can be more confident.

Types of sample
- **Quota** – a researcher is given specific characteristics, e.g. forty people over 30, and then finds people who meet these criteria. This is a non-random sample, e.g. if the researcher stands on a street corner, he or she can only ask people who happen to be passing. Other people have no chance of being asked.

- **Random** –every member of the population has an equal chance of selection

- **Systematic samples** – this sampling technique selects every *n*th item, e.g. every 100th item on a production line might be tested; every 10th person on a list of people in the target population may be interviewed.

- **Stratified samples** – a sampling technique which has pre-determined proportions of respondents, e.g 20% male, 80% female, 50% aged 16–24, 50% over 24. Within these proportions respondents may be chosen randomly – this would be a stratified random sample.

- **Cluster samples** – respondents are drawn from a small geographical area selected to represent the target population as a whole; makes sampling quicker and easier as respondents are in one area.

- **Convenience samples** – the interviewer simply finds someone available for interviewing. Easy to do but unlikely to be reliable.

Market research and customer buying

Effective market research

Market research is most likely to be useful when:

- the information is available when it is needed

- the information is available at an appropriate cost

- the information is accurate

- data is understandable

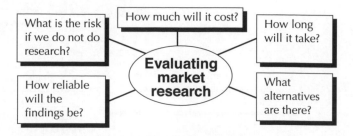

Cost of market research

How much should a firm spend on market research? This depends on:

- urgency for information

- required quality of information needed

- nature of decision (e.g. degree of risk)

Typical problems of market research

- bias e.g. due to poor interviewers and questionnaires or because it is looking for a particular result (e.g. entrepreneurs want to be convinced that their idea works)
- sample too small and unrepresentative
- results take too long to arrive and so are out of date

Value of market research

Research does not guarantee success but can help to reduce the risk.

Not all decisions use formal researching methods. Some decisions are based on intuition or hunch.

Value of intuition

It may be appropriate/necessary to follow intuition if:

- there is no information available

- market conditions are rapidly changing

- the firm wants a creative/novel solution

Consumer buying behaviour: the acts of individuals involved in buying goods and services. By studying this behaviour marketers can develop appropriate marketing strategies.

Consumer behaviour

Market research will try to find out more about consumers and the market place including:

- Occupants — Who is in the market already?
- Objects — What are consumers buying?
- Objectives — Why is the market buying these goods and services?
- Organisation — Who is involved in the buying process?
- Operations — How does the market buy?
- Occasions — When does it buy?
- Outlets — Where does it buy?

Six buyer readiness stages

awareness e.g. of name, of product

knowledge e.g. of product features

liking i.e. think about the product favourably

preference i.e. actively prefer it to alternatives

conviction i.e. consumers are sure they want it

purchase i.e. consumers buy it

Promotional actions will vary according to the stage consumers are at.

Influences on customer buying behaviour

- Personal influences such as individual needs, perceptions, attitudes and experiences; age; stage in the personal life cycle; economic circumstances.

- Interpersonal determinants such as cultural, social and family influences.

Stages in consumer decision making

recognition of problem or opportunity (decide you need/want something)

search process (look for alternatives)

evaluation of alternatives (weigh up the alternatives)

decision to purchase

act of purchase (buy the goods/services)

post-purchase evaluation (was it value for money? Was it worth it?)

feedback

Buyer's purchase decision

Based on:

- choice of product
- choice of brand
- choice of outlet
- decision when to buy
- decision about how much to buy

Outside influences on the customer buying decision

Marketing mix:

- price
- product
- place
- promotion

External environment:

- political/legal
- economic
- social/cultural
- technological

Categories of consumer as they buy the product over time

Innovators: willing to try new ideas; willing to take risks in this market; this group may buy the product first

Early adopters: opinion formers in this market; they buy after innovators

Early majority: adopt new products before the average person; need to think about a product before buying it

Late majority: only adopt after many others have already; sceptical buyers

Laggards: very late to adopt new products/services; only accept it when it has proved itself for some time in the market; the last group to buy

Segmentation

Segmentation
Identifying groups of relatively similar needs and wants within a market. The firm can then develop an appropriate marketing mix for each segment. The aim is to meet customer needs more precisely. The problem is that it may cost more to develop new versions of a product or service.

Segmentation is part of the market analysis stage of the marketing process

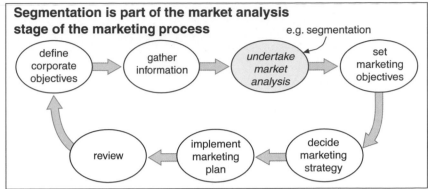

Methods of segmentation

• Age	e.g. magazines for different age groups (e.g. Just 17); adult snacks (e.g. Phileas Fogg); Landmark Express offers cheaper car insurance for people over 45; Club 18–30 holidays obviously target a particular age-group.
• Gender	e.g. certain cars are targeted at women drivers; some toys are aimed more at boys (e.g. Action Man), others target girls (e.g. Barbie).
• Socio-Economic groups	e.g. newspapers target different Socio-Economic groups.

A	upper middle class	higher managerial/professional e.g. lawyer
B	middle class	middle managerial/administrative/professional e.g. manager
C1	lower middle class	supervisors, clerks, junior managers e.g. shop assistant
C2	skilled working class	skilled manual worker e.g. mechanic
D	working class	semi skilled/unskilled manual e.g. cleaner
E	subsistence level	unemployed or state pensioner

• Location	e.g. board games sell better in colder climates; outdoor games are more popular in warmer regions
• An individual's stage in the life cycle	e.g. the housing market consists of first time buyers, people trading up and retirement buyers; magazines – *Practical Parenting, The Oldie*
• Family size	e.g. family packs of food, design of houses
• Usage rates	e.g. frequent wash shampoo
• Lifestyle	e.g. convenient, microwaveable food for young, single working people
• Benefit	e.g. people buy toothpaste for different benefits, including the taste, fresh breath and to keep their teeth white
• Psychographical (motives for buying)	e.g. reasons why people buy chocolates include to reward themselves, to relax, to share, to give to others.

Advantages of segmentation
- can identify requirements of different groups more precisely
- can meet needs of these groups more effectively than the competition
- avoids wasteful marketing activities which are not targeted

What makes a segment attractive?
- one which is accessible i.e. the firm can provide the goods and services which are required
- one which is profitable i.e. the rates of return justify the investment and risk
- one which is sustainable i.e. will justify long term involvement

Problems of segmentation
- May reduce possibilities of economies of scale if the firm produces for many different markets

Targeting
Targeting: selecting which segments to aim for. This depends on the size and expected profitability of a segment and its fit with the firm's resources and objectives.

Undifferentiated marketing: one product for the whole market, e.g. WD40 is used by a range of buyers to stop doors squeaking, protect engine parts from damp, loosen rusty bolts, loosen limescale, etc.

Concentrated marketing: a particular segment is targeted, e.g. Club 18–30 holidays target this particular age group

Differentiated marketing: a separate mix is developed for each segment, e.g. full fat milk, semi skimmed, skimmed, breakfast milk, goat's milk

Product life cycle

Product life cycle

Shows stages in a product's life; highlights the typical sales of a product over time. This is a model used to aid decision making.

It is part of the marketing planning process:

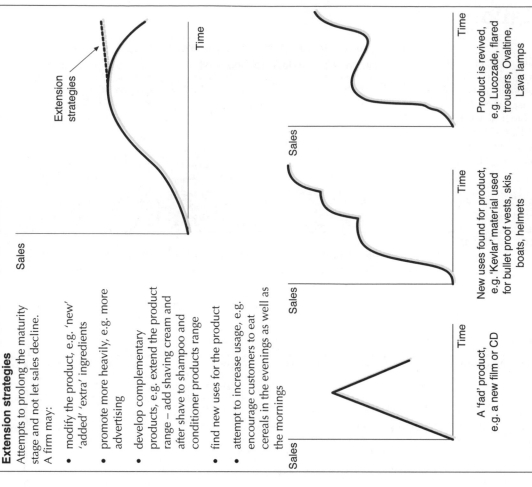

- define corporate objectives
- gather information
- *undertake market analysis*
- set marketing objectives
- decide marketing strategy
- implement marketing plan
- review

The life cycle model

The shape and length of the product life cycle will differ from one product to another. Some life cycles last years (e.g. Kellogg's Cornflakes); others are more short-lived (e.g. Teenage Mutant Ninja Turtles.)

Stages of the life cycle include: development, introduction, growth, maturity, decline

	Develop-ment	Intro-duction	Growth	Maturity	Decline
		electric cars	CD ROMs	colour TVs	black & white TVs
		video 'phones	fax machines	washing machines	typewriters
			mobile phones		

Development Product is being developed and tested. This may takes years, e.g. new car or new film, or may take hours, e.g. a new recipe in a restaurant. Losses are often made due to heavy development costs.

Introduction Sales often slow. Distributors may be reluctant to take a new unproved product. Heavy promotion may be necessary to make consumers aware of the new product. High level of risk. High unit production costs – no economies of scale.

Growth Sales begin to grow rapidly. Competition beginning to enter the market. Cost per unit falling due to economies of scale. Profits usually made.

Maturity Sales growth is slower. More competition. Promotion needs to stress differences with competition. The firm will try to develop/maintain brand loyalty.

Decline Sales declining. Profits falling. Substitutes appear.

Extension strategies

Attempts to prolong the maturity stage and not let sales decline. A firm may:

- modify the product, e.g. 'new' 'added' 'extra' ingredients
- promote more heavily, e.g. more advertising
- develop complementary products, e.g. extend the product range – add shaving cream and after shave to shampoo and conditioner products range
- find new uses for the product
- attempt to increase usage, e.g. encourage customers to eat cereals in the evenings as well as the mornings

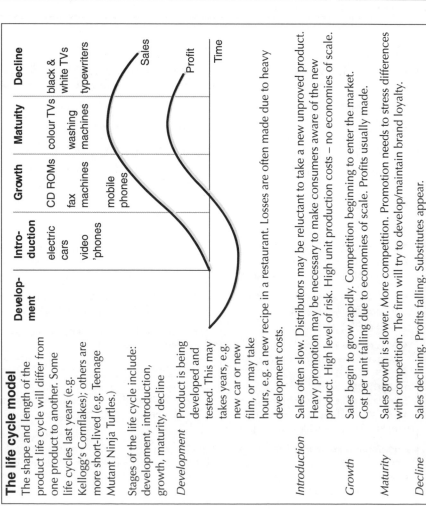

A 'fad' product, e.g. a new film or CD

New uses found for product, e.g. 'Kevlar' material used for bullet proof vests, skis, boats, helmets

Product is revived, e.g. Lucozade, flared trousers, Ovaltine, Lava lamps

Value of the product life cycle model

This highlights different stages in a typical life cycle and the need to adjust marketing strategies and tactics at each stage. However, it is only a model. The decision maker must take account of different markets and different ways in which products may develop. There is a danger of it become self fulfilling, e.g. because firms expect a decline in sales they fail to devote enough resources to a product to enable sales to be maintained.

Stages of the product life cycle

	Introduction	Growth	Maturity	Decline
Marketing objective	attract innovators	develop distribution channels and broaden product range	differentiate	rationalise
Sales	low but increasing	rapidly increasing	slowing up	falling
Degree of competition	low	some	increasing	falling
Profit margins	low	high	falling	falling
Customer group	innovators	mass market	mass market	laggards
Product	basic models	expanding number of product lines	full product line	rationalise to focus on main products
Distribution	often limited	expanding	expanding	falling
Price	could be skimming or penetration policy	may increase	high	often falling
Promotion	informing	persuading	competing/ differentiating	reminding

Is the decline of a product inevitable?

It may be inevitable due to:

- changing social climate
- changing tastes e.g. boredom factor
- developments in technology
- product innovation

but arguably much of the decline is due to poor marketing e.g. failing to react to changing market conditions, failing to anticipate change

The life cycle of a product is likely to be shorter if:

- the rate of technological change is rapid
- there is a high degree of innovation in the market
- customers' tastes are changing rapidly
- the product is marketed badly

Product life cycle and cash flow

In the early stage of the life cycle cash is leaving the business and not coming in. Cash is being spent first on researching and developing the product and then on launching it. At this stage there are no sales. Even once launched, cash flow may be negative because the promotional expenditure is likely to be high (e.g. the first few days after a new film is launched). As sales increase cash flow should become positive and grow. When sales decline cash flow will fall.

	Sales, cash	
	Positive	Sales
		Cash
	Negative	Time
Development high outgoings e.g. R & D	**Introduction** heavy promotion; low sales	**Growth** Sales increase; cash flow becomes positive

Problems of the life cycle model

- only considers one product rather than taking an overview of a firm's portfolio
- backward looking e.g. can only really tell whether or not you are in decline once it has happened
- may be self fulfilling (deterministic) e.g. if you think sales will fall you invest less in marketing, so sales do fall.

Product life cycle and capacity utilisation

When a product is first launched capacity utilisation is likely to be low. The firm is likely to have capacity to produce far more than is actually being sold when the product is first launched. This increases the unit cost and can reduce the profitability of the product. As sales increase, capacity utilisation increases. At some point the firm may have to decide to increase capacity again.

Product life cycle and prediction

It is difficult to predict future sales using the product life cycle model because:

- a firm cannot easily tell where the product is in the life cycle until much later (e.g. a fall in sales may turn out to be the decline phase but may simply be a temporary decline)
- not all life cycles are the same – there is considerable variation in the length of each phase and so it is difficult to extrapolate based on other products or past experience

Product portfolio analysis

Product portfolio analysis
Used to examine the existing position of the organisation's products in their markets to enable better decisions to be made.

Part of the marketing planning process:

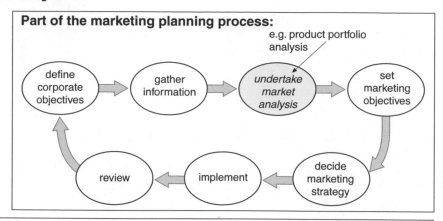

e.g. product portfolio analysis

Boston Box Model
One of the most well known methods of product portfolio analysis is the Boston Box (also called the Boston Matrix). It shows what percentage of the market each product has (from high to low) and the rate at which the market as a whole is growing (from high to low).

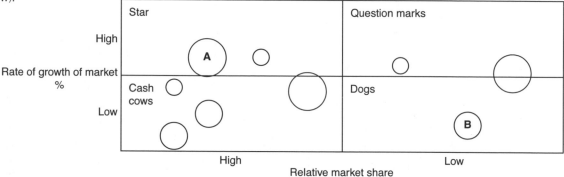

Each circle in the above diagram represents a particular product produced by the firm. The area of the circle represents the value of its sales, e.g. product A has higher sales than product B

Stars: high share of fast growing market e.g. Vodaphone mobile phones
May require considerable amounts of cash to keep it competitive.

Question marks (also called problem children or oil rigs):
small share of fast growing markets; potentially successful but need protection and investment. May become stars but may be pushed out.

Cash cows: large share of slow growing market such as a market which has matured, e.g. Marmite, Oxo cubes, Heinz Ketchup. These products have already been developed, and promoted, and generate relatively high levels of cash. This cash can be used to develop and protect other products.

Dogs: small share of slow growing market
Could be revived (e.g. Lucozade) but may be dropped. Dogs often take up more management time than they are worth.

Options for decision makers
- Hold   attempt to maintain existing market position, e.g. with strong cash cows
- Build   invest to develop position, e.g. with question marks. May involve sacrificing short term profits.
- Harvest   aim for short term profits, do not invest long term, e.g. possible with cash cows
- Divest   get rid of product, e.g. with dogs

Value of portfolio analysis
- examines all the firm's products together
- provides an overview
- helps with marketing planning e.g. ensuring a balanced portfolio

Balanced portfolio
Appropriate mix of cash cows, stars, dogs and question marks. With a balanced portfolio a firm can 'milk' its cash cows to provide the finances to stimulate and build the question marks and support the stars.

Unbalanced portfolio
- too many dogs – high risk of failure; no products for the future
- too many cash cows – likely to be profitable at present but not investing for the future
- too many question marks – high risk and may drain finances

Price

Price is an element of the marketing mix:

High price
The price is more likely to be high if:

- the product is heavily branded
- there are limited competitors
- incomes are high
- demand is price inelastic
- there are few substitutes
- the product/service has a USP

- unit costs are high
- the item is exclusive
- distribution is limited
- the good is at the growth stage of the life cycle
- the firm is following a skimming strategy

Factors influencing price
The price of a good or service may depend on:

- costs – organisations will generally want to cover their costs to make a profit for investment and to reward their owners
- demand and price elasticity – i.e. what is the level of demand and how sensitive is demand to price?
- competition – i.e. how similar are their products? What price are they charging?

- government – e.g. the government places indirect taxes (such as VAT) on most goods, which increases costs
- objectives – e.g. short term or long term profits
- stage of the life cycle – e.g. the price is more likely to increase in the growth phase and fall in decline
- rest of the mix – e.g. is it positioned as a more exclusive item than competitors' products?

Methods of pricing

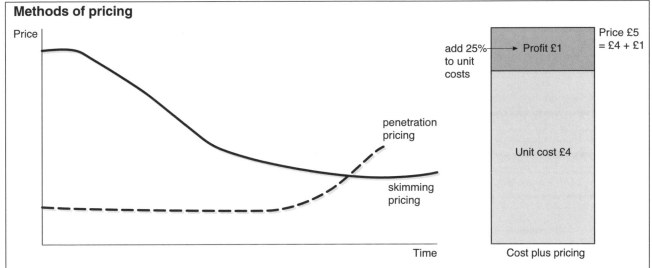

Price skimming – high initial price to cover initial research and development costs quickly. Suitable for an innovative or protected product (e.g. a patent) and where demand is price inelastic.

Penetration pricing – low price to gain market share quickly. Suitable when there are substantial economies of scale or when demand is price sensitive.

Competitor based pricing – suitable when the market is competitive and price comparisons are easy, e.g. shopping goods.

Demand based or perceived value pricing – firm tries to estimate what people are willing to pay. This is the most market oriented approach, but it can be difficult to discover what people are willing to pay.

Cost plus pricing – the firm adds an amount on to unit costs to decide on the price. This is a simple and, therefore, popular pricing method, but ignores demand conditions (see diagram).

Predatory pricing – a firm undercuts competitors to remove competition; once competitors leave, the price is increased again. This policy can lead to a price war in which all firms try to undercut each other.

Price discrimination – charging different prices for the same product/service, e.g. some taxis charge different prices late at night, rail fares are often higher at peak times; and some bars have 'happy hours' when drinks are cheaper. The firm will increase the price in segments where demand is price inelastic and decrease the price when demand is price elastic.

Loss leader – product sold below cost to generate orders for other product e.g. retailers put well known brand in shop windows and sell at a loss to attract people into the store.

Psychological pricing – focuses on consumer's perception of price, e.g. charging high prices to convey quality, charging £2.99 rather than £3.00 because people regard it as 'over £2' rather than in the £3 band, and stressing a reduction in price (e.g. was £20, now £12).

Product

The product is an element of the marketing mix:

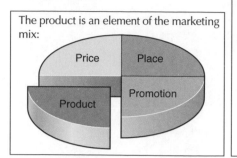

Examining the product

A product can be examined on three levels:

- **Core** – the benefits of the product, e.g. microwave = convenience, after shave = attraction

- **Tangible** – the actual features of the product, e.g. what it looks like, what it weighs, what it does, how it is packaged

- **Augmented** – other services or benefits that are obtained, e.g. delivery, guarantees, servicing

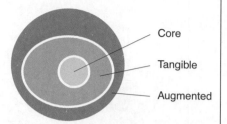

Product quality

The quality of a product depends on its:

- performance – e.g. the speed of a car, the power of a microwave

- features – The extras, e.g. air conditioning or sunroof on a car

- ease of servicing – How easy is it to fix?

- reliability – How likely is it to go wrong in, say, the first year?

- durability – How long will it last?

- aesthetics – What does it look like?

- economics – What does it cost to produce? Can it be sold at a profit?

- brand name

- ease of manufacture

Product design

Design should consider
- target costs
- method/ease of production
- customer requirements

Getting the design right is crucial. UK firms are often criticised for not spending enough time or money on design; as a result the product is more difficult to manufacture, scrap levels are higher and good quality is more difficult to achieve.

Product differentiation: anything which distinguishes one product from another in the eyes of the consumer.

Product cannibalisation: when the sales of one product which a firm has launched reduce the sales of another of its existing products.

New product development process

Generate ideas – these may be from internal sources or external

↓

Analysis e.g. are the ideas viable? Do they fit with the firm's objectives? Will it work?

↓

Development e.g. developing the idea; building prototypes

↓

Test marketing e.g. trying the product out in the market; firms may not do this because it gives competitors time to react

↓

Launch and commercialisation – the product is launched

The process of new product development is a filtering process; the firm often starts off with many ideas but gradually reduces these down to the few they think will survive and succeed. Even so many products still fail.

Value analysis

- Examining all aspects of a product or service to decide whether they genuinely add value, i.e. what would be lost if this part of the product was not offered?

- Considering how much it costs to provide a particular feature in relation to the extra the consumer will pay for it.

Types of product – consumer goods (i.e. goods/services bought to be consumed)

Convenience items
Consumer searches for nearest shop and does not take long thinking about the purchase decision. Extensive distribution.

Types include:

- **staple items** – regularly bought, e.g. milk, newspaper
- **emergency items** – e.g. plasters
- **impulse items** – chewing gum: consumer may not have gone into the shop to buy it; afterthought

Shopping goods
Consumer shops around, e.g. for TV, washing machine
Often distributed in city centres or out-of-town shopping centres.

Consumers take time to buy; think about it; compare goods and prices; look for the best value

Speciality goods
Unique/'special' goods; consumers willing to make special effort to buy, e.g. Porsche, Armani suits.

Exclusive distribution.

Consumer durables
bought by households but not consumed immediately when used once e.g. television

Consumer non durables
bought by households and consumed immediately when used once e.g. food

Types of product – industrial goods (i.e. goods bought by firms to use in the production process)

- **Raw materials**
  e.g. oranges, oil. Prices may fluctuate with supply and demand; often traded on world-wide markets. Little distinction between products; limited branding.

- **Manufactured parts**
  Usually sold directly to manufacturer; price and service very important; branding and advertising less important.

- **Supplies**
  e.g. light bulbs, soap. Little time spent in purchase; bought from intermediaries; price important; little brand preference.

- **Installations**
  Capital goods, e.g. factories or new production equipment; long purchasing process; personal selling is important; often a long negotiation period; the technical aspects of the product are vital; price inelastic. Bought direct from manufacturer. Sellers have to be willing to design to order.

- **Accessory equipment**
  e.g. desks. Often bought from wholesalers; competitive market; buyers likely to 'shop around'. Many buyers; small orders.

	Industrial goods	Consumer goods
Number of customers	Relatively few, professional buyers	Many
Relations with customers	Close	Often distant
Promotion	Often personal selling	Advertising more important
Distribution	Direct; few if any intermediaries	More intermediaries

Copyright: creator's or legal owner's rights in creative works such as paintings, writings, photographs or TV commercials. Copyright occurs automatically and does not need registering.

Trademark: a symbol used by a producer to identify a product. A trademark is legally protected under Trade Marks Act 1938 and Trade Marks (amendment) Act 1984. Trademarks must be registered with Patent Office.

Patent: a licence which prevents the copying of an idea; aims to protect inventors of a new product or process. New inventions protected for 15 years. Must be registered with Patent Office. This protection encourages research, allows inventors monopoly profits to reward their ideas, and encourages more products to be developed.

The American Can Co.'s patent for the ring pull has earned them over £50m.

Logo: visual symbol of a product or organisation e.g. Shell's 'shell'; Apple's 'apple', MGM's lion.

Why do products fail?
- Poor market research
- Poorly developed
- Inappropriate mix
- Competitors' actions
- External environment

Distribution

The channel of distribution describes how the title of ownership passes from the manufacturer to the consumer.

Distribution is an element of the marketing mix.

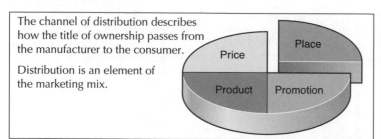

Distribution targets:
A firm is likely to set distribution targets such as:

- number of areas in which a product is distributed
- number of outlets in which a product is available
- number/value of sales per type of outlet or per region

Levels of distibution

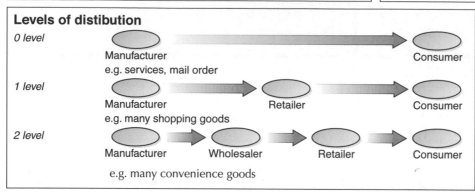

0 level

Manufacturer — Consumer
e.g. services, mail order

1 level

Manufacturer — Retailer — Consumer
e.g. many shopping goods

2 level

Manufacturer — Wholesaler — Retailer — Consumer
e.g. many convenience goods

Changing nature of distribution
Major retailers such as Sainsbury's have become much more important in recent years, becoming 'channel captains', i.e. they dominate the channel compared to manufacturers. They have also reduced the role of wholesalers and increased one level rather than two level channels.

Intermediaries
Intermediaries reduce the number of transactions between retailers and producers:

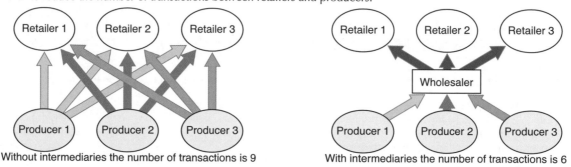

Without intermediaries the number of transactions is 9

With intermediaries the number of transactions is 6

Wholesalers: 'break bulk' i.e. buy in large quantities from manufacturers and break into smaller quantities for retailers.

Agents: do not take ownership of the goods. They represent a firm and try to gain sales for it. Receive a commission. Often used to enter overseas markets.

Distribution strategies

Push strategy
Manufacturer forces goods through channels by giving intermediaries incentives, e.g. discounts, higher margins, display items.

manufacturer ⟶ intermediaries

Pull strategy
Focus is on consumers, by appealing to consumers directly. The aim is to make them demand the product and force intermediaries to stock the goods.

customer ⟵ intermediaries ⟵ manufacturer

Choosing a distribution channel
Consider:

- costs
- alternatives – when Avon could not distribute cosmetics through department stores it sold door to door.
- type of product – industrial products tend to have shorter channels as they have fewer customers and a more complex product which needs detailed explanation. Fragile products are also likely to have a direct channel.
  Basic low value items, with many consumers widely spread geographically, are likely to have long channels with many intermediaries.

Types of channel

Exclusive
Very limited number of outlets; suitable for speciality goods

Selective
Selected outlets with suitable environments and image; suitable for shopping goods

Extensive
Widespread distribution; suitable for e.g. convenience goods

Promotion

Promotion involves communication about the product or service.

It is an element of the marketing mix.

Promotional objectives

- to make consumers aware, e.g. of new product launch
- to remind consumers; to reinforce a message
- to persuade consumers

How much should a firm spend on promotion?

Depends on
- overall marketing budget
- promotional objectives
- stage of the life cycle, e.g. likely to spend more at launch stage
- spending of competitors

Promotional messages

May have:
- rational appeal; appeals to consumers' self interest. Based on logic e.g. on the basis of quality, economy or function.
- emotional appeal; appeals to emotions such as guilt, fear, love.
- moral; appeals to consumers' sense of what is right.

Methods of promoting

- **Sales promotion:** short term incentives to increase sales, e.g. coupons, competitions. Effect is often to destroy loyalty to other brands and encourage brand switching; when promotion ends consumers often switch to another brand's offer.
- **Advertising:** is a paid for means of communication, e.g. buying advertising space in newspapers, buying advertising slots on TV.
- **Public relations:** involves managing relations with different publics, e.g. the media, consumers, pressure groups, investors. May involve getting media coverage of an event or product launch or generally creating a favourable impression

and generating word of mouth interest. The difficulty is that it is not easy to control what others write or say.

- **Personal selling:** use of sales representatives.
- **Direct mailing:** information is sent through the post
- **Exhibitions and trade fairs**
- **Merchandising:** an attempt to influence consumers at point of sale, e.g. display material
- **Packaging:** e.g. design, shape, information displayed on it
- **Branding:** name or design which identifies the products or services of a manufacturer and distinguishes them from competitors.

Above the line v below the line promotion

Above the line:	ADVERTISING
Below the line:	all other forms of promotion apart from direct advertising

Above the line promotional activities: direct advertising through independent media such as television, newspapers and radio.

Below the line promotional activities include all other promotional activities apart from direct advertising, e.g. direct mail, special offers, in store displays.

Brands

Own label (own brand) – retailers use own name (e.g. Sainsbury's), rather than a manufacturer's.

Family brand – business name on a number of products, e.g. Heinz beans, soup, spaghetti

Individual product branding – each product has a different brand name, e.g. Van den Bergh produces Flora, Delight, Krona, Stork, Blue Brand and Echo margarines.

Brand leader – brand with the highest market share

The value of brand loyalty

- may be able to earn high profit margins
- may be able to keep customers more easily
- may be able to launch new products more easily
- could extend the brand

Promotion continued

Advertising

Advertising should seek to :

- **A** increase <u>awareness</u>
- **I** create <u>interest</u>
- **D** develop a <u>desire</u>
- **A** lead to <u>action</u> (purchase)

Awareness – make consumers know the product or service exists

Interest – make consumers want to know more

Desire – make consumers want it

Action – make consumers buy it

This is known as the **AIDA** model.

Advertising occurs on posters, in newspapers, in magazines, on TV, and radio.

When deciding on the appropriate medium, advertisers should consider: the cost, the target audience, and the appropriateness of the chosen medium.

Using the promotional mix

Industrial goods are generally sold to a few professional buyers. Advertising is less important apart from e.g. the trade press, whereas personal selling is vital.

With consumer goods, such as jeans, advertising to the final consumer is more common. Personal selling is important to get the items distributed but advertising pulls the consumers into the shops.

Controls on advertising

1. Advertising Standards Authority is a voluntary body which seeks to ensure adverts are 'legal, decent, honest, truthful and do not cause widespread offence'.

2. Independent Television Commission – controls advertising on TV and radio.

3. Laws such as the Trades Description Act (whereby the goods advertised for sale must be as described).

Corporate advertising: promoting the company as a whole rather than a particular product

The personal selling process

This relies on the 5 Ps:

- **Preparation:** staff need to be trained and familiar with the product or service and what the firm has to offer

- **Prospecting:** identifying possible prospects, i.e. those likely to buy

- **Pre-approach:** finding out about customers' needs

- **Presentation:** presenting to the client

- **Post sale:** follow up to the sale to ensure the customer is satisfied and will come back for more!

Assessing advertising

The **DAGMAR** model highlights how advertising can be assessed by a firm.

- **D** defining
- **A** advertising
- **G** goals for
- **M** measured
- **A** advertising
- **R** results

In other words, it is important to define what it is you are trying to achieve so that you can measure whether or not you have been successful.
(If you do not set a target, how do you know if you have succeeded?)

Arguments for advertising
- informs
- creates jobs
- creative/art form

Arguments against advertising
- adds 'unnecessary' costs
- persuades people to buy goods/services they do not really want
- encourages the 'wrong' kind of values and behaviour, e.g. greed

Media selection

Depends on:
- **coverage:** i.e. the number of potential customers the advertiser wants to reach
- **frequency:** how often the advertiser wants the message to be transmitted
- **costs**

Media	Examples and benefits
• printed materials	e.g. newspapers, magazines Allows accurate targeting since each publication has its own customer profile
• broadcast media	e.g. TV and radio Very powerful media reaching very high percentage of households
• outdoor media	e.g. posters, advertising on buses, trains
• direct mail	Sent through the post; can target certain households
• cinema	Can use colour, movement and sound; can have local adverts but impact tends to be short lived; message may only be seen once

Elasticity of demand

Elasticity of demand
Measures the responsiveness of demand to a change in a variable such as price, income or advertising. It measures how much demand changes (in %) compared to the variable.

Elastic and inelastic
If demand changes more than the variable (in %), it is sensitive or elastic.
e.g. if demand increases 30% following a 10% price cut, the price elasticity of demand is 3. It is elastic because demand has changed three times more than price has changed (in %).

If demand changes less than the variable, it is insensitive or inelastic.
e.g. if demand changes 5% following a 10% price cut, the price elasticity of demand is 0.5. It is inelastic because demand changes half as much as the change in price.

Elastic:
% change in demand is greater than % change in variable

Inelastic:
% change in demand is less than % change in variable

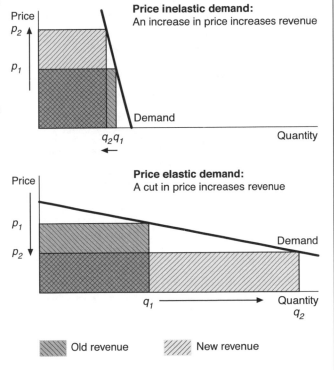

Price elasticity: sensitivity of demand to changes in price

Measured by the percentage change in demand compared to the percentage change in price:

$$\text{Price elasticity} = \frac{\text{\% change in demand}}{\text{\% change in price}}$$

If demand is not sensitive to price (price inelastic) the firm is more likely to increase price to increase revenue, because the increase in price leads to a smaller decrease in quantity demanded (in %).

If demand is sensitive to price (price elastic) the firm will lower price to increase revenue because a lower price will lead to a larger increase in quantity demanded (in %).

Whether an increase in revenue will also increase profit depends on what happens to costs as output changes.

Price inelastic demand:
An increase in price increases revenue

Price elastic demand:
A cut in price increases revenue

Old revenue   New revenue

The price elasticity will usually be given as a negative number. This is because when price goes down demand usually goes up and vice versa, i.e. price and quantity move in opposite directions. This results in a negative answer. When considering the price elasticity in business studies the sign is not usually important and should be ignored. i.e. –4 = 4 (elastic) and –0.7 = 0.7 (inelastic). The size of the number (>1 or <1) regardless of the sign, shows whether it is elastic or inelastic.

Goods are likely to be price inelastic if:

- only a small percentage of income is spent on them, e.g. milk

- there are few substitutes, e.g. innovative products, protected by patents

- they are addictive goods, e.g. cigarettes

- they are paid for by someone else, e.g. business travel paid for by the firm

- they are heavily branded

Elasticity of demand continued

Income elasticity: shows the sensitivity of demand to income

Measured by the percentage change in demand compared to the percentage change in income.

$$\text{Income elasticity} = \frac{\%\ \text{change in demand}}{\%\ \text{change in income}}$$

Some goods will be income elastic (i.e. sensitive to income changes), others will be income inelastic.

Income elastic goods and services may include: overseas holidays, sports cars, washing machines, dishwashers and houses.

Income inelastic may include: potatoes, pencils, milk, and newspapers.

Industries such as the holiday industry are therefore more sensitive to booms and slumps in the economy than the pencil industry.

A *positive* sign shows that when income increases, demand increases as well (or vice versa), i.e. both demand and income move together. This is true for NORMAL GOODS.

A *negative* sign occurs if demand falls when income increases (i.e. demand and income move in opposite directions); this happens with INFERIOR GOODS – as consumers get more income they switch to more luxurious options. A bicycle may be an inferior good for *some* consumers; with more income consumers switch to a car.

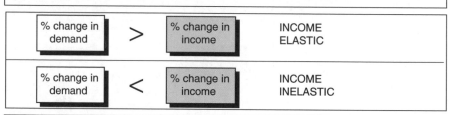

Cross elasticity: shows how responsive demand for one good (A) is to changes in the price of another good (B)

$$\text{Cross elasticity} = \frac{\%\ \text{change of demand for A}}{\%\ \text{change in price of B}}$$

The larger the value of the cross elasticity, the greater the relationship between the two goods, e.g. demand for *The Times* is likely to be more sensitive to changes in the price of *The Independent* compared to changes in the price of *The Sun* as the first two are more similar.

If the cross elasticity has a *positive* sign, the goods are SUBSTITUTES. An *increase* in the price of one good leads to an *increase* in demand for the other and consumers switch, e.g. IBM and Compaq

If the cross elasticity is *negative* the two goods are COMPLEMENTS. An *increase* in the price of one good leads to a decrease in demand for it and a *decrease* in demand for the other good, e.g. personal computers and computer disks.

Advertising elasticity: shows how responsive demand is to changes in advertising

$$\text{Advertising elasticity} = \frac{\%\ \text{change in demand}}{\%\ \text{change in advertising expenditure}}$$

The larger the value of the advertising elasticity, the greater the relationship between advertising and demand. A value of 3 means that demand changes 3 times more than the change in advertising expenditure elasticity (elastic); a value of 0.3 means demand changes 0.3 times as much.

If the answer has a *positive* value this means that demand increases with more advertising; if it is *negative,* demand decreases with advertising (e.g. a 'Don't drink and drive' campaign).

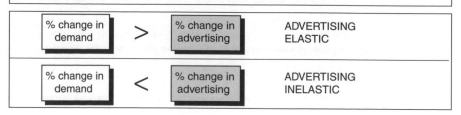

Elasticity, revenues and profits

If demand is price elastic a price fall will increase revenue; whether profit increases depends on what happens to unit costs. If unit costs increase (perhaps because the firm has had to expand capacity or because material costs increased) the profit margin and indeed overall profits may fall.

If income increases and the good is a 'normal' good then demand will rise. This will increase revenue (assuming price is unchanged); profits may rise but this again depends on unit costs.

How useful is the concept of elasticity?

Helps with planning: can estimate the impact of changes in price and income on demand. This will allow the firm to plan for:

- sales

- staffing

- cash flow

- production and stock levels

However:

- depends how reliable the estimate is

- other things can change, e.g. the price elasticity shows the effect of a change in price on the quantity demanded; however many other things may also change at the same time (such as income levels, competitors' advertising and technology which will also affect demand and so change the results).

How is elasticity estimated?

- past data (e.g. what happened when the price was changed in the past?). However, conditions may have changed significantly since then making the figure inappropriate.

- test market e.g. the price may be changed in one area and the effect measured. But is this market representative? Have competitors changed their marketing activities to distort the results?

- intuition – managers may simply estimate the price or income elasticity taking account of present conditions. Risky as it relies on individuals' judgement.

Sources of finance

Short term finance

Used for day-to-day requirements, e.g. buying supplies
- Overdraft – very flexible; interest is paid when the account is overdrawn and is usually lower than a bank loan. However, the amount owed can be demanded back at any moment.

Medium term finance

Used for e.g. new advertising campaign

- Bank loan – borrowed over a fixed period of time. Loan is repaid in regular instalments.

- Hire purchase – often used to buy equipment. Usually involves a down payment and then regular instalments.

- Trade credit – buying items from suppliers and paying later, e.g. paying 30 days after invoice arrives.

- Leasing – equipment is rented. This avoids a large initial outflow and equipment may be repaired and updated easily.

- Debt factoring – firms borrow money using their debtors (i.e. the amount owed) as security. Debt factor lends to firm and takes over responsibility for debtors.

Long term finance

Used for major expenditures, e.g. buying new premises

- Issue share capital – may involve more owners and loss of control; shares may be sold to existing shareholders (rights issue), to the general public (public or direct issue), to a merchant bank which then sells them to the general public (offer for sale) or to private clients (placing).

- Debentures – IOU certificates; the buyer is paid interest each year and receives the amount they lent back after a fixed period of time; the buyer is not an owner of the company.

- Mortgage – borrowings using property as collateral (security) to guarantee the loan.

- Government assistance – e.g. grants.

- Venture capital – money lent to small firms (usually combination of loans and share capital) to finance new firms which are risky and may have difficulty getting finance from elsewhere.

Sources of internal finance
- Profit
- Sale of fixed assets
- Working capital (e.g. reduce stocks)
- Sale and lease back

Sources of external finance
- Sale of shares
- Loans
- Debentures
- Venture capital

Long term debt *v* share capital

The gearing ratio measures long term borrowing as a percentage of the firm's long term finance (capital employed); highly geared = high percentage of borrowings.

Debt
- Interest must be paid before owners receive dividends
- Lenders can force liquidation
- Higher risk – interest must be paid, even if profits are low

Sell shares
- Lose ownership and control with new investors
- Owners expect dividends although may be possible to delay

Deciding how to raise finance
This depends on:
- whether the needs are short term, medium term or long term
- the present and expected rates of interest
- the desire to keep control

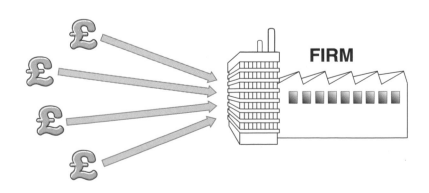

FIRM

Problems with different sources of finance
- Asset sales: may not have any assets to spare! May need assets to continue production and sales
- Loan capital: interest has to be paid even if profits are low; this can be risky
- Working capital: may reduce liquidity if cash is used up; may lose supplier goodwill if supplier payments are delayed; may upset debtors if they are chased
- Ordinary share capital: may lose control

Accounting

Accounts
Numerate information to help decision making. Accounting collects data of a firm's activities, turns this into monetary values, and presents findings in a suitable form for the decision maker.

Accounting is part of the decision making process:

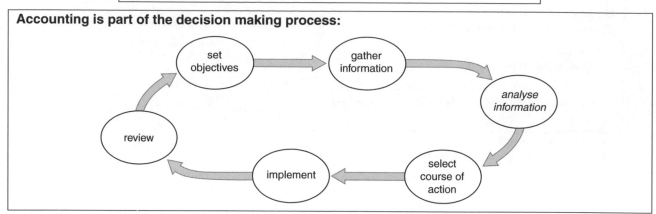

Accounting information is used by:

- outsiders   e.g. potential investors, lenders, government, suppliers
- insiders   e.g. managers, employees

Types of accounting

Financial accounting
essentially backward looking; mainly concerned with record keeping

Management accounting
to aid management's decisions and planning; concerned with the future, e.g. what price to set?

Accounting principles

Realisation: a sale is realised when a good is delivered; i.e. when goods are delivered they can be recorded as revenue even if cash has not been received.

Matching: costs must be matched to the period when they are incurred, e.g. if a firm buys £300 of materials and only uses up one third in this period, the costs are £100; £200 is left in stock.

Materiality: deciding whether an item is worth treating as an asset and depreciating, e.g. if only a third of a £1.50 jar of coffee has been used by the end of the period, the cost should be entered as 50p and the remaining value of the asset recorded as £1. However, items as small are this are often 'written off', i.e. all of the £1.50 would be put as a cost in one go. This is because they are not material enough for a firm to bother measuring exactly how much has been used up.

Prudence: accountants should be conservative when producing accounts; if in doubt they should underestimate revenue and overestimate costs.

Consistency: accounting information should be consistently gathered and presented from one year to the next, e.g. a firm should not simply change its depreciation policies from one year to another just to make its results look better.

The accounting profession and the interpretation and development of accounting principles is regulated in the UK by the Accounting Standards Board (ASB).

The ASB is responsible for producing:

- *FRED* Financial Reporting Exposure Drafts – draft versions of proposed new accounting standards
- *FRS* Financial Reporting Standards – agreed accounting standards.

Balance sheet 1

Balance sheet
Shows the financial position of an organisation at **a particular moment in time**. It shows what the business owns and how this has been financed **as at** a particular date.

Balance sheet as at (a certain date)

This is what the company owns	**Fixed Assets** *provide a benefit for more than 12 months*	Tangible	e.g. buildings, factories
		Intangible	e.g. brand name, goodwill, patents
		Financial	e.g. investments in other firms
	Current assets *provide a benefit for less than 12 months*	Stock	e.g. raw materials, works in progress, finished goods
		Debtors	the amount owed to the firm; also prepayments (advanced payments)
		Cash	(or money in the bank)
	TOTAL ASSETS		
These are the sources of finance used to acquire the assets	**Current Liabilities**		e.g. creditors of less than one year, overdraft, tax and dividend due
	Long term liabilities (creditors of more than a year)		e.g. loans
	Reserves } *Together these are called Shareholders' Funds*		e.g. retained profit
	Issued shares		i.e. finance raised through selling shares
	TOTAL LIABILITIES AND SHAREHOLDERS' FUNDS		

These items can be rearranged to give:

Balance Sheet as at (a certain date)

      Fixed assets

plus **Current assets** } *Called 'Working capital'*
less **Current liabilities** } *or 'Net current assets'*

      ASSETS EMPLOYED or NET ASSETS

      Long term liabilities

plus **Reserves** } *Together these are called Shareholders' Funds*
plus **Issued share capital**

=   **CAPITAL EMPLOYED**

CAPITAL EMPLOYED	⟶	ASSETS EMPLOYED
Sources of finance	Used to acquire	e.g. buildings, factories, stocks, cash

Balance sheet 2

Fixed assets and depreciationn

> FIXED ASSETS
> + CURRENT ASSETS
> = TOTAL ASSETS

A fixed asset will depreciate over time. Depreciation is the cost of a fixed asset. It is entered each year in the profit and loss account and reduces the value of the asset on the balance sheet.

Depreciation – straight line method

If an asset is bought for £500 and it is estimated it will be sold for £100 after 4 years, it will cost the firm £400. A decision must be made about how to allocate this cost. The simplest method is to allocate it in equal amounts i.e. £100 each year. This is the STRAIGHT LINE METHOD of depreciation.

Year	Value of asset on balance sheet (called Net Book Value) £	Annual cost of asset (depreciation) (appears on profit and loss) £	Accumulated depreciation (i.e. total depreciation) £
0	500	0	0
1	400	100	100
2	300	100	200
3	200	100	300
4	100	100	400

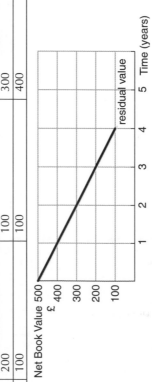

Historic cost = original cost of the asset

Accumulated depreciation = total depreciation to date

Net Book Value
= historic cost − accumulated depreciation, i.e. value of asset left on balance sheet

Residual value = value of asset at the end of its life, i.e. on disposal

Significance of depreciation
- reduces the value of assets on balance sheet
- is a cost on the profit and loss
- depreciation policy can be changed to window-dress the accounts

Depreciation – reducing or declining balance method

This method of depreciation depreciates a fixed asset by a constant percentage each year (rather than a constant amount). The result is that the asset will depreciate by a bigger amount in the early years and less later on. (As a result profits will be less in the early years and more in the later years compared to the straight line method).

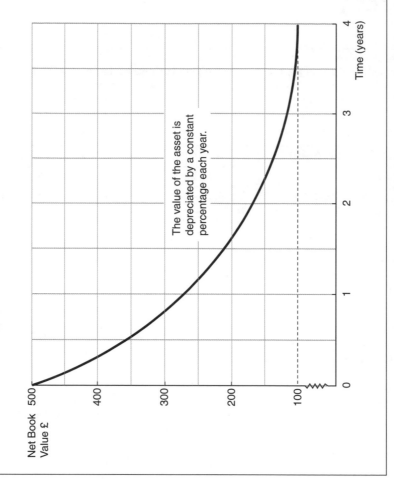

The value of the asset is depreciated by a constant percentage each year.

Subjectivity of depreciation
The initial cost of an asset is known. However the accountant must estimate:
- how long it will last (i.e. the expected life span)
- what it will be worth at the end (residual value)

This involves judgement i.e. subjectivity.

The depreciation per annum will be smaller:
- the smaller the residual value
- the longer the expected life span

Stocks

These appear as current assets on the balance sheet

FIXED ASSETS
+ CURRENT ASSETS
= TOTAL ASSETS

Should be valued at the lower of cost or net realisable value (i.e. what they would be worth if sold). Problems occur when trying to estimate what their realisable value is and when estimating their cost.

Example of problem estimating costs

A firm buys 10 units of materials in January at £30 each and another 10 units in February at £40 each. In March 10 units are used up but the firm may not know exactly which ones were used. Were they the ones bought in January or in February? If it does not know, the firm must make an assumption.

Under the FIFO principle the **first in** are assumed to be the **first out** i.e. the January materials are assumed to be used up. The cost of materials is therefore £300 (10 × £30) and the stock left is worth £400 (10 × £40).

If LIFO (**last in first out**) is used then it is assumed the February ones are used. The costs are therefore £400 and the stocks left are worth £300.

Some firms might assume that a mixture of January and February stocks had been used and take the average price. In which case the costs would be £350 and the stock left would be worth £350.

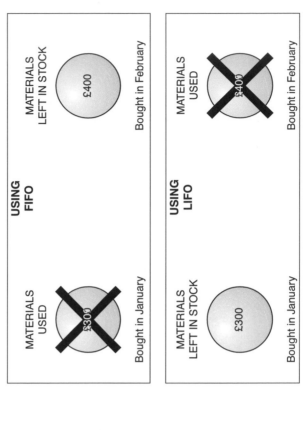

USING FIFO

MATERIALS USED
£300
Bought in January

MATERIALS LEFT IN STOCK
£400
Bought in February

USING LIFO

MATERIALS LEFT IN STOCK
£300
Bought in January

MATERIALS USED
£400
Bought in February

Aged stock analysis: analyses the age of the stock a firm holds, e.g. if stock has been held for a long time it may have become more difficult to sell.

Intangible assets

Brand name: intangible asset; no agreed method of valuation.

Reasons to include brands as assets in the balance sheet

- Help generate future sales and revenue.
- Enable higher prices to be charged and higher profits to be earned.
- Make the firm less vulnerable to recession.
- Can boost balance sheet and make the firm less vulnerable to takeover.

Reasons not to include brands as assets in the balance sheet

- No agreed method of valuation, so it is difficult for investors to compare companies' figures.
- Valuations are volatile – subject to trends.
- Investors will have already taken the brands into account and they will be reflected in the share price regardless of whether they are listed separately in the balance sheet.

Goodwill: occurs when a firm pays more for another firm than its book value, e.g. if Firm A spends £100m buying a company worth only £90m in its accounts then £10m of 'goodwill' has been acquired. This is listed as an intangible asset; it represents the value of the location, skill, reputation, and management of the acquired organisation. Goodwill is the difference between the value of a business as a whole and the aggregate of a fair value of its separable net assets.

Balance sheet 2 continued

Debtors

These appear as current assets in the balance sheet.
They represent money which is owed to the firm.

An analyst should try to find out more about who owes the firm money, e.g. if the money is all owed by one firm it may be riskier than if it is owed by several firms. It would also be useful to have details of the track record of the debtors, and information about how long they have owed the company money, e.g. 2 days or 11 months?

Aged debtors analysis: analyses the debtors of the firm in terms of how long they have owed money. Money which has been owed for a long time may be more likely to be bad debts.

Significance of debtors

* affect cashflow e.g. 'buy now, pay later' may attract more business

* amount of credit given may influence sales

Credit control

Firm needs policies regarding:
* how much credit to give

* payment terms and conditions

Influences on policy:
* likelihood of bad debts

* cashflow/liquidity

FIXED ASSETS
+ *CURRENT ASSETS*
= TOTAL ASSETS

Asset structure

The proportions of various types of asset held by a firm as shown on the balance sheet, e.g. a large manufacturing company is likely to have high levels of fixed assets (e.g. equipment).

Asset structure depends on:

* technology – advanced technology firms are likely to have a larger proportion of fixed assets

* the nature of the business, e.g. retailers are likely to have relatively high levels of stock

* the size of the business, e.g. small firms may not be able to afford the available technology

* stage of development, e.g. in the early stages a firm may not hold many fixed assets (e.g. cannot afford large premises)

* objectives, e.g. a firm pursuing a lean production policy is likely to hold relatively low stock levels

Reserves

Issued Share Capital } Shareholders'
+ Reserves   } Funds
+ Long term liabilities (or creditors for more than one year)
= CAPITAL EMPLOYED

* **Revaluation reserves:** occur when assets, such as land, increase in value. The fixed asset value is increased and to reflect the increased worth of the business a revaluation reserve is created.

* **Share premium reserve:** occurs when a share is issued at a price which is greater than its nominal (or face) value, e.g. if a 25p share is sold for 30p then the cash received is 30p, but the issued share capital will be recorded as 25p; the difference of 5p is listed in the share premium reserve.

* **Retained profits:** this records the total profit the firm has made up until now. Remember that reserves are not all sitting in cash; they will also be held in other forms of assets such as stock and buildings.

Working capital (net current assets)

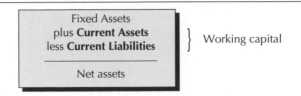

Fixed Assets
plus **Current Assets**
less **Current Liabilities**
_____
Net assets

} Working capital

Working capital (also called 'Net current assets')
Day to day finance of the organisation = current assets – current liabilities

Managing working capital
Involves decisions regarding:

- stock levels; a firm will want enough stock to ensure continued production and sales but at the same time will want to reduce stock levels to reduce the opportunity cost, warehousing costs

- debtor levels; a firm may want to offer credit to attract more business but at the same time having too many debtors may be bad for its cash flow

- cash levels: a firm may want cash because it is so liquid; at the same time holding cash has an opportunity cost

- creditors; a firm may want to delay paying creditors because this means it holds on to its cash for longer. At the same time this may lose the goodwill of suppliers

Improving working capital
- Manage cash effectively, e.g. control spending

- Try to increase credit period from suppliers

- Try to get goods produced and sold as quickly as possible (this minimises time between spending money to produce and receiving the cash from a sale)

- Effective credit control i.e. do not have too many debtors, collect money efficiently, make sure debtors can pay

- Manage stocks effectively (stocks represent tied up money), e.g. try to adopt JIT

Credit control
Controlling credit policy and terms and conditions
involves:

- assessing future customers to decide whether they are credit worthy

- determining credit terms and conditions (e.g. payment terms, number of days of credit given, interest charged)

- policies to deal with late payers

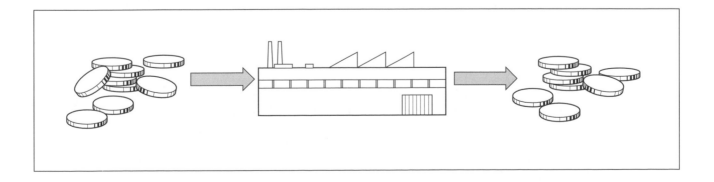

Profit and loss statement

Profit and loss statement

Shows the profit or loss generated by a business over a given period.

It involves:

Revenue or turnover: this measures the value of the sales; it may not be in cash since the firm is often owed money (debtors).

Costs: this is the value of items used up in the process; it is not necessarily the same as the cash paid out; e.g. if a firm pays for £300 of materials in cash but only uses up one third, the costs are £100 since the other £200 of materials remain as assets of the firm.

Profit and loss for the year ending 31 March 200X:

		£
Turnover	also called "revenue" or "sales"	100
Less Cost of sales	cost of producing the goods/services	40
Gross profit		60
Less Expenses	cost of marketing, administration	25
Operating profit		35
Non operating income	e.g. dividends from shares in other companies	2
Profit before interest and tax		37
Interest payable	to repay loans	5
Profit on ordinary activities before tax (tax on profits)		32
Corporation Tax		7
Profit after tax	also called "profit attributable to shareholders"	25
Dividends paid to shareholders		14
Retained profit		11

Other items/terms which may be listed on the profit and loss statement:

Extraordinary item: a cost or revenue which is 'out of the ordinary', i.e. not part of ordinary activities, e.g. the closure of a factory or restructuring costs.

Exceptional items: costs or revenues which are unusually large, e.g. an exceptionally large bad debt.

Profit and cash

Profit is not the same as cash: e.g. if goods are sold on credit this creates revenue but no cash. If materials or equipment are bought in cash, this leads to a cash outflow, but no cost is involved until they are used up. Imagine a £450 asset is purchased for cash, is used for four years, and is then sold for £50. The overall cost is £400 (£450 − £50). Using the straight line method, the cost is £100 p.a.

Year	0	1	2	3	4
Cash flows £	(450)	0	0	0	50
Costs £ (annual depreciation)	0	100	100	100	100

Profit v cash example

A firm buys £300 of materials in cash and uses up £200 of them to produce goods which are sold on credit for £1000. Labour is paid £50 in cash. No other costs are involved.

		£
Turnover		1000
Costs (labour)	50	
(materials)	200	250
Profit		750

		£
Cash in		0
Cash out (labour)		50
(materials)		300
Cash		(350)

The importance of cash flow and profit

If the firm's cash flow is poor it may not survive (due to liquidity problems). If the firm is not making a profit it may not be worth continuing in the long run (because the value of the sales is is less than the value of the inputs so why undertake this activity at all?)

Profit quality

The quality of a firm's profit depends on whether it is regarded as sustainable or not in the long term. For example, if a retailer makes a one-off profit from selling some of its shops this is not good quality profit because it cannot be repeated next year. Good quality profit is ongoing, e.g. profit generated from daily trading.

Revenue v capital items

Revenue items appear on the profit and loss. Capital items appear on the balance sheet. If, for example, a firm purchases equipment, this is an asset and appears on the balance sheet (capital item). If a firm uses up materials this is a cost and appears on the profit and loss (revenue item). Sometimes there is debate about an item, e.g. research and development. Some firms treat this as an investment, list it on the balance sheet and depreciate it over a number of years. Others 'write it off' in one year, i.e. treat it as something which has been used up and so put it all as a cost in one go (revenue item).

Net profit

This is the profit once the expenses and overheads have been taken away from gross profit.

Turnover

Less Cost of sales

= **Gross Profit**

Less Expenses   e.g. advertising

Less Overheads   e.g. rent

= **Net profit**

'Net profit' is often called 'operating profit'.

Is profit a good indicator of a firm's success?

Yes :

- generates rewards for owners
- generates funds for investment

But depends on:

- how much profit has been made
- how much is invested to begin with (e.g. return on capital employed)
- the quality of the profit made (is it sustainable?)
- the amount of profit other firms are making
- the trend, i.e. are profits increasing or decreasing?

Profit utilisation

The way in which profit is used; e.g. is it used to pay dividends or to invest into the business? This can sometimes be a source of conflict between the owners and the managers.

If a firm takes a long term view it may retain more profits for investment and pay out less to shareholders.

If a firm takes a short term view it may pay out higher dividends.

The amount paid out as dividends depends on:

- total profits
- share price (do the managers need to protect this by paying out more dividends?)
- the need for investment
- whether the firm is pursuing a long term or short term strategy

The profit and loss and the balance sheet

The profit and loss statement shows the profit for a given period (usually a year). It shows how it was achieved,

The retained profit figure in the balance sheet shows the TOTAL retained profit to date (i.e. since the firm began). If the firm makes a profit of £5m this year of which £2m is retained, the retained profit figure in the balance sheet will increase by £2m. If the firm makes a loss the retained profit figure on the balance sheet will fall.

Analysing a firm's profits

Rather than simply looking at a firm's overall profits you may want to analyse this figure in more depth. The annual accounts will provide information on whether the profits were made from businesses which continue in existence or ones which have been discontinued (e.g. closed down or sold off). They may also provide a segmental analysis showing how much was made in different countries or by the different parts of the business. Even so, analysts usually want even more information e.g. how much profit was made by individual products or brands? How much profit was made by new compared to old products? This is not generally available publicly.

Remember!

Profit is not necessarily cash. Profit simply shows that the revenue exceeded the costs. The profit could be in the form of debtors (i.e. not received as cash yet) or in stocks, buildings or other assets. It is unlikely to be just sitting as cash.

Ratios

Ratio analysis compares one figure with another to place it in context and assess its relative importance. It helps analyse data and aids decision making.

It is part of the decision making process:

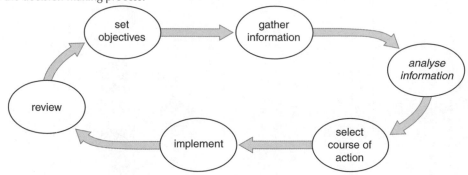

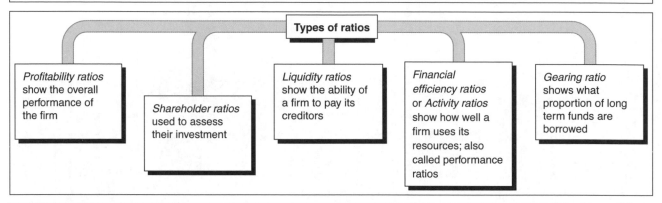

Types of ratios

Profitability ratios show the overall performance of the firm

Shareholder ratios used to assess their investment

Liquidity ratios show the ability of a firm to pay its creditors

Financial efficiency ratios or *Activity ratios* show how well a firm uses its resources; also called performance ratios

Gearing ratio shows what proportion of long term funds are borrowed

---

Profitability ratios: measure how well the firm is doing. One of the most common is *return on capital employed* (%) (profit before interest and tax ÷ capital employed) x 100

Assuming firms are aiming for profit, the higher the ratio the better. It measures the rate of return being generated by managers and can be compared to other rates of return, e.g. interest rates in banks.

The overall return depends on the value of the sales and how much profit is made per sale.

- The profit per sale is measured by the *profit margin* (%) (profit before interest and tax ÷ sales) x 100

- The value of the sales compared to the assets of the firm (i.e. the *asset turnover*) is measured by:
  sales ÷ assets employed.

Return on capital employed (ROCE)

Return on capital employed (ROCE) = $\dfrac{\text{profit before interest and tax}}{\text{capital employed}}$ x100 = %

shows overall return on investment.

Assuming profitability is the objective, firms will want to increase the ROCE.

High ROCE can be achieved by:
- increasing sales
- increasing profit margins

ROCE is likely to be lower if
- the markets are in decline
- unit costs are increasing and the firm cannot increase price
- sales are falling

The return on capital employed is likely to be higher when:
- the market is growing
- the firm is increasing its efficiency
- demand is high

Profit margin
The profit margin is likely to be higher when:
- there is limited competition
- there is strong brand loyalty
- lower unit costs
- high price (e.g. price inelastic product or exclusive item)

A high profit margin does not guarantee a high return on capital employed; return on capital employed also depends on how much is sold

Profit margin % = $\dfrac{\text{profit before interest and tax}}{\text{sales}}$ x 100

Gross profit v net profit

Gross profit is turnover (also called sales or revenues) minus cost of sales (i.e. overhead costs have not been deducted).

Net profit is turnover (= sales = revenue) minus cost of sales *and* overhead costs.

If gross profits are rising over time but net profit is falling this is due to increasing overheads.

Profit margins

$$\text{Gross profit margin} = \frac{\text{gross profit}}{\text{sales}} \times 100$$

$$\text{Net profit margin} = \frac{\text{net profit}}{\text{sales}} \times 100$$

If a firm decreases the price then if all other things are unchanged the gross profit margin will fall. However, with more sales the overhead cost per unit will fall and so the net profit margin may increase.

Liquidity ratios

These measure the ability of an organisation to meet its short term liabilities.

Current Ratio $\dfrac{\text{current assets}}{\text{current liabilities}}$

Typically between 1.5 and 2

Acid test ratio Current assets without stocks ÷ current liabilities
(also called 'quick ratio')

The acid test is a tighter test of liquidity than the current ratio. It measures the ability of the firm to meet its current liabilities if it could not sell its stock. Usually 0.8 to 1.

Acid test ratio

Do not want this ratio to be too high because:
- this could mean too many debtors (i.e. too much money outstanding); this may lead to bad debts and/or cashflow problems
- could mean too much cash; cash represents idle money which could be earning a higher return elsewhere

Do not want this ratio to be too low because:
- could mean liquidity problems i.e. may not be able to pay current liabilities

Some successful firms have lower acid test ratios than many textbooks suggest. This is because
- they are powerful enough to delay payment to suppliers if necessary
- they are confident they will sell their stock quickly and generate cash
- they can raise cash quickly (e.g. bank finance)

Dividend per share
The amount paid as dividends will depend on:
- the firm's profits
- the pressure to reward shareholders, e.g. if share price is falling, may need to increase dividends to boost it
- the amount that other firms are paying
- rewards available elsewhere, e.g. rates of interest
- amount shareholders expect, e.g. may have been promised high returns in earlier press statements

Shareholder ratios

Return on equity (%): (profit attributable to ordinary shareholders ÷ ordinary share capital and reserves) x100

Shows profit attributable to ordinary shareholders compared to their investment; the higher the figure the greater the rate of return earned for shareholders.

Price/earnings ratio: The earnings are the profits of the company which could be paid out to shareholders (i.e. which are attributable to ordinary shareholders). The price is the share price. The ratio measures how much investors are willing to pay for a share compared to the profits of the company per share. If this is a high figure then investors are willing to pay more to buy the share; this suggests confidence in the future performance of the business.

Dividends per share (pence): dividends ÷ number of shares; this is the amount received by shareholders on each share.

Dividend yield (%):
(dividend per share ÷ market price) x100.
Shows the dividends as a rate of return compared to the price of buying a share; this should be compared with rates available elsewhere.

Dividend cover (number of times):
(Profit attributable to ordinary shareholders ÷ dividends)
This measures the ability of the firm to pay out dividends.

Ratios continued

Financial efficiency ratios

Also called 'activity ratios'. Show how well the firm is using its resources.

1. Stock turnover measures the value of the firm's stock compared to its sales $= \dfrac{\text{cost of sales}}{\text{stock}}$

e.g.

Cost of sales — STOCK — Stock will be used up 3 times. Stock turnover is 3.

Cost of sales — STOCK — Stock turnover is 4.

With just in time production techniques, many firms are managing with less stocks. This increases the stock turnover ratios as the stock is used up and replaced (or turned over) more frequently.

The stock turnover is likely to be higher when:
- the firm adopts a just in time policy
- the lead time is low
- the product is perishable

Stock turnover will depend on:
- reliability of suppliers; if they can be relied on the firm may hold less stocks and have more deliveries. Stock turnover will be higher
- nature of the product; if the product cannot be stored easily, firms cannot hold many stocks and so stock turnover will be higher (e.g. food, milk, flowers)
- policy of the firm e.g. if it is adopting a just in time policy it will hold less stock at any moment and stock turnover will be high

---

2. Debtor days: the amount that is owed in terms of the number of days' worth of sales. e.g. if the firm is owed £1000 and in a year sells £10,000 then it is owed

(£1000/£10,000) x 100 = 10% of its sales
10% of 365 days = 36.5 days

i.e. the firm is owed the equivalent of 36.5 days' worth of its sales.

You can use the formula: Debtor days $= \dfrac{\text{debtors}}{\text{sales}}$ x 365

If debtor days is too high the firm may have liquidity problems. However the 'right' level of debtor days will depend on:
- the industry – in some industries the payment period is typically longer than others, e.g. shipbuilding v launderette
- the firm's policy – in some cases firms may deliberately

allow customers longer to pay to encourage sales
- interest rates – any money outstanding is not earning the firm interest; the higher the interest rate the more likely it is that the firm will want to chase up this money

Firms can reduce debtor days by:
- insisting on cash payment
- including penalties for late payment
- including incentives for early payment
- using debt factors

But firms need to be careful
- chasing debtors may lose their goodwill
- customers may chose firms which allow a long payment period

Gearing measures how much the firm has borrowed compared to other forms of long term finance. 'Highly geared' means a high percentage of the firm's funds are borrowed.

Interest cover shows how many times the profit before interest can cover the interest payments. If it is equal to 1, it means all the profits are needed to pay off the interest on debts. Generally it is 3 to 4, i.e. firms can cover their interest payments 3 times over.

High gearing
Advantages
- borrowing may have enabled profitable projects to be undertaken
- borrowing can be a cheaper source of finance than shares (pay interest before tax whereas shareholders paid after tax; to pay £1 to shareholders the firm has to earn more than this because tax is paid first; to pay £1 interest has to earn £1)

Disadvantages
- may involve risk – if profits are low the firm may struggle to repay interest
- may be difficult to borrow more finance

Increasing gearing can be risky for firms because of the interest payments BUT if a firm refuses to borrow it may miss out on market opportunities. Increasing gearing is acceptable provided the profits earned more than cover the interest payments. So the firm needs to consider interest cover as well as the gearing ratio.

A typical gearing ratio for UK firms is around 50%. However firms are more likely to be highly geared:
- in the early years (as they borrow to set up and expand)
- if interest rates are low (so firms exploit this by borrowing and fixing interest rates)
- if the owners are reluctant to lose control by bringing in outside finance

Balance Sheet

as at 17th June 200X		£m
Fixed assets		190
Current assets		
stocks	10	
debtors	6	
cash	4	20
less		
Current Liabilities		10
Assets employed (or net assets)		200
Issued share capital of £1 shares		100
Reserves		50
Long term liabilities		50
Capital Employed		200

Profit and loss for the year ending 17th June 200X

	£m
Turnover (or sales)	400
cost of sales	300
Gross profit	100
expenses	80
Operating profit	20
non operating income	0
Profit before interest and tax	20
interest payable	4
tax	1
Profit attributable to ordinary shareholders	15
dividends	10
Retained profit	5

Calculations

The shareholder ratios cannot be calculated without the share price. This cannot be found in the published accounts because it will change daily. Assume a share price of £2.00 for the calculations below.

Ratio	Equation	Measurement	Workings	Answer
return on capital employed	(profit before interest and tax ÷ capital employed) × 100	%	(20 ÷ 200) × 100	10%
profit margin	(profit before interest and tax ÷ sales) × 100	%	(20 ÷ 400) × 100	5%
asset turnover	(sales ÷ assets employed)	number of times	400 ÷ 200	2
current ratio*	current asset ÷ current liabilities	number of times	20 ÷ 10	2
acid test (or 'quick')	current assets without stocks ÷ current liabilities	number of times	10 ÷ 10	1
gearing	(long term liabilities ÷ capital employed) × 100	%	(50 ÷ 200) × 100	25%
interest cover*	profit before interest ÷ interest	number of times	20 ÷ 4	5
stock turnover	cost of sales ÷ stock	number of times	300 ÷ 10	30
debtor days	$\frac{\text{debtors}}{\text{sales}}$ x 365	number of days' worth of sales	$\frac{6}{400}$ x 365	5.5 days
dividend cover*	profit attributed to ordinary shareholders ÷ dividend	number of times	15 ÷ 10	1.5
dividend per share	dividend ÷ number of shares	pence	10 ÷ 100	10p
dividend yield	(dividend per share ÷ market price) × 100	%	(10 ÷ 200) × 100	5%
earnings per share*	profit after interest and tax ÷ number of shares	pence	15 ÷ 100	15p
price earnings ratio*	market share price ÷ earnings per share	number of times	200 ÷ 15	13.3
return on equity*	(profit attributable to ordinary shareholders ÷ shareholders' funds) × 100	%	(15 ÷ 150) × 100	10%

* **Note** the ratios marked with an asterisk are **NOT** needed for AQA examinations

Ratios continued

Limitations to ratio analysis

- Ratios are only as reliable as the underlying data, i.e. if the accounts have been 'massaged' or 'window dressed' to create a favourable impression, then the ratios may also flatter. In addition, ratios are often calculated using out of date information, e.g. data from last year's accounts. Ratio analysis based on past data will not necessarily help predict the future.

- Ratios are only based on quantitative data. It is also important to consider qualitative factors, such as the skill of management, the rate of change in the market, and the industrial relations record of a firm.

- Need to consider the type of firm, the stage in its development, and the objectives of the owners, e.g. a low profitability ratio may be acceptable in the early stages of growth when the owners are investing heavily in equipment and training.

- Typicality – the figures in the balance sheet show a particular day; this may not be typical and consequently any ratios calculated using these figures are not necessarily representative.

- Need to consider what the ratios are for other firms (inter firm comparison) and what ratios have been in the past (intra firm comparison); e.g. a 12% ROCE may seem high but it is not as impressive if others are earning 14% and last year the firm earned 16%.

- Need to consider the context, e.g. is the market growing or declining? Is the economy booming or not? For example we may expect profitability to be higher in a growing market.

- The usefulness of ratio analysis depends on the skill of the user; the more experienced and able the user the more likely he or she will be to interpret the ratios effectively, place them in context, and understand their significance.

Auditors' report: companies must get independent accountants to check their accounts. They then produce an auditors' report. This usually states that in their opinion the annual accounts represent a 'true and fair view'.

Window dressing

Presenting accounts in a favourable manner. Window dressing is not illegal.

The ability to window dress occurs because accounting principles can be interpreted in different ways.

Methods include:

- depreciating an asset over a longer period of time to reduce the depreciation cost per annum.

- including a valuation for brands as a fixed asset.

- deciding when to recognise revenue, e.g. if a company delivers a machine to a client, installs it and gives a trial period during which the client can return the machine, the revenue might be declared on delivery, after installation or after the trial period.

- sale and leaseback to increase liquid assets and improve liquidity position.

When analysing a firm's accounts it is important to check the Notes to the Accounts and the Statement of Accounting Policies to find out more about the way the accounts have been produced.

Why window dress?

To produce impressive results to attract investors, maintain share price, and gain favourable press coverage.

Break-even analysis

Break-even is part of the decision making process. It is an aid to decision making.

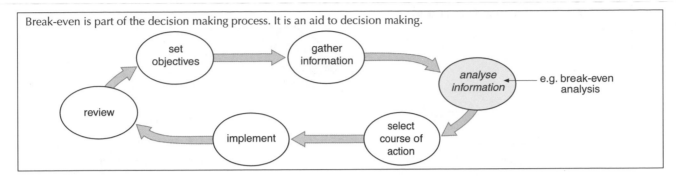

Break-even is the output at which revenue equals costs, i.e. no profit or loss is made.

- Total revenue = price x quantity
- Total costs = fixed costs + variable costs

Fixed costs do not change with output, e.g. rent
Variable costs vary directly with output, e.g. materials

- Profit = total revenue – total costs

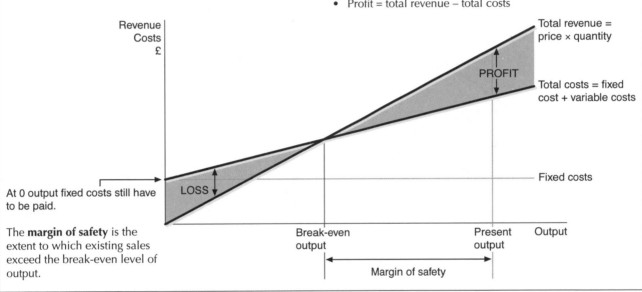

At 0 output fixed costs still have to be paid.

The **margin of safety** is the extent to which existing sales exceed the break-even level of output.

Calculating break-even output

> Number of units which must be sold to break even
> = fixed costs ÷ contribution per unit

1. Find the contribution per unit. This is selling price – variable cost per unit

2. This gives the contribution per unit towards fixed costs. Find how many units must be sold for these contributions to cover fixed costs.

Example: Price per unit £10; Variable cost per unit £4; Fixed costs £12,000; maximum output 5000 units.

Contribution per unit = £10 – £4 = £6

Fixed costs/contribution = £12,000 ÷ £6 = 2000 units i.e. 2000 units must be sold to get a large enough contribution to meet the fixed costs.

Plotting the break-even graph

Produce a table which calculates Total Costs and Total Revenue.

Example: Price per unit £10; Variable cost per unit £4; Fixed costs £12,000; maximum output 5000 units.

Quantity	Total revenue (price × quantity) £	Fixed costs £	Variable costs (variable cost per unit × quantity) £	Total costs £	Profit/loss £
0	0	12,000	0	12,000	(12,000)
1000	10,000	12,000	4000	16,000	(6000)
2000	20,000	12,000	8000	20,000	0 = break-even
5000	50,000	12,000	20,000	32,000	18,000

The graph is plotted at the top of page 62.

Break-even analysis continued

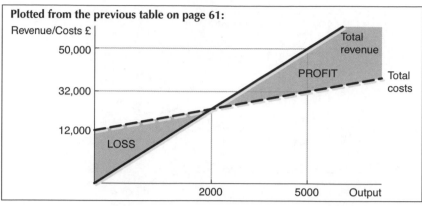

Plotted from the previous table on page 61:

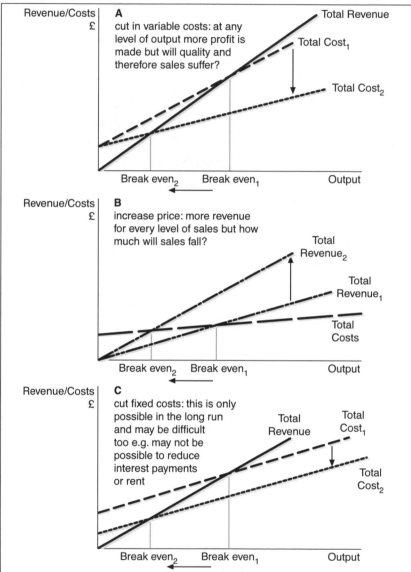

Break-even helps the firm to analyse what happens if:

- output is changed
- price is changed
- variable costs are changed
- fixed costs are changed

A cut in variable costs: at any level of output more profit is made but will quality and therefore sales suffer?

B increase price: more revenue for every level of sales but how much will sales fall?

C cut fixed costs: this is only possible in the long run and may be difficult too e.g. may not be possible to reduce interest payments or rent

The value of break-even analysis

- helps with planning e.g. whether to change price
- helps with identifying the effect of changes in costs e.g. what happens if variable costs increase by 10%?
- can be used for sensitivity analysis, i.e. comparing the impact of a 5% price fall to a 3% variable cost increase to a 2% fixed cost increase; this highlights how sensitive the firm is to different conditions

But:

- depends on the underlying reliability of the data
- depends on whether managers can bring about particular conditions, e.g. can managers keep variable cost per unit at the given level?
- depends on reactions of competitors and the external conditions, e.g. a specific level of sales may not be hit because of competitors' actions
- assumes all the output is sold; in fact sales may not equal output – sales could be lower than output so stocks increase, or sales could be higher than output so stocks decrease
- assumes output is all sold at one price; in reality the firm may have to lower the price to sell more
- assumes variable costs are constant per unit; in reality they may vary with discounts or changes in productivity

Special order decisions

Imagine a firm is offered a price by a customer for a special order which covers the direct costs and contributes to the indirect costs. The price is lower than 'normal' customers pay and does not cover direct and indirect costs combined. Should the firm accept the order?

The answer depends on:

- how existing customers would react (would they find out, what would they think, what would be the impact on future sales?)
- whether the firm has the capacity to produce the special order (if not it would be sacrificing the higher priced sales to existing customers)
- whether this may lead to higher priced orders in the future
- whether the new customers will always expect this lower price

Costing

Cost and profit centres

Cost centre: a business unit to which costs are allocated. It may be an individual, division, product or region. The measurement of costs for different units enables management to keep control and make better decisions as well as providing employees with targets which are relevant to their particular area of the business.

Importance of cost centres

- Can track costs of different parts of the organisation e.g. particular departments

- Can set budgets to control costs

Profit centre

A business unit to which costs *and* revenues are allocated. It may be an individual, division, product or region.

Profit centres:

- May be motivating as you can give people control over their own revenues and costs.

- Could be associated with delegation and giving employees greater authority.

If the firm does not use profit centres, individual managers are simply looking at overall profit figures and may feel very little link to these.

Problems of cost and profit centres

- May encourage individual units to pursue own objectives/own success at expense of the whole organisation

- May result in disputes over the allocation of indirect costs

Standard costing

Establishes estimates of costs and sales and compares these with actual costs and sales. The difference between the standard cost and the actual cost is the variance.

Advantages of standard costing:

- Helps with setting budgets

- Can be used to review performance

- Can motivate staff

Types of costs

Variable costs: change directly with output, e.g. raw materials

Fixed costs: do not change with output, e.g. rent. Fixed costs can change (e.g. interest rates may increase, rent may increase) but are not linked to the amount produced.

Semi variable costs: vary with output but not directly; e.g. supervision costs, maintenance costs

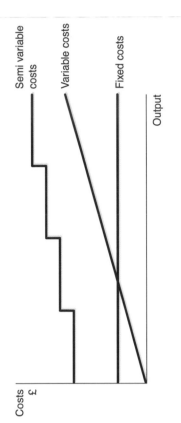

Direct costs: costs which can be identified with a particular cost centre (e.g. a product or process) and which vary directly with activity or output, e.g. the materials used in one process or labour directly involved in one product.

Indirect costs: costs which cannot be directly identified with a particular cost centre, e.g. general marketing costs or administration. Also called **overheads.**

Indirect costs may be fixed (e.g. rent) or variable (e.g. variable overheads such as maintenance costs; these are not directly associated with a cost centre, and, although more maintenance is likely to be needed with expansion, these costs will not change directly with output).

Average cost: This is the unit costs or cost per unit. e.g. if the total costs are £200 and 50 units are made the average cost is £4.

$$\text{Average cost} = \frac{\text{total cost}}{\text{output}}$$

Marginal cost: This is the extra cost of a unit. This is important when considering a special order: what extra costs are incurred? Will the revenue cover the extra costs? Marginal costing is another name for contribution costing.

Costing continued

Costing statements: used to analyse the performance of different parts of the business. There are three types of costing statements: marginal costing, full costing and absorption costing.

1. Marginal costing/Contribution costing

Total contribution = total revenue − total variable costs

In this type of costing statement fixed costs are left unallocated. The contribution of each centre is calculated. This contributes towards the fixed costs.

£	Product A	Product B	Product C	Total
Revenue	100	60	30	190
Less Variable costs	60	30	10	100
= Contribution	40	30	20	90

	£
Total contribution	90
Less Fixed costs	60
= Profit	30

Contribution costing is useful for deciding whether to accept one-off orders (known as 'special order decisions'): provided the order makes a positive contribution towards indirect costs it will increase profits or reduce losses.

2. Full costing

Overheads are divided (apportioned) between the various cost centres. Firms have to decide on an allocation rule. In the example below, indirect costs of £60 have been apportioned in the ratio 60% : 30% : 10% i.e. the same proportion as direct costs.

	A £	B £	C £
Turnover	100	50	40
Direct costs	60	30	10
Indirect costs	36	18	6
Profit/loss	4	2	24

3. Absorption costing

Based on the same idea as full costing but does not allocate all indirect costs using the same rule. Different allocation rules are used for different types of indirect costs, e.g.

- rent may be apportioned on the basis of the area occupied by each cost centre.
- heating costs may be apportioned on the basis of the amount of space taken up by a given centre.
- insurance costs may be apportioned on the basis of the value of the assets in each centre.

Advantages of full and absorption costing:

- Makes managers aware of the total cost of a product.
- Provides a full cost to enable a suitable price to be set, i.e. a price which will cover all costs and ensure a profit.

BUT

- The costs may be apportioned in different ways which will give different results; there is no set way of apportioning costs and changing the rule will give different results for each cost centre.

The decision whether to produce

It is important to remember that many of the indirect costs must be paid whether or not a particular product is produced.

	A £	B £	C £
Turnover	100	50	40
Direct costs	60	30	10
Indirect costs	50	5	5
Profit/loss	(10)	15	25

Although product A makes a loss, it makes a contribution of 40 (£100 − £60) towards indirect costs. If the firm stopped producing A many of the £50 of indirect costs would now have to be covered by the other products, e.g. the rent of the factory will not stop just because one type of product is no longer made. In the short run, at least, production of A should continue because it makes a positive contribution. In the long run it might be possible to reduce indirect costs, e.g. sell/lease out part of the factory space.

Budgeting

Budgets: a financial target for a given period of time, e.g. there may be a budget for how much can be spent on materials over the next six months, or the target level of sales revenue.

Budgets:
- help planning
- help coordinate different activities so that e.g. overall costs are not too high
- allocate responsibilities and communicate to subordinates what they have to achieve
- motivate employees by setting targets
- enable superiors to review performance by referring back to the set budget at the end of the period.

Types of budget:

Sales budget: sets sales estimates for each product in terms of number of units or value

Production budget: sets output targets

Cash budget: cash flow forecast

Master budget: summarises estimated income, expenditure and profit.

Fixed and flexible budgets: A fixed budget gives a target for a given level of activity, e.g. costs of £1000 for 200 units. A flexible budget shows figures at different levels of activity, e.g. costs for different *levels of output.*

Zero based budgeting

Before a budget is set for any activity it is critically reviewed. The assumption is that there will be no money available; managers then have to justify why they should have a budget.

Value of zero based budgeting

- Forces budget setters to examine every item each year and decide if necessary
- Prevents creeping budgeting whereby budgets automatically increase each year because managers simply add a percentage on for inflation
- Makes managers think about each item in the budget each year, rather than just assuming that because it was there last year it should be there again.

BUT
- Can be very time consuming
- Can lead to extensive paperwork and bureaucracy

Setting a budget

A budget may be based on:
- the past; there is a tendency for managers to look at what they spent before and add on a bit to cover inflation
- other firms; what are they spending? If they have increased their spending you may be able to justify a bigger budget
- objectives: what is it you are trying to achieve? What are the expected returns?
- resources; what can you afford?

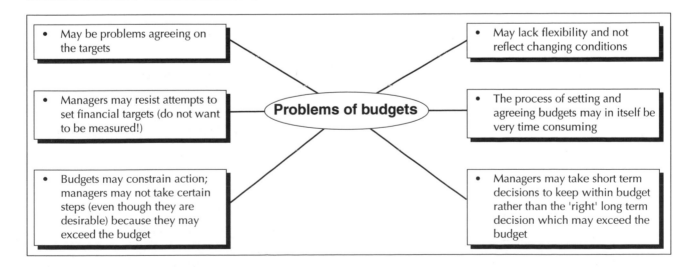

- May be problems agreeing on the targets
- Managers may resist attempts to set financial targets (do not want to be measured!)
- Budgets may constrain action; managers may not take certain steps (even though they are desirable) because they may exceed the budget

Problems of budgets

- May lack flexibility and not reflect changing conditions
- The process of setting and agreeing budgets may in itself be very time consuming
- Managers may take short term decisions to keep within budget rather than the 'right' long term decision which may exceed the budget

Budgeting continued

Budgetary control
Measuring and analysing the actual outcomes compared to the budgeted figures.

The difference between the forecasted figure in the budget and the actual figure is called the **variance**.

Positive or favourable variance: occurs when actual costs are lower than forecasted or revenue is higher than expected, i.e. profits are higher than expected.

Negative or adverse variance: occurs when actual costs are higher than expected or revenue is lower than budgeted, i.e. profits are lower than expected.

Item	Budgeted	Actual	Variance
Sales of product A	£100	£120	POSITIVE: should increase profit
Direct labour costs	£300	£350	NEGATIVE: should decrease profit
Indirect costs	£400	£350	POSITIVE: should increase profit

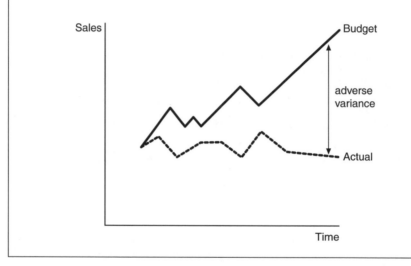

Should managers be concerned about a variance?
- Depends on whether it is positive or adverse.
- Depends on whether it could be/was foreseen e.g. natural consequence of higher level of sales.
- Depends on the cause e.g. are costs higher than expected because we sold more than expected?
- Depends on the size of variance.

Budget effectiveness
Effectiveness of budgets depends on:
- how they are set (e.g. imposed *v* agreed)
- whether they are realistic
- how they are perceived, e.g. are they welcomed or resisted by staff?

Causes of variance
Labour costs could be higher than expected because:
- employees took longer than expected to complete the job
- more employees were needed than expected
- wage rates were higher than expected
- the firm produced more than expected

Material costs could be higher than expected because:
- usage rate higher than expected
- wastage rates higher than expected
- material costs higher than expected, e.g. suppliers increased price

Do budgets control or empower employees?
This depends on how they are used.
- May be used to ensure managers do not overspend, to ensure spending is constrained; then used to review performance. Part of a Theory X approach where employees are not trusted.
- May be used to give managers more control, e.g. agree on a budget (rather than impose it on them) and then they are empowered to put plans into action and decide how to use money effectively and achieve revenue targets.

Depends on whether managers are simply told their budgets or whether they can influence the size of the targets.

Cash flow

Cash
Cash is a tangible money asset. It is shown in the current assets on the balance sheet. Cash flow statements show the flows of cash into and out of the business. Cash flow forecasts attempt to predict flows to highlight when cash might have to be borrowed or when it could be invested.

Cash flow forecasts
These are an essential part of a firm's financial planning. If a firm is short of cash it may be illiquid and struggle to remain solvent. A firm must estimate expected inflows and outflows of cash and ensure it has planned effectively.
- If it is short of cash it can try to find alternative sources.
- If it has too much cash it can try and invest this to earn a higher return.

Cash flow forecasts
Example:

Opening balance is £1050 (opening balance is the amount the firm starts the period with).

Sales for January, February and March are £300, £600 and £1200. One third is paid in cash; the remainder is paid one month later.

Materials each month are £300 paid for in cash. Wages are £200 in cash each month. Rent is paid 3 months at a time in January, April, July and October. It is £600 for three months.

£	January	February	March
Opening balance	1050	50	(50)
Cash in:			
cash sales	100	200	400
cash from earlier credit sales	–	200	400
Cash out:			
materials	300	300	300
wages	200	200	200
rent	600	–	–
Closing balance	50	(50)	250

- **Cash inflows:** cash coming into the business. Some of this period's sales may be paid in cash; also cash might be paid from previous credit sales
- **Cash outflows:** cash leaving the business e.g. cash payments this month on labour or materials
- **Closing balance:** amount of cash left at the end of the period. This becomes the opening balance for next period.

Problems with cash flow forecasts
Cash flow forecasts may be wrong if:
- the sales forecast is wrong e.g. due to changing external conditions
- customers are slow to pay
- suppliers demand to be paid more quickly
- there are unexpected increases in input prices
- the planning is poor
- internal factors change, e.g. unexpected wage increases or production problems

Investment appraisal

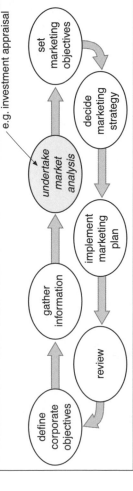

e.g. investment appraisal

set marketing objectives → decide marketing strategy → implement marketing plan → review → gather information → define corporate objectives → undertake market analysis

Investment appraisal

This involves quantitative techniques to assess the attractiveness of different capital projects. These projects usually involve a high level of expenditure and cannot be easily reversed. They involve a high degree of risk. Investment may be e.g. in factories or plant or equipment.

When considering an investment a firm will consider:

- the initial cost
- the expected benefits and costs
- the risk involved
- the alternatives

If a firm was considering financial factors only it would select the project with:

- the lowest payback
- the highest average rate of return
- the highest net present value

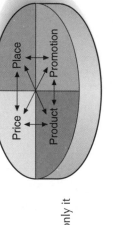

Place — Product — Price — Promotion

Methods of investment appraisal

1. Payback:
This is the length of time it takes for the firm to recoup its initial investment.

2. Average rate of return (ARR):
This is the average profit per year as a percentage of the initial investment.

(average return p.a. ÷ initial cost) × 100

3. Net Present Value:
This method takes account of the 'time value of money'. £1 in a year's time is not as desirable as £1 now; £1 in five year's time is even less desirable – firms would prefer to have the money today. Therefore when firms estimate the expected inflows an investment project will bring in the future, these figures must be discounted (reduced) to calculate what they are worth today, i.e. their present values. Discount factors are used to calculate a discounted cash flow,

e.g. Year Discount factor

1   0.909 – this means the firm thinks that £1 in one year's time is equal to 90.9p now

2   0.826 – this means the firm thinks that £1 in 2 years' time is equal to 82.6p now

Calculation of investment appraisal

EXAMPLE:

Year	£	Discount factors	Calculation	Present value £
0	(200)	1	(200) × 1	(200)
1	50	0.909	50 × 0.909	45.45
2	50	0.826	50 × 0.826	41.3
3	100	0.751	100 × 0.751	75.1
4	160	0.683	160 × 0.683	109.28

1. Payback = 3 years
£50 in year 1 + £50 in year 2 + £100 in year 3 = £200 which covers (pays back) the initial outflow.

2. Average rate of return (ARR) = 20%

Calculation:

total inflows = 50 + 50 + 100 + 160 = £360
initial cost = 200
overall return = net inflows – initial cost
= £360 – £200 = £160

average return per year = overall return ÷ number of years = £160 ÷ 4 = £40 p.a.
average rate of return = (average return per year ÷ initial cost) ×100 = (40 ÷ 200) ×100 = 20%

NOTE: the average rate of return method is also called the accounting rate of return

3. Net Present Value (NPV)
The present value of the future expected inflows = £45.45 + £41.3 + £75.1 + £109.28 = £271.13. This what the firm believes the future earnings of the project are worth in today's terms.
The initial outflow = £200
Net present value = discounted inflows – initial outflow
= £271.13 – £200
= £71.13

In today's terms the project is expected to be worth £71.13 more than it would cost; therefore it is worth investing. The higher the net present value, the more the project is worth compared to its cost.

The discount factor depends on issues such as the interest rate, expected inflation, and risk. If the interest rate is high, firms would rather have the money now than later so future inflows are discounted more than if the interest rate is low. If the project is high risk and the value of money is expected to be much lower in the future, the firm will again discount future expected earnings to a greater extent.

Internal and external costs and benefits

When assessing a project, a firm will usually consider its internal (or 'private') costs and benefits, such as the cost of labour, rent, equipment and the revenue from sales. These are the financial costs and benefits it will pay or receive and which affect its financial accounts. Firms do not usually include the 'external effects' of what they do, e.g. the effect on the environment or the impact on the community. To find the cost or benefit of any action to society as a whole (rather than just to the firm) the external effects should be included.

Social costs = internal costs + external costs
Social benefits = internal benefits + external benefits

Cost benefit analysis

This is an investment appraisal technique which attempts to measure the social costs and benefits of a project, not just the private costs and benefits. It would, for example, try to estimate the 'external cost' of a motorway in terms of the pollution, the noise and damage to wildlife. This method is often used by the Government but it can be difficult to quantify external costs and benefits.

When is investment appraisal used?

Investment appraisal may be used for decisions such as:

- location
- purchasing factories
- purchasing equipment
- marketing campaign

Limitations of investment appraisal

- Only considers quantitative factors. Ignores qualitative factors such as employee and community reaction to any proposal.

- Only as reliable as the data. Because some of the calculations are complicated, it is tempting to think they are correct. In fact the figures are all based on expectations and so cannot be guaranteed.

- Depends on the skill of the user. The usefulness depends on how well managers can use these techniques and interpret the results.

Investment criteria levels

Criteria set by the firm which any new project must meet if it is to be accepted e.g. payback of less than five years and average rate of return of over 20%.

Opportunity cost

The cost of the next best alternative. For example, if a firm invests in a new promotional campaign, then the money and resources used for this could have been used for something else, e.g. new equipment. When considering an investment, a manager should always consider what is being sacrificed, i.e. the opportunity cost.

Internal rate of return (IRR)

This is the discount rate which equates the present value of a project's expected future net inflows with the supply price (i.e. it makes the net present value = 0). When considering an investment project the firm may compare the internal rate of return with the interest rate. If the interest rate is less than the IRR this means the project would have positive net present value and so it is worth investing. If the interest rate is more than the IRR the project would have a negative net present value and so should not be undertaken. (NOTE: this method is not on the AQA specification.)

Discounted cash flow (DCF)

This technique is used for the net present value and internal rate of return methods of investment appraisal. It takes account of the time value of money (e.g. the fact that £1 next year is worth less than money can grow over time) and discounts future expected inflows to work out their present value (i.e. what they are worth in today's terms).

Qualitative factors in an investment decision:

(i.e. non financial) factors might involve:

- employee reaction to any plan
- the environmental impact of any action
- the social consequences of any plan
- the ethics of a plan
- whether the projects fit with the firm's objectives

Human resource management (HRM)

INPUTS ⟶ PEOPLE ADD VALUE ⟶ OUTPUTS

Human resource management (HRM): regards people as an important resource of the organisation which needs to be managed effectively.

People add value to the organisation by:

- increasing productivity
- improving quality
- innovating
- improving customer service

People can differentiate one organisation from another and are an important source of competitive advantage. Human resource management aims to enhance the contribution of individuals and groups towards the organisational objectives now and in the future.

This involves:

- attracting the right numbers of employees with the right skills and attitudes
- developing individuals to meet the challenges of their jobs now and in the future
- providing a safe and healthy environment in which to work
- enabling employees to contribute to the organisation
- developing an environment in which people are used to their full capacity and potential

Human resource management is a 'staff' function (i.e. advisory); it seeks to enable managers to manage their own employees more effectively.

Effectiveness of human resource (people) management
Can be measured by:
- absenteeism rates (likely to be higher if people are badly managed)
- labour turnover (likely to be higher if people are badly managed)
- accident rates (likely to be higher if people are badly managed and do not take proper safety measures)
- productivity (likely to be lower if people are badly managed)
- quality (likely to be lower if people are badly managed and so do not take care over their work)
- customer satisfaction (likely to be lower if people are badly managed, because they then pay less attention to customers)

Human resource management and other functions
The management of people will affect:
- operations, e.g. how much can be produced, by when, at what quality, and at what cost
- marketing, e.g. certain skills may provide a USP, may help develop innovative products, may attract customers, may generate more sales
- finance, e.g. will affect costs and revenues

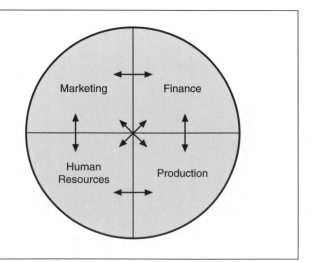

Workforce planning

Planning for future human resource requirements.

Involves an assessment of future expected demands and supply. This may lead to plans regarding training, transfers, redundancies, recruitment or promotion.

Depends on other functions e.g. marketing decisions may affect the number and type of product to be produced; production decisions may affect training requirements and staffing levels.

Workforce planning is affected by:

- objectives of the firm, e.g. expansion or retrenchment
- changes in technology
- changes in working practices
- impact of training
- impact of transfers, retirements, sickness
- population changes, e.g. changes in number of employees in a local area and/or a given age range
- competitors' actions, e.g. how successful are they likely to be at recruiting?
- financial resources

Workforce (human resource) planning

Systematic process of planning human resource requirements for the organisation.

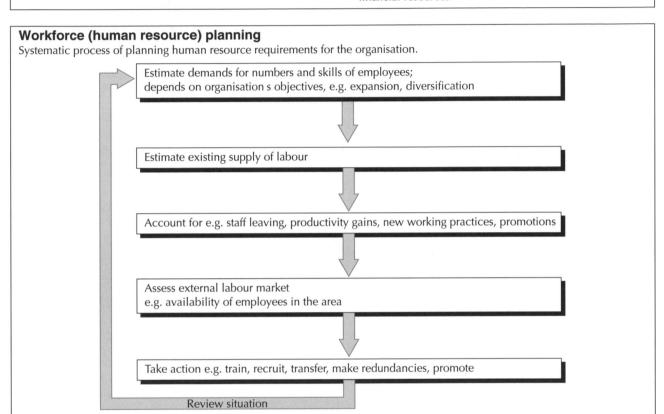

Estimate demands for numbers and skills of employees; depends on organisation s objectives, e.g. expansion, diversification

Estimate existing supply of labour

Account for e.g. staff leaving, productivity gains, new working practices, promotions

Assess external labour market e.g. availability of employees in the area

Take action e.g. train, recruit, transfer, make redundancies, promote

Review situation

Labour turnover

Measures the number of employees leaving a firm in a given period compared to the average number employed, as a percentage.

$$\frac{\text{Number of employees leaving}}{\text{Average number employed}} \times 100 = \%$$

High labour turnover

Possible causes:

- poor working conditions
- low pay/benefits
- bad management style
- more attractive alternative offers, e.g. from competitor

Impact of high labour turnover:

- cost of recruiting new staff
- cost of training new staff
- may be disruptive, e.g. to teams if members keep changing
- may discourage future applicants and may make it more difficult to recruit
- may lose production whilst recruiting

Management structure and organisation

Authority: legitimate power.

Responsibility: obligation to complete a task effectively.

Chain of command: line of command from top to bottom of organisation.

Hierarchy: level of responsibility.

Span of control: number of subordinates directly responsible to a superior.

A narrow span enables managers to keep control and reduces risk.

A wide span develops subordinates and enables them to have greater freedom; allows for fewer levels of management.

Size of span:
depends on ability of subordinates to complete the task, whether the task is simple or complex; the ability of the superior to oversee employees; and the quality of communication.

Narrow span
More likely if:
- the manager wants to keep a tight control
- communication systems not very effective
- employees lack skills/training
- employees want direction e.g. new to the job
- jobs are closely interrelated and need regular meetings/discussion

Wider span
May mean:
- fewer levels of hierarchy needed
- greater delegation

Organisational chart: represents the organisational structure. It shows reporting relationships but does not show the authority of each position.

Formal organisation: deliberately planned authority relationships and communication channels.

Informal organisation: network of relationships and communication established by employees themselves. Not shown on an organisational chart.

Organisational design
Includes:
- deciding how to 'group' jobs
- reporting relationships, i.e. who reports to whom
- the span of control/layers of hierarchy
- the degree of centralisation/decentralisation

Consequences of badly designed organisations
- low motivation and morale
- late and slow decision making
- conflict
- poor coordination
- communication problems
- failure to respond quickly to external change
- high costs

Types of structure
- **Tall, thin organisation**, e.g. the army

This type of structure has a small span of control and many levels of hierarchy.

Number of employees at each level

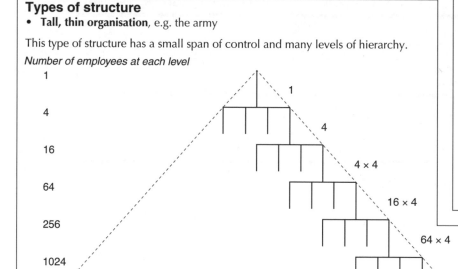

1	
4	1
16	4
64	4 × 4
256	16 × 4
1024	64 × 4
	256 × 4

To oversee 1000 employees with a span of 4, 5 levels of hierarchy are needed.

- **Wide, flat organisation**, e.g. the church. This type of structure has wide spans of control but few layers of hierarchy. There are fewer chances of promotion but employees are likely to have more authority.

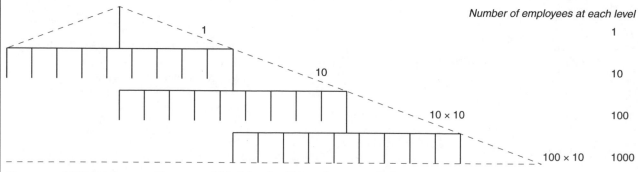

Number of employees at each level

1	1
10	10
10 × 10	100
100 × 10	1000

To oversee 1000 employees with a span of 10, 3 levels of hierarchy are needed.

A recent trend is **delayering** = fewer levels of hierarchy and wider spans; this increases the responsibility of employees and reduces the need for middle management.

Departmentalisation
The grouping of jobs within an organisation

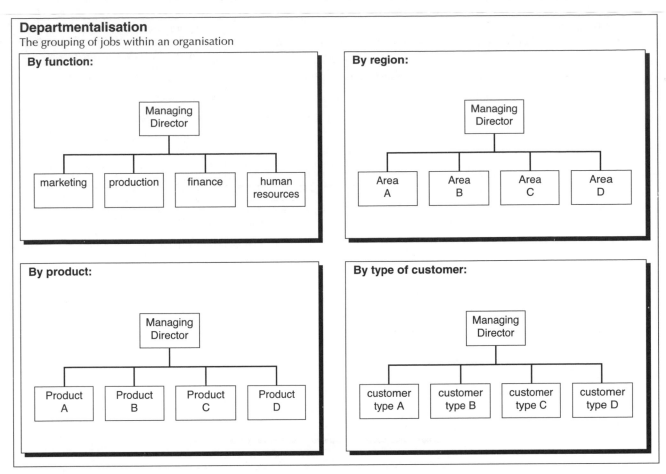

By function:

Managing Director
- marketing
- production
- finance
- human resources

By region:

Managing Director
- Area A
- Area B
- Area C
- Area D

By product:

Managing Director
- Product A
- Product B
- Product C
- Product D

By type of customer:

Managing Director
- customer type A
- customer type B
- customer type C
- customer type D

Matrix structure
This cuts across the usual functional roles. Individuals have two or more superiors, e.g. if a project team is created, the marketing manager involved may be responsible to the project leader and to the marketing director.

	Production Director	Marketing Director	Human Resources Director	Finance Director	Research and Development Director
Product Manager A		●			
Product Manager B					

A sales manager for product A will report to the Marketing Director and the Product Manager.

Functional v matrix management
Functional management: managers are organised according to their function, e.g. all the marketing managers are grouped together, all the finance managers work together and so on. The advantage of this approach is that it keeps specialists working together so they can share their expertise.

Matrix management: brings together employees who can help solve a particular problem, e.g. someone to deal with the marketing, someone to focus on the finance and so on. This brings together people from different functions who can benefit from each other's skills and experiences. The disadvantage is that employees have two bosses (one is the project leader, the other is their functional manager); this can cause communication problems because there can be confusion over who is in charge.

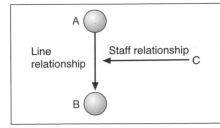

A
Line relationship
Staff relationship
C
B

Line relationship: A to B; direct authority relationship, e.g. production manager to production supervisor.

Staff relationship: C to A; advisory relationship which has no direct authority over the line; an expert or specialist who provides information to the line manager, e.g. market research or human resources function.

'Staff' sometimes get frustrated because they can only advise; 'line' may not pay any attention.

Management structure and organisation continued

Centralisation
Occurs when authority is kept at a senior level in the organisation.
Advantages:

- easier to implement a common policy throughout the organisation

- easier to keep control and coordinate policies

- may lead to cost savings (avoids duplication of resources within business units/division)

- possibly better decision making (by those with overview)

- in times of crisis may be able to act quickly

If the organisational structure is wrong:
- motivation may decrease – people do not know what is happening or why

- decision making can be slow

- lack of coordination

- costs can rise

- failure to share ideas

Decentralisation
Occurs when authority is widely dispersed throughout the organisation.
Advantages:

- decisions made closer to the market and to the customer

- may make the organisation more flexible/more able to respond to customers/markets/local conditions

- develops people for the future, e.g. builds management skills

- may reduce some of the workload of senior management because authority is delegated

BUT
- may lead to conflicting objectives/policies

- individual business managers may feel stressed/may lack necessary skills

The trend in the 1980s and 1990s was to decentralise to provide greater flexibility.

Objectives

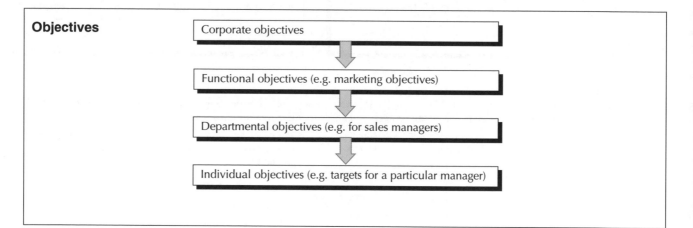

Corporate objectives

Functional objectives (e.g. marketing objectives)

Departmental objectives (e.g. for sales managers)

Individual objectives (e.g. targets for a particular manager)

Management by objectives
A system by which individuals throughout the organisation are set objectives to ensure they are working towards the overall corporate objectives.

Benefits of management by objectives
- Sets targets which can motivate.

- Means of control/review – can assess performance relative to agreed objectives.

- Means of forcing discussion of aims.

Problems of management by objectives
- Employees may focus purely on the agreed targets and not use initiative elsewhere.

- Objectives may become out of date or inappropriate so employees are aiming for the wrong thing.

- May be difficult to agree targets.

- Process of target setting and reviewing can be time consuming and expensive.

- Targets may be imposed on employees rather than agreed.

Recruitment and selection

Hiring a new employee is an investment; it is important to get the right person for the right job. The right person will add value to an organisation; the wrong person can increase costs and reduce quality. Organisations can never be sure that they have selected the right person until he or she starts work, but an effective recruitment and selection process can reduce the risk.

Recruitment and selection process

Job analysis:	process of examining the various elements of a job, e.g. its responsibilities, tasks, duties
Job evaluation:	assessment of the relative worth of a job; undertaken to ensure that the rewards of one job are fair compared to others in the organisation
Job description:	broad statement about a job, e.g. its job title, reporting relationships, duties, tasks
Person specification:	defines the requirements of the job holder, e.g. experience, qualifications, disposition
Attract applicants:	e.g. advertise (internally or externally) contact job/employment centres contact colleges/universities headhunt (i.e. recruit from other companies; also called poaching)
Applicants send:	curriculum vitae or fill in firm's application form or make direct contact
Selecting:	e.g. interview psychometric testing (personality test) aptitude testing (test skills e.g. word processing) intelligence testing medical – check health

Advantages of recruiting

Internally
- know the employee already
- employee knows organisation already
- may be quicker
- may be cheaper
- motivates employees

Externally
- more choice
- can benefit from the experience of employees who have worked for other firms.

Internal recruitment or external recruitment?
Depends on:
- time available
- skills available internally
- impact on morale if recruit externally
- nature of job, e.g. does it need particular skills which are not available internally? Does it need wide range of experience?
- amount of money available
- external labour market

Factors in recruitment
Consider:
- how much time is available before vacancy has to be filled?
- how much money should be/can be spent?
- what is the most effective means of attracting applicants? e.g. unlikely to advertise nationally for a very junior post
- what is the state of the labour market?
- what is an appropriate reward package?

Assessing the effectiveness of the recruitment and selection process
- Ratios, e.g. number of applicants : number manager felt were suitable to be interviewed
- Performance in the job once recruited
- Cost
- Time taken
- Retention rates, i.e. how long do people stay once they have been recruited?

Employment

Offering the job

Employees are entitled to a written contract of employment within 13 weeks of starting work. It includes: job title, rate of pay and method of pay, normal hours of work, holiday arrangements, sick pay and pension arrangements, disciplinary and grievance procedures, and the length of notice due to and from the employee.

Policies and procedures

Grievance procedure: process by which employees can complain about the way in which they are treated.

Discipline procedure: process by which employees are disciplined, e.g. verbal warning, written warning, final written warning and dismissal.

Equal opportunities policy: provides employees with the same opportunities regardless of race or colour or gender, i.e. does not discriminate.

Social Chapter

An attempt by EU countries which are part of it to agree on terms and conditions of employment across states. The agreement covers areas such as:

- hours of work
- health and safety
- equal opportunities
- access to training
- workers' involvement in decision making

Under the Social Chapter workers are guaranteed :

- the right to join a trade union
- the right to take industrial action
- the right to be consulted and informed about company plans
- the right to equal treatment for men and women
- the right to a minimum wage and a maximum week of 48 hours' work

The UK opted into the Social Chapter in 1997.

Training

Induction training: introduces employees to their job and the organisation as a whole, e.g. history, mission, rules.

On the job training: employees learn whilst undertaking the job.

Off the job training: employees trained away from the actual job; may be within firm or at outside college.

Training and Enterprise Councils: government funded organisations which coordinate training in their regions.

The value of training

- Increases employees' skills in their present jobs
- Prepares employees for change
- Increases the organisation's flexibility
- Motivates employees
- Can reduce mistakes and improve profits

Evaluating training

Consider:

- costs
- employee reaction
- impact on performance

Investment in training

Depends on:
- effectiveness of training
- impact on skills and motivation
- alternatives e.g. opportunity costs
- resources available
- need for training, e.g. is there a skills gap?

Market failure

Managers may be unwilling to train staff because they may be recruited by other firms and their investment will be wasted. (When other firms take away your employees this is called 'poaching' – it is an example of market failure.)

Appraisal

Assessing an employee's performance in his or her job. This should be an ongoing process but some organisations also have a formal appraisal process. Used to identify training needs.

Value of appraisals

- Provides opportunity to review progress (good for communication)

- Identifies achievements of individuals (which may be linked to rewards and promotion)

- Identifies training needs

- Potential control mechanism

Depends on:
- how introduced

- how perceived

- how used (e.g. is pay linked to it or not?)

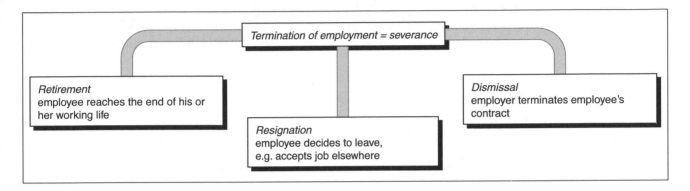

Termination of employment = severance

Retirement
employee reaches the end of his or her working life

Resignation
employee decides to leave, e.g. accepts job elsewhere

Dismissal
employer terminates employee's contract

Unfair dismissal

If employees feel unfairly dismissed they might:
- settle with the employers directly

- complain to an industrial tribunal

Industrial tribunals

An industrial tribunal might order the firm to:
- reinstate the employee in the same job

- re-employ the employee in another job

- pay compensation

Redundancy

An employee is made redundant because of the closure of all or part of the business. An employee who has worked full time for the organisation for more than two years, or part time for five years, is entitled to statutory redundancy pay. (Full time is defined as more than 16 hours per week.) Firms may pay more than the legal requirement.

Outplacement services

These are provided by some firms to help employees find alternative employment. May involve information, advice and the provision of various facilities (e.g. reference books, newspapers, word processors).

Issues with redundancy:

Employers must consider:

- which jobs to cut

- how to select employees

- the amount of notice to be given

- the degree of consultation

- redundancy payment

Voluntary redundancy: occurs when individuals are willing to be made redundant (i.e. they volunteer for it).

Employment continued

Employment patterns

Changes in the UK labour market in recent years include:
- older population
- fewer younger people entering workforce
- more women workers
- more part time workers
- more jobs in the service sector
- more flexible working patterns

Flexible working patterns
Include:
- flexi-time: employees have some freedom over what hours they work
- temporary workers: employees work for a few days or a few weeks at a time
- multi-skilling: employees trained in a variety of tasks. Important aspect of flexible production so employees can cover for each other if anyone is absent. Also means employees can be switched from one part of the process to another to meet changing demand.
- homeworking: working at home, e.g. teleworking – working from home via information technology, e.g. computer
- part time jobs: employees work a few hours each week
- job sharing: two or more people share a job, e.g. one works mornings, another works afternoons.
- removal of job demarcation (demarcation line defines the tasks involved in one job; by removing these employees can undertake more tasks)

Advantages
- Allow firms to increase or decrease their output more easily. This means that firms can match supply to demand more effectively. This is important for Just in Time production.
- Allow individuals to develop work patterns which suit their own lifestyles e.g. part time work whilst raising children.

Importance of flexible workforce
If a firm has a flexible workforce it can adjust its labour input to meet demand. This enables it to adopt a just in time production approach: as demand increases and falls the firm increases and decreases its labour force, e.g. it hires more temporary employees, increases the hours worked, moves employees to areas where there is a shortage from areas where demand is lower.

Problems introducing flexibility
- Employees may want long term, full time contracts
- Employees may not want to learn new skills
- Employees may not want to be moved from one job to another to meet changes in demand
- Flexibility may lead to feelings of insecurity – employees do not know where they will be working (e.g. in which part of the firm) or what they will be doing. Also employees may be upset by the constant change and possible need to keep learning new skills
- The lack of security may make it difficult to plan effectively

Possible benefits to employees of flexibility
- More variety in their work; potentially motivating
- More challenging
- Learn new skills – may create opportunities for the future

Employment type	1985 %	1995 %	2005 (estimated) %
Permanent	84	82	79
Part time	21	24	25
Self employed	11	13	13.5
Temporary	5	6	8

Source: Business Strategies

Communication

Communication networks

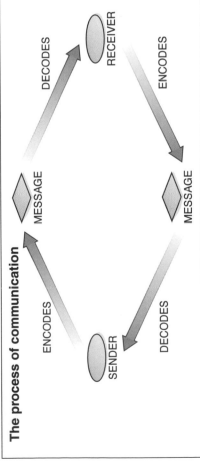

Wheel

'Y'

Circle

Used to examine the effect of information flowing in different ways between people.

Networks such as the wheel and the Y are centralised: information must pass through a central position (labelled A). The circle is decentralised – information passes around. For complex problems decentralised networks tend to produce a quicker solution, fewer mistakes, and a more satisfied group. (In centralised networks A becomes overloaded and members do not all have effective input.)

For simpler problems a centralised structure is usually quicker and makes fewer errors.

Barriers to communication

- Jargon — words or phrases not known to the receiver
- Noise — any form of interference which makes it difficult to receive, e.g. actual noise or use of complicated words
- Emotional state — if the receiver is upset, angry or depressed he or she can misinterpret
- Distrust — if employees do not trust their employer, this affects their interpretation of the message
- Suitability of the channel — e.g. a long list of sales figures might be easier to understand if written down
- Location — e.g. communication is more difficult if parts of the business are on different sites

Results of poor communication

- Low morale
- High level of errors
- Hostile relations
- Slow decision making
- Poor decisions
- Lack of control

The process of communication

ENCODES

MESSAGE

DECODES

RECEIVER

SENDER

DECODES

MESSAGE

ENCODES

Types of communication

Vertical: up and down the organisation; downward is from superiors to subordinates, e.g. giving orders, setting targets; upward is employee to employer, e.g. presenting a report.

Horizontal or lateral: communication across the organisation, e.g. one team member to another.

Verbal: using words (whether they are spoken or written down).

Non verbal: not using words, e.g. body language.

Formal: using the channels of communication established by the organisation.

Informal: using channels established by the employees themselves. Often called the grapevine. Passes information around quickly but information is often distorted.

SENDER

RECEIVER

SENDER

RECEIVER

One way: sender does not receive feedback, e.g. manager puts up notice on noticeboard.

Two way: sender receives feedback, e.g. manager discusses an issue with an employee at a meeting.
Slower than one way communication but sender gains more information.

Communication continued

Communication is important

- To let people know what to do
- To let people know how they are doing
- To coordinate activities
- To gain from employees' experience and benefit from their ideas
- To utilise people's assets
- To be able to identify any possible problems before they develop
- To keep customers informed
- To listen to customers and anticipate changes in the market
- To keep investors informed

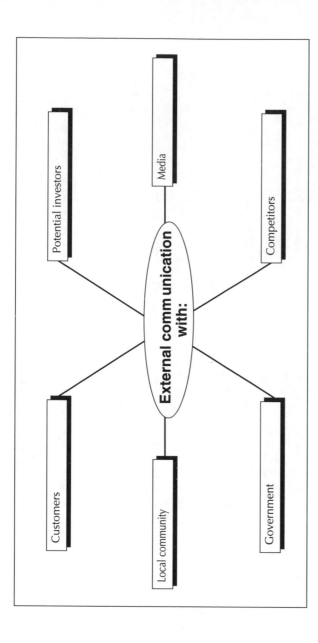

External communication with:

- Customers
- Potential investors
- Media
- Local community
- Competitors
- Government

Problems of communication for larger organisations

- Overload of managers; cannot make effective decisions as they have too much work.
- Too many layers of hierarchy leading to slow decisions, alienation of the workforce and distorted messages.
- Over-reliance on written communication; failure/inability to deal with issues face to face.
- May need to invest in information technology; may need to invest in training (even then more IT may simply lead to more communication, not necessarily good communication).

Improving communications

- More use of information technology as long as staff are trained.
- More decentralisation enabling individuals/departments to make decisions for themselves without always referring to senior management for advice.
- Delayering, i.e. removing levels of hierarchy (may make communication easier between senior and junior staff although morale may be affected adversely, making communication worse).
- Better motivation – makes people more willing to talk to each other

Motivation in theory

Motivation is the extent to which an individual makes an effort to do something. It is when someone wants to do something for him/herself, rather than being made to do it.

Key elements

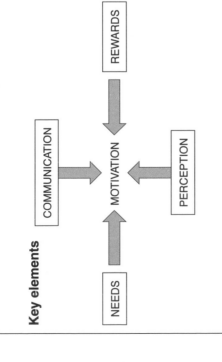

To motivate:

- appropriate rewards must be offered
- individuals must know how to achieve these rewards
- individuals must believe they are capable of achieving the rewards
- individuals must perceive the rewards are fair

Motivated employees are likely:

- to be more productive
- to have better attendance rates
- to be more co-operative and open to change
- to produce better quality work.

Maslow

Maslow's hierarchy of needs:

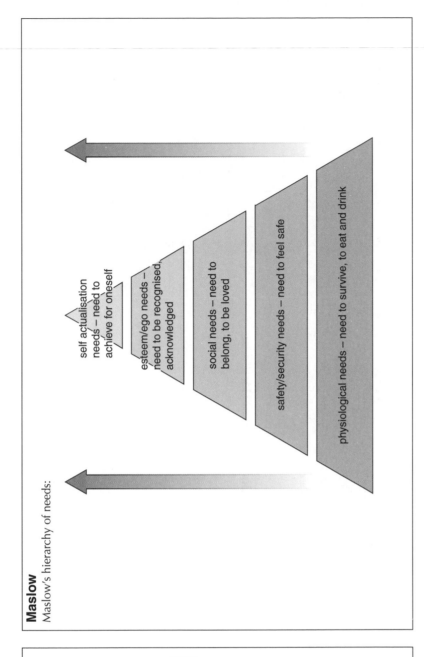

- self actualisation needs – need to achieve for oneself
- esteem/ego needs – need to be recognised, acknowledged
- social needs – need to belong, to be loved
- safety/security needs – need to feel safe
- physiological needs – need to survive, to eat and drink

According to Maslow:

Individuals will be motivated if the reward satisfies an unfulfilled need. Once satisfied a need no longer motivates; individuals will want the next level of need satisfied.

Implications of Maslow's hierarchy

- employees may have different needs, therefore the firm may need to offer a range of rewards
- the reward must be matched to need
- self actualisation needs cannot be completely fulfilled, therefore they are potentially very powerful motivators; firms could consider the intrinsic nature of the job, e.g. job enrichment to continually offer new challenges.

Motivation in theory continued

Herzberg's Two Factor Theory

Hygiene factors: prevent dissatisfaction if they are present but do not actually satisfy, e.g. acceptable working conditions, rules, basic pay

Motivators: factors at work which actually satisfy if they are present, e.g. responsibility, recognition, the chance of promotion

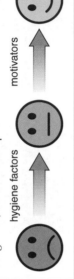

hygiene factors   motivators

Herzberg

A key point about Herzberg's work is that HYGIENE factors prevent dissatisfaction (they do not actually motivate). MOTIVATORS satisfy. i.e. the factors necessary to motivate people are different from the factors which prevent dissatisfaction.

Hygiene factors are generally extrinsic to the job i.e. related to factors outside the job itself

Motivators are related to the job itself. They are intrinsic to the job.

Herzberg highlighted the difference between Motivation and Movement.

Movement occurs when you do something because you have to or are made to.
Motivation occurs when you do something because you want to.

Significance of Herzberg:

Need to ensure 'hygiene' factors are present to prevent dissatisfaction before providing 'motivators' to satisfy. To motivate need to pay attention to job design.

BUT some argue his results are based on relatively small sample of professionals in the US therefore not necessarily applicable elsewhere or for different types of employees.

Vroom's Expectancy theory:

The extent to which individuals believe that they can achieve the rewards offered affects their motivation. If they have a high expectancy (i.e. are confident they can achieve the rewards) motivation is likely to be higher. If their expectancy that a reward can be achieved is low, they will be less motivated.

Equity theory: Rewards must be seen to be fair compared to what others get for their efforts.

Taylor

Scientific Management. Individuals are motivated by money. Show them the best way to do a job so they can increase productivity. Reward them for higher output. This approach meets lower level needs.

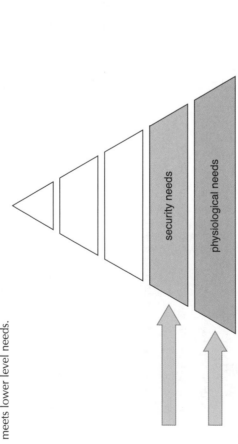

Mayo

Hawthorne Works; Human Relations School. Individuals have social needs. They respond to being involved, working in teams, being listened to. Highlighted importance of informal leaders within groups; the manager may not be the person people listen to!

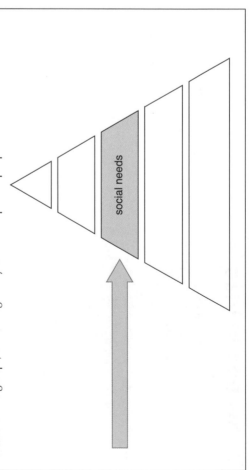

Motivation in practice

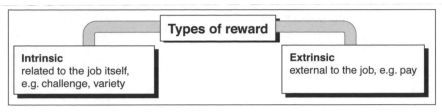

Types of reward

Intrinsic
related to the job itself,
e.g. challenge, variety

Extrinsic
external to the job, e.g. pay

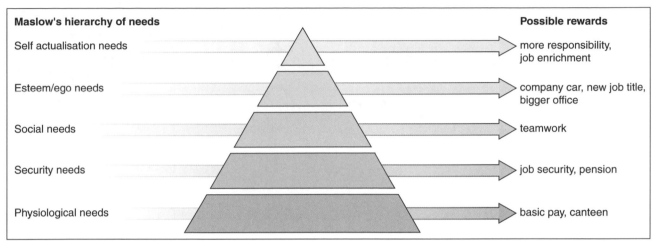

Maslow's hierarchy of needs

Possible rewards

Self actualisation needs → more responsibility, job enrichment

Esteem/ego needs → company car, new job title, bigger office

Social needs → teamwork

Security needs → job security, pension

Physiological needs → basic pay, canteen

Motivating jobs should:

- provide variety

- allow individuals some responsibility

- provide employees with feedback

- provide employees with a complete unit of work, not just a small part of a job

- have a sense of purpose

Motivation and needs
Remember:
- employees' needs are likely to change at different stages of their lives

- individuals are likely to have different needs

Designing motivating jobs

- Job enrichment – employees are offered a more challenging job, with more responsibility. Called 'vertical loading'.

- Job enlargement – employees are offered more tasks to do; similar level of responsibility. Called 'horizontal loading'.

- Job rotation – individuals systematically moved from one job to another; provides variety and gives them a view of other areas of the firm.

- Autonomous work groups – teams set up and allowed to make their own decisions on, e.g. who does what. The team as a whole is held responsible for results.

- Delegation – subordinates entrusted with tasks by superiors. This frees management time and allows employees more responsibility.

- Empowerment – giving employees power over their own work.

Job enrichment
Hackman and Oldman identify three psychological states:
- experienced meaningfulness of work

- experienced responsibility for the outcomes of the work

- knowledge of the actual results of the work activities

These psychological states are created by five core job dimensions:
- skill variety – extent to which a job entails different activities and involves a range of different skills and talents

- task identity – extent to which a job involves the completion of a whole piece of work with a clear outcome

- task significance – extent to which a job has a meaningful impact on other people

- autonomy – the extent to which a job provides freedom, independence and discretion in determining what has to be done, how it has to be done

- feedback – the extent to which the job results in feedback about performance

From this Hackman and Oldham have developed the Motivating Potential Score (MPS) from which it is possible to calculate an overall measure of job enrichment.

Motivating Potential Score (MPS)

$$MPS = \left(\frac{\text{skill variety} + \text{task identity} + \text{task significance}}{3} \right) \times \text{autonomy} \times \text{feedback}$$

Motivation in practice continued

Should managers delegate more?
Depends on:
- ability of subordinates

- willingness of subordinates to accept extra authority and to take responsibility

- willingness of managers to 'let go'; some may fear loss of control

Manager · resources · required standards · deadlines · authority Subordinate

Value of delegation
- develops employees for the future

- can motivate (if employees want the extra authority)

- can make use of specialist skills

- can free up management time to focus on more strategic issues

- can share workload

Depends on:
- what is being delegated (e.g. is it meaningful work or just odd jobs?)

- how it is perceived (is it seen as exploitation or being given a chance to progress?)

- how it is done (e.g. is it forced on employees or discussed and agreed with them?)

- the rewards available

Reward or remuneration systems

Payment systems
- **Time** – pay by the hour, e.g. shop assistants. Relies on individuals using their time productively.

- **Piece work** (employees paid for each unit of output). Should be motivating but quality can suffer as individuals rush to complete work. 'Commission' occurs when individuals are paid a percentage of sales. 'Measured day work' occurs when individuals agree a target output and are paid assuming this work is done. At the end of the period adjustment is made depending on actual output. BUT it can be difficult to measure output in some jobs, e.g. receptionist.

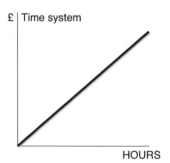

- **Performance related pay** – rewards could be linked to individuals' achievement in terms of agreed criteria, e.g. could be team building, achieving targets, success hitting the budget, quality of work. Often performance is reviewed through appraisals. It enables a wider range of criteria to be used than just output, say. However the measurement of performance may be subjective and open to different opinions.

- **Salary** – set amount per year; paid monthly. Shows that employers trust employees to use their time effectively.

Incentive schemes:
- Profit sharing – individuals receive a proportion of company profits

- Bonus scheme – additional payments if set targets are exceeded

Rates of pay
Pay is likely to be higher if:
- employees are well organised (e.g. strong union power)

- employees are difficult to replace (e.g. highly skilled)

- inflation is high

- there is a labour shortage

- the firm is doing well

Factors in a good reward system
- Cost efficient

- Motivating

- Easy to administer

- Easy to understand

Reward or remuneration systems

resources of the firm

competition's rates

inflation rates

Influences on pay

union/employee bargaining power

Government: in some countries there is a minimum wage; the Government may introduce an incomes policy to control inflation and this limits employees' pay increases.

Value of pay as motivator
- Can meet a variety of needs, e.g. physiological and security
- Firms do not need to identify employees' needs
- May be simple to administer compared to offering a range of different rewards

Fringe benefits
- Company car
- Contributions to pension schemes
- Subsidised canteen
- Contributions to health schemes
- Relocation allowance if an employee is moved from one area to another

Does share ownership motivate?
Depends on:
- how many shares are given to employees
- whether the value of the share is increasing or not
- extent to which employees feel they can influence the share price

Problems of pay as a motivator
- Employees may want other rewards
- Costs money – firm may lack financial resources
- Increases costs – impact on profits
- May have short term effect
- Next time may have to pay even more to have same effect
- May encourage others to demand more pay

Profit sharing
A proportion of the firm's profits are distributed to employees.
Benefits:
- may motivate – employees may feel more closely linked to the business
- employees may gain high rewards if the business does well

BUT
- can be difficult to agree on how to divide profits and how much of profits to pay out
- individuals may see no clear link between their own efforts and the overall profits of the business

Successful reward systems
Successful reward systems will:
- attract and retain sufficient numbers of suitable employees
- reward employees for effort, experience, loyalty and achievement

Motivation and communication

Communication can improve motivation because:
- letting people know what they are supposed to be doing
- letting people know what others are doing
- letting people know how they are doing/how they have done
- involving people in decision making

Communications is important for social and esteem needs.

Motivation can improve communication because:
- motivated people are more willing to discuss issues
- motivated people are more open to new ideas
- motivated people are more interested in discussing work

Leadership

Leadership is the process of influencing others towards a shared goal.

Trait theories

These believe that leadership depends on personal qualities (traits), e.g. a leader is naturally extrovert, charming, single minded. Studies have been unable to identify the same traits in all leaders, so the theory may have limited practical use for firms.

Leaders can affect

- Motivation within the team
- How long a job takes
- The way the job is done
- The quality of the work
- Whether the job gets completed
- The degree of creativity used

The Tannenbaum Schmidt continuum

Highlights the range of management styles available.

- **Tells**   leader presents final decision to subordinates
- **Sells**   leader persuades subordinates why a decision has been made
- **Consults**   leader asks for subordinates' opinions and then decides
- **Participates** leader involves subordinates and decision is made jointly

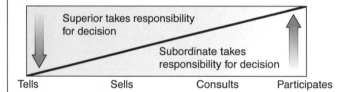

Superior takes responsibility for decision

Subordinate takes responsibility for decision

Tells   Sells   Consults   Participates

Democratic leadership approach

This is most appropriate if:
- employees are skilled and trained
- employees are motivated
- leader is accepted
- there is no immediate time pressure
- the job needs discussion and a variety of inputs e.g. the task is a new one and employees are able to contribute

Style theorists

These believe that effective leadership depends on the way in which people are led, e.g. autocratic or democratic.

- **Autocratic:** leader tells employees (or authoritarian)

- **Democratic:** leader discusses with employees and involves them in decisions

- **Laissez-faire:** leader has little direct input; leaves subordinates to make decisions

- **Paternalistic:** 'fatherly' style of leadership; employees treated as family members; leader tries to guide them; will tend to decide for them ('I know best')

- **Team-based management:** the team is given authority to make decisions. This avoids an 'us' and 'them' situation developing. Often linked to single status, i.e. no differentiated conditions for employees.

Authoritarian style

This is most appropriate when:
- there is a high degree of risk
- the superior likes a high degree of control
- the group respect the leader
- time is short
- the existing approach is not working successfully
- employees lack the necessary information/skills themselves and need direction
- the job itself is not intrinsically motivating
- jobs are repetitive, narrowly defined jobs
- there is an emergency situation
- there is a need to act quickly
- employees do not want responsibility

Blake Mouton's managerial grid

Shows a range of managerial styles

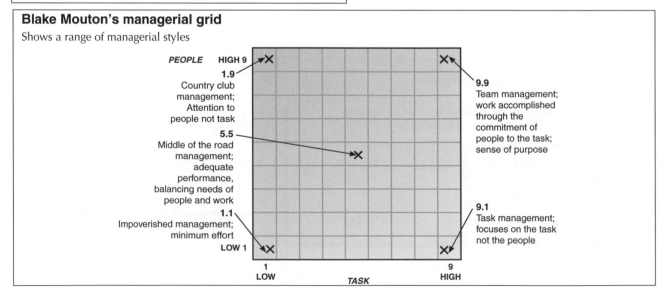

1.9
Country club management; Attention to people not task

9.9
Team management; work accomplished through the commitment of people to the task; sense of purpose

5.5
Middle of the road management; adequate performance, balancing needs of people and work

1.1
Impoverished management; minimum effort

9.1
Task management; focuses on the task not the people

McGregor's Theory X and Theory Y: management theory
Highlights the different assumptions which managers hold about employees.

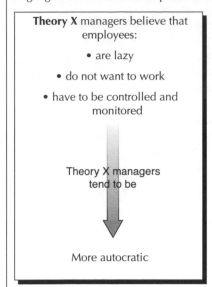

Theory X managers believe that employees:

- are lazy
- do not want to work
- have to be controlled and monitored

Theory X managers tend to be

More autocratic

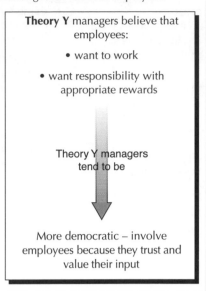

Theory Y managers believe that employees:

- want to work
- want responsibility with appropriate rewards

Theory Y managers tend to be

More democratic – involve employees because they trust and value their input

Likert's model of management:
Again shows management styles

System 1: exploitative authoritative power and direction from the top; threats and punishment used

System 2: benevolent authoritative; some opportunities for consultation

System 3: consultative; subordinates consulted; rewards rather than threats used

System 4: participative; subordinates fully involved in decisions

A Theory X manager believes:
- the average person is lazy and has an inherent dislike of work
- most people must be coerced, controlled, directed and threatened with punishment if the organisation fails to achieve its objectives
- the average person avoids responsibility, prefers to be directed, lacks ambition and values security most of all
- motivation occurs only at the physiological and security levels

A Theory Y manager believes
- for most people work is as natural as play or rest
- people will exercise self-direction and self-control in the service of objectives to which they are committed
- commitment to objectives is a function of rewards with their achievement
- given the right conditions, the average worker can learn to accept and to seek responsibility
- the capacity for creativity in solving organisational problems is distributed widely in the population
- the intellectual potential of the average person is only partially utilised
- motivation occurs at affiliation, esteem and self actualisation levels, as well as the physiological and security levels

Situational approach
This believes that there is no one best way of leading – it depends on the situation and a number of variables.

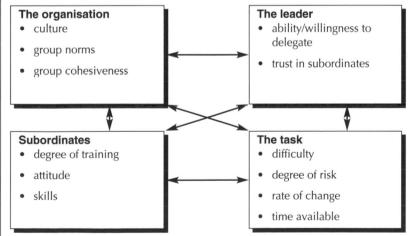

The organisation
- culture
- group norms
- group cohesiveness

The leader
- ability/willingness to delegate
- trust in subordinates

Subordinates
- degree of training
- attitude
- skills

The task
- difficulty
- degree of risk
- rate of change
- time available

For example, if it is a complex task with a high degree of risk, with unwilling and untrained subordinates, and a tight deadline, then an autocratic style is likely to be appropriate. If subordinates are willing and able, the manager is trusting, and the task is routine, a more democratic style might be the most successful.

The 'best' style of leadership/ management
Depends on:
- the attitudes and skills of employees
- employees' training
- the nature of the task
- the degree of risk involved
- the group norms
- the superior's tolerance for ambiguity (i.e. to what extent does he/she need to know exactly what is happening?)
- the time horizon

Employee participation and involvement

Methods of employee participation

- **Worker Directors** – employee representative on the Board of Directors. Occurs in Germany and other continental countries but rare in UK. Often the worker director has little power.

- **Works councils** – employee representatives form a committee. Called a 'Betriebsrat' in Germany. They have a right to influence policies involving employees and appoint a director to the main board. Known as "codetermination" because of employees' right to codetermine (agree and formulate policy on) issues involving people. Some UK companies are setting up works councils, e.g. BT and ICI in line with EU policy (see below).

- **Consultative committees** – employee representatives are consulted on issues such as health and safety or new developments; deal with issues affecting the whole firm.

- **Quality circles** – voluntary group of employees, e.g. 5–12; meet during working hours to discuss problems relating to their work rather than company-wide issues; present ideas to management.

- **Team briefings** – Manager meets with employees regularly to discuss issues relevant to their work. Objective is to make sure employees know and understand what they are doing and why.

European Works Council Directive

Aims "to improve the right to information and to consultation of employees" in large businesses which operate in two or more European countries.

European Works Councils are made up of representatives from each country and management representatives. May discuss issues of common interest such as:

- health and safety

- major changes such as restructuring

- job security

Value of employee participation

- May avoid conflict by raising grievances and sorting out disputes before they become too serious.

- May motivate employees because they feel their ideas are respected and important (e.g. meet employees' ego needs).

- May lead to new ideas (and from those who know their jobs and the problems they face).

- May build a more open culture in which discussion and feedback is encouraged.

- May build a common view of the firm's mission, objectives and strategy.

BUT
- Can slow up decision making

- Can be expensive

- Can be difficult defining and keeping limits of participation e.g. employees may want more of a say

Depends on:
- method of participation

- perception of employees

- commitment of senior management e.g. are decisions actually implemented?

Effective employee participation

May require:
- a democratic management style
- a workforce which is not dissatisfied, e.g. its Hygiene factors are met (Herzborg)
- a reward system that shows trust and encourages participation (e.g. not piece work which makes employees focus on producing more output all the time)
- a management willing to act on workers' ideas (otherwise workers may lose heart)
- appropriate mechanisms for involvement.

Industrial democracy

Occurs when employees are involved in the decision making process either on an individual level (through consultation or delegation) or on a collective level (e.g. through works councils). The degree of democracy depends on the extent to which employees are involved in decisions.

Teams

'A small number of people with complementary skills who are committed to a common purpose, performance goals and an approach for which they hold themselves accountable'
Jon Katzenbach and Doug Smith *The Wisdom of Teams* (1993)

Teamwork

Positives:
- may meet social needs and be motivational
- individuals can benefit from each other's resources (synergy)
- the team can take responsibility for areas such as recruitment, production scheduling and quality. This can develop individuals and remove the need for layers of supervisory management (cutting costs)

Negatives:
- individuals may not work well together; may lack cohesion
- decision making may be less effective (if individuals not able or trained) and may be slower

A good team

- Has a clear understanding of its objectives
- Cooperates
- Shares ideas/generates ideas
- Is motivated to complete the task
- Supports members
- Appreciates each other's role

Team effectiveness

Depends on:

- **group size**

Can be difficult to manage a large team; difficult for everyone to agree; sub groups often form; leader may need to take control.

BUT: large groups potentially have more skills

- **communication within the group**

If communication is centralised (i.e. works through central people) these groups:

- are very effective at making and carrying out clear, predictable, straightforward tasks
- group becomes dependent on those with greatest access to information

BUT:
- levels of satisfaction relatively low compared to decentralised groups

If communication is decentralised:
- group not so dependent on key individuals
- satisfaction usually higher

BUT:
- decision making may be slower

Team (or group) roles

An effective team usually has members playing different roles. According to Belbin, roles within a group include:

- **chairperson:** coordinates efforts of the group; makes sure team makes best use of resources
- **shaper:** sets objectives and priorities and pushes team forward
- **plant:** comes up with new ideas
- **monitor/evaluator:** analyses problems and evaluates progress
- **resource investigator:** extrovert; explores and reports on developments outside the group.
- **company worker:** administrator rather than a leader and good at carrying out plans
- **team worker:** supports the team, helps to keep it together and tries to get members to work together
- **finisher:** maintains momentum and has important role in getting the task finished

Effective teams

Have:
- enough members to have the right skills but not too many to make the team difficult to manage
- positive atmosphere
- clear objectives
- effective, focused discussion
- consensus decision making

Stages of team development

- **forming:** individuals come together; exchange ideas and information; explore each other's roles and what behaviour is accepted
- **storming:** group begins to exchange ideas as they try to reach agreement on objectives and strategy; often conflict and disagreement at this stage
- **norming:** group begins to share ideas; group cohesion develops and members start to work together
- **performing:** group focuses on the task; a way of working is established; members contribute to the task

(Tuckman and Jensen)

Groups/teams

Can:
- be costly
- be time consuming
- gain members' acceptance of a decision; i.e. bring about commitment

BUT
- can pool resources
- bring together complementary skills
- working together, the group can bounce ideas off each other and provoke further thoughts

Groupthink

Group norms: this is the behaviour the group members decide is acceptable, e.g. the work rate, the emphasis on quality, the attitude to days off sick. Anyone deviating from the group norm will face peer pressure to change.

According to Janis, groups can work ineffectively and make poor decisions due to:

- sense of invulnerability; leads to excessive optimism and risk taking
- members forced to conform to group norms

Risky shift

People making decisions in groups can make riskier decisions than they would if asked to make the decision individually. Shown in test with juries which gave tougher penalties than they would individually.

Formal groups: established by the business to carry out specific tasks, e.g. management teams. They are part of the organisation with arranged meetings and a defined role.
Informal groups: established by employees themselves; they are not a formal part of the business. They do not have formal meetings or a defined role within the organisation. Examples of informal groups could be a group of friends or people who meet in the canteen at lunchtime for a chat.

Why are firms making more use of teams?

- Can see benefits, e.g. greater creativity, higher levels of motivation.
- To meet expectations of staff to be more involved (e.g. team-based management).

Trade unions

Represent, protect, inform, and provide services for employees on a factory, local, and national level. Employees cannot be prevented from joining a union.

Types of unions
- Craft – for employees with a particular skill, e.g. electricians AEEU
- Industry – for employees in particular industry, e.g. coalminers NUM
- General – broad union for wide range of employees usually unskilled or semi-skilled, e.g. TGWU
- White collar – for clerical, professional or managerial staff, e.g. NUT (teachers)
- Staff associations for employees in a particular organisation, e.g. Marks and Spencer

Union recognition
Occurs when an employer agrees to discuss human resource issues with a union over e.g. wages. Employers have to recognise unions which represent a majority of the workforce.

Industrial relations
Also called employer:employee relations. The state of the relationship between employer, unions and employees.

Benefits of unions

To employers
- channel of communication
- can highlight human resource implications of any action
- provide ideas/information

To employees
- provide power
- provide advice
- provide services, e.g. legal advice if dismissed
- provide protection

Employees' views of what a trade union should try to do:

	%
protect existing jobs	37
improve working conditions	20
improve pay	15
have more say over management's long term plans	14
have more say over how work is done day to day	5
reduce pay differences at the workplace	4
work for equal opportunities for women	2

Source: British Attitudes Survey, Social and Community Planning Research

Consultation with unions
Managers ask union representatives for their opinions; managers make final decision.

Bargaining with unions
Managers negotiate with unions; final decision depends on negotiation.

Collective bargaining
Union representative negotiates on behalf of a group of employees. Employees have more power as they are bargaining as a group rather than individually.

Forms of industrial action
- Overtime ban – can make it difficult for a firm to meet its orders
- Sit in – employees occupy premises
- Go slow – employees work at a slow rate
- Work to rule – employees stick to their contracts absolutely; this often slows up their work considerably.
- Strikes – employees refuse to work. To be official employees must have a secret ballot and gain a majority.

Determinants of union strength
- The percentage of employees who are members (called the 'unionisation rate' or 'union density')
- The degree of public support
- Management attitude
- Legal environment
- The ability of management to find alternative labour
- Union and management resources

Recent developments in employer:employee relations

- **No strike agreements** – trade unions agree not to strike in the case of a dispute; usually agree that if they cannot reach a solution the dispute will go to arbitration. Arbitration occurs when a third party decides how to settle the dispute.

- **Single union deals** – management only recognise one union for the purpose of bargaining.

- **Beauty contests** – competition between trade unions to gain recognition by an employer, e.g. firm announces it will only bargain with one union so unions must compete for that right.

- **Pendulum arbitration** – a third party solves a dispute by choosing one side or the other; cannot compromise between the two sides; the idea is that this makes the two sides make more realistic claims in the first place.

Single union

One union represents all employees within the firm who want to be union members (rather than having several unions within the firm).

This can:

- speed up the negotiation process

- give employees more power as they have a more unified voice

- be part of an overall deal, e.g. single union in return for job security

- reduce conflict (e.g. between unions)

ACAS: Advisory Conciliation and Arbitration Service. Independent body set up by the Government in the 1970s. Provides advice to employers and employees on industrial relations. If asked it will attempt to bring the two sides in a dispute together (conciliate). If this does not work, ACAS (if asked by both sides) will solve the dispute by making the decision itself (arbitration).

CBI: Confederation of British Industry. Represents firms in private sector; attempts to influence public opinion and the government; attempts to promote image of industry; provides information on industry for members.

Organisations concerned with employer : employee relations

TUC: Trades Union Congress. Represents most unions at national and international level; attempts to influence public opinion and Government.

Employers' associations: represent employers' views and interests in a particular industry, e.g. EEF (Engineering Employers' Federation).

Employment law

Discrimination

Under the Sex Discrimination Act 1976 and Race Relations Act 1976 it is unlawful to discriminate on the basis on sex, marital status, race, colour or ethnic origin.

- **Direct discrimination** – relates to how people are treated e.g. not interviewing applicants because of their gender, paying people less because of their marital status or ethnic origin.

- **Indirect discrimination** – relates to terms or conditions which certain groups are less likely to fulfil than others e.g. insisting applicants must not have a beard or having a dress code which would have an adverse effect on some groups.

Genuine occupational qualifications

Situations where it is possible to discriminate include:

- roles in a play which require specific gender or ethnic group

- serving in a restaurant where people of a particular racial group are required for authenticity (e.g. a Chinese restaurant)

- because of decency or privacy (e.g. working as a toilet attendant)

Need to be aware of possible discrimination in all areas of human resource management including:
- job description

- person specification

- interviews

- selection

- selecting for training

- promotion

Commission for Racial Equality and Equal Opportunities Commission have developed Codes of Practice to monitor and promote equal opportunities.

Positive action: in the UK firms cannot positively discriminate, e.g. discriminate in favour of women at work; they can however take steps to encourage certain groups to apply for positions and take advantages of opportunities open to them.

Equal Pay Act 1970: right of men and women to receive equal treatment when it comes to terms and conditions of employment when engaged in the same or broadly similar work or work of equal value.

Code of Practice for Age Diversity in Employment 1998: aims to protect older workers against discrimination on the basis of their age. **Note:** this is a voluntary code, not a legal requirement.

Disability

Disabled Persons (Employment) Act 1944 and 1958: firms of more than 20 people must employ a quota of disabled people (at present 3%). Not an offence to be below this but employer has duty to engage suitable disabled people if anyone is available.

Disability Discrimination Act 1995

An employer with 15 or more employees must not discriminate against current or prospective employees with disabilities. Cannot justify less favourable treatment if by making a 'reasonable adjustment' it would remove the reason for that treatment.

2000: government launched the **Disability Rights Commission** empowered to undertake formal investigations and to bring cases of alleged discrimination against employers who have breached the Act. Also acts as an advice and information service.

Equal opportunities policy

An Equal Opportunities policy means employees are treated equally regardless of e.g. gender, marital status or ethnic origin in areas such as recruitment, payment and promotion
Equal opportunities could involve:
- Equal chance, i.e. when applying for a job everyone has the same opportunities and is considered equally.

- Equal access, i.e. everyone has the same access to training, promotion and staff development.

Benefits of an equal opportunities policy

May include:

- acting legally

- more people to choose from – can recruit better quality staff

- more motivated staff

- positive corporate image

Minimum wage

Introduced in the UK in 1998 (National Minimum Wage Act)
Possible benefits:
- 'fair' reward for employees

- may motivate staff

- may attract more employees

BUT
- may increase costs (leading to higher prices)

Rehabilitation of Offenders Act 1974: designed to wipe clean the record of offences; people who have had a police record for certain offences do not have to declare these after a certain period of time.

Working Time Directive (1995)

Includes provisions that:

- there is a minimum daily rest period of 11 consecutive hours

- at least 1 day off a week

- mandatory daily rest breaks after 6 hours

Health and Safety at Work Act 1974

The act covers many areas including:

- the provision of safety equipment and clothing

- providing hygienic conditions

- providing breaks

- providing protection for the use of hazardous substances

The Health and Safety at Work Act includes provisions that:

- adequate toilet and washing facilities must be provided

- the inside of buildings must be properly heated and ventilated

- suitable lighting must be provided wherever people work or walk

- floors must not have slippery surfaces

- fire doors must not be locked or obstructed

Employers must take reasonable steps to protect employees as well as visitors and customers to the premises.

If a firm fails to take appropriate action it may be taken to court and fined. Alternatively it may be instructed to change its behaviour.

The Act is enforced by the Health and Safety Executive.

Why is a healthy and safe environment important?

- To be legal (and therefore avoid being sued).

- To protect the workforce and therefore reduce illness and time off work.

- To prevent employees leaving (and therefore the costs of recruiting others).

- Because of social responsibilities.

- A good working environment may increase productivity.

Data Protection Act, 1984

To 'regulate the use of automatically processed information relating to an individual'.

All users of personal data must register with the Registrar. Law states that e.g. data should be adequate, relevant and not excessive; individuals are entitled to reasonable access; data should be accurate and up to date.

Employment laws and unions

Major changes affecting unions include: 1980, 1982, 1988, 1989, 1990 Employment Acts, 1984 Trade Union Act, Trade Union Reform and Employment Rights Act 1993.

The effects of changes in the laws in the 1980s and 1990s include:

- a union must hold a secret ballot before it can have an official strike

- a union is liable for damages if a strike is unofficial

- a code of practice recommends a maximum of 6 official pickets (employees who protest outside a factory to persuade others not to go to work)

- secondary picketing is illegal (i.e. workers can only protest at the place of work where the original dispute occurred; cannot try to influence employees at other places, e.g. suppliers or distributors)

- senior union officials must be elected at least every five years

- unions must provide at least seven days notice of official industrial action

Union membership has declined since the late 1970s. A major reason is the growth of employment in sectors where unions are not traditionally very strong, e.g. part timers, the service sector, in the south east, and women workers.

Union recognition

Under laws introduced in 2000 a union can now have statutory recognition if it can provide clear evidence that it has the support of employees in the relevant bargaining unit.

This can happen in two ways:

- a union has more than 50% of the bargaining unit already in membership

- in a specific ballot of relevant workers the union wins the support of the majority of those actually voting and at least 40% of those entitled to vote.

Once recognition is granted, managers must consult unions over issues such as pay and holidays.

NOTE: these regulations do not cover companies or 'bargaining units' of 20 or fewer employees (this amounts to 90% of all UK enterprises).

Employment law continued

Employment rights
Redundancy Payments Act 1965
Employees who have worked continuously for an organisation for a given period (currently 1 year full time) are entitled to notice and statutory redundancy pay (approximately 1 week for every year worked).

In the case of redundancy employees are entitled to:
- pay (based on how many years they have worked for the business)
- notice
- time off work to attend interviews for a new job

Dismissal
Fair dismissal: termination of an individual's employment contract for a fair reason according to the law.

Fair reasons include:
- illegality, e.g. employee lied about qualifications
- incapability – employee is incapable of doing the work
- job no longer exists (redundancy)
- any other substantial reason, e.g. physical assault

Unfair dismissal: the reason for the termination of employment is regarded as unfair in law, e.g. a firm cannot dismiss someone for being a member of a union or for being pregnant.

Constructive dismissal: the organisation creates a situation in which the employee feels he or she has to resign, e.g. because of harassment.

Summary dismissal: employee dismissed on the spot without a further warning. Only occurs when there has been a severe breach of the organisation's rules (called 'gross misconduct').

Industrial tribunals
If employees feel they have been unfairly dismissed or discriminated against, they can appeal to an **industrial tribunal**; this is an industrial court which judges whether or not the employer behaved fairly.

Results of an industrial tribunal may be:
- case fails
- employee is reinstated in the same job
- employee is re-employed but in a different job
- employee is compensated

Recent employment laws
These include:
- 48 hour limit to the number of hours an employee can be forced to work in one week
- right of parents to parental leave
- right to trade union recognition
- greater rights for time off work
- right for employees in firms operating in two or more EU countries to be represented on works councils

Impact of employment legislation on firms
- May increase costs, e.g. minimum wage.
- May affect the way production is scheduled/organised.

BUT
- May make employees feel more secure (e.g. provide hygiene factors (Herzberg)).
- May improve employees' welfare and motivation.

Depends on:
- how the firm was behaving before
- what the law says
- the impact of the law on other firms, e.g. in other countries

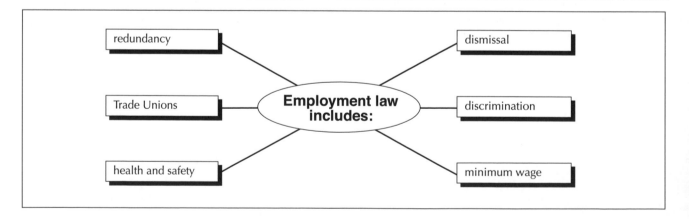

Operations management

Types of production
- *Primary:* extractive industries, e.g. coal mining
- *Secondary:* manufacturing sector, e.g. car makers
- *Tertiary:* services, e.g. travel agents

The UK has a small primary sector and has a growing tertiary sector.

Operations management objectives
Operations management may set objectives including:
- reduce unit cost given set quality criteria
- meet quality targets
- meet output targets
- provide appropriate range of products

Productive efficiency
refers to the efficiency of the process of transforming inputs into outputs.
It depends on:
- the nature of the process, e.g. job, batch, flow
- the existence of economies of scale
- capacity utilisation
- investment in R & D

The more efficient the process, the lower the cost per unit (given a particular quality standard). The firm may be able to lower the price or may keep the price and benefit from higher profit margins.

Research and development (R & D)
Involves activities to improve either the product or the way it is made. To be competitive firms need to research into new ideas and develop these ideas into products. R & D may be undertaken by firms themselves or bought in from e.g. universities. R & D represents an investment for the long term. It is a vital source of new ideas, innovation and competitive advantage. UK firms are often criticised for not undertaking enough research and development.
Remember: R & D is not the same as market research. Market research identifies customer needs. R & D focuses on X using scientific methods to improve the product/and or the process.

Innovation
The successful exploitation of new ideas; getting new ideas to the market and into production. Research and development without innovation means ideas are wasted and not turned into actual products and services.

Budgeting for research and development
- Can be difficult as results often not linked to spending; more spending does not guarantee better results
- Long term and so sometimes resisted, e.g. people want short term results and are not prepared to invest for the long term

Value of research and development
R & D may:
- improve production processes
- improve quality
- reduce costs
- improve the product and offer better value to consumers
- provide USP
- provide competitive advantage
- create new markets
- lead to faster development times/lower lead times

Should a firm spend more on research and development?
Depends on:
- resources
- desire for long term *v* short term success
- rate of innovation in the market
- its strategy e.g. to be the market innovator or a 'me too' producer

Value analysis
Each aspect of a product is examined to see if costs could be reduced without affecting the value placed on the final good by the consumer.

Production process and international competitiveness
The choice of process will affect a firm's competitiveness abroad by influencing :
- its unit costs
- its lead time
- its quality
- its ability to meet demand

Operations management continued

Methods of production
- **Job** one off or project production, e.g. building a dam or a ship

- **Batch** items are produced in 'batches', i.e. they all undergo one operation before being moved on to the next operation, e.g. baking bread. Often involves high stock levels as items wait to be transferred from one stage of the process to the next; needs careful planning to organise scheduling and routing of the products; some flexibility – machines can be adjusted to produce different versions. However, down time (as machines are switched over) can be expensive.

- **Flow** continuous production process; each unit moves from one operation on to the next without waiting for a batch to be completed. Requires heavy initial investment and a constant, high level of demand to justify the investment

- **Mass** large scale production

Job, batch, flow
Job production is more flexible to customer needs but tends to have a high cost per unit. Flow production has much higher productivity and lower unit costs because of the high volumes but is less flexible.

Flow production produces standardised products.

Factors to consider before adopting flow production:
- What is the size of the market?

- To what extent do customers want variety?

- What investment is required?

- How will employees react?

- What is the expected rate of return?

- What is the impact on costs and quality?

Choosing the 'right' production method
Consider:

- expected sales

- desired degree of variety/flexibility, e.g. job is very flexible

- marketing strategy, e.g. niche v mass, job suits niche

- the nature of the product, e.g. standardised or unique, flow produces standardised product

- costs of setting up and operating, e.g. flow requires heavy investment

Capacity
The amount the firm can produce

- **Capacity utilisation:**
the percentage of productive capacity which is being used, e.g. a capacity utilisation of 50% means half of its productive capacity is being used.

- **Overcapacity:**
the maximum capacity of producers is greater than the demand; often leads to price cutting and a very competitive market.

Impact of operating under full capacity
- Likely to mean higher unit costs as fixed costs cannot be spread over so many units. This may lead to lower profit margins or the firm may have to increase prices which may reduce sales further.

Reactions to being under capacity
- May sell off assets and reduce capacity if the belief is that demand will not increase again.

- May try to boost demand, e.g. promotional campaigns.

- May try to subcontract, i.e. produce for other firms.

Capital intensive production
Involves a high level of capital equipment compared to the labour input.

Factors to consider before becoming more capital intensive include:
- cost of finance

- availability of finance

- impact on output levels and quality

- demand levels

- impact on employees – will redundancies occur? Have employees been consulted?

Labour intensive production: high level of labour input compared to capital, e.g. retailing

Work study (Taylor's approach to job design)
Examination of work to improve methods and establish suitable standards to assess performance.

Involves:
- **Method study** – systematic process of recording and analysing existing and proposed methods of doing work to develop more effective and easier methods.

- **Work measurement** – techniques to establish the time for a qualified worker to carry out a job at a given level of performance.

Subcontracting
Using other producers to meet an order. Why? To make use of specialist skills; because a firm is at full capacity and cannot meet the order; because it may be cheaper. Consider: the subcontractors' reliability, price and quality.

Idle time
Occurs when the production process is not operational, e.g. broken down or waiting for materials to arrive or machines being retooled (reset) to produce a new product. Also called 'down time'.

Operations management and technology

Modern production techniques

- **Cell production:** small number of closely co-operating machines; equipment and people are grouped to produce parts which are then moved to the next cell. This makes each cell focus on quality and feel responsible as a team for its output. This can motivate individuals, give them a clearer link with their output (because each cell produces a complete section of the finished product) and a sense of empowerment.

- **Lean production:** waste-saving measures such as Just in Time production and shorter product development times (see page 103). Aim: to save time, money, materials and people.

- **Kaizen:** (continuous improvement); an approach which stresses that improvement can come from small and gradual developments; seeks to establish a continuous process of improvement through discussion and review

- **Time as a competitive advantage:** firms can gain a competitive edge by developing products more quickly (shorter product development times) and delivering more quickly.

Just in time production (JIT): firms produce 'just in time' when goods or service are ordered. They do not hold stocks.

Advantages	Disadvantages	Why might JIT not be adopted?
- Minimises stock holding costs - Money not tied up - Focuses effort on quality as finished goods sent to customer immediately, not left in stock	- May not be able to meet sudden increase in demand - Very reliant on suppliers and employees - May lose bulk-buying discounts - Vulnerable to breakdowns	- Costs of changing systems/equipment - Cost of training - Inability to find suitable suppliers - Loss of bulk order discounts - Very seasonal demand and need to stock up, e.g. fireworks for 5 November - fear! (of what happens if it goes wrong)

Choosing suppliers

The choice depends on the quality, the reliability, when they can deliver and the price. In the past firms tended to use many suppliers and switch from one to the other depending on which one offered the lowest price. Firms tended to 'bully' suppliers to get the price down. The modern approach is to use fewer suppliers and build long term, co-operative relationships with them.

Automation: use of machines to replace employees; leads to transfers or redundancies. Can lead to higher productivity and lower unit costs.

When investing in new technology consider:
- initial costs
- running costs
- depreciation
- impact on quality, reliability, flexibility and volume
- reaction of workforce

CAM: (computer aided manufacture) use of computers to support the manufacturing process. Affects speed, quality and costs.

CNC: computer numerically controlled machines, e.g. for cutting and shaping metal. Can be more reliable than human operatives; can improve quality and reduce wastage.

Operations technology

CAD: (computer aided design) use of computers to assist in the production of designs and drawings and data for use in the manufacturing process. Increases flexibility and speed.

Computer integrated manufacture: (CIM) use of information technology to integrate various elements of manufacturing process, e.g. design and production (CAD and CAM).

Manufacturing resource planning: (MRP II) computerised planning system for production. Turns sales forecasts into purchasing requirements for materials, components, and production scheduling. Used to order supplies.

Location

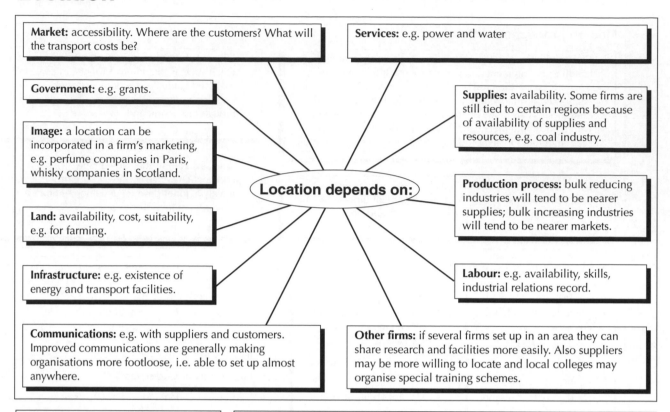

Market: accessibility. Where are the customers? What will the transport costs be?

Government: e.g. grants.

Image: a location can be incorporated in a firm's marketing, e.g. perfume companies in Paris, whisky companies in Scotland.

Land: availability, cost, suitability, e.g. for farming.

Infrastructure: e.g. existence of energy and transport facilities.

Communications: e.g. with suppliers and customers. Improved communications are generally making organisations more footloose, i.e. able to set up almost anywhere.

Location depends on:

Services: e.g. power and water

Supplies: availability. Some firms are still tied to certain regions because of availability of supplies and resources, e.g. coal industry.

Production process: bulk reducing industries will tend to be nearer supplies; bulk increasing industries will tend to be nearer markets.

Labour: e.g. availability, skills, industrial relations record.

Other firms: if several firms set up in an area they can share research and facilities more easily. Also suppliers may be more willing to locate and local colleges may organise special training schemes.

Types of location decision
- Where to set up initially
- Opening up a new facility
- Relocating

Locational inertia: firms stay in an area even if the original reason for locating there has gone.

Greenfield site: location which has no previous experience of a given type of industry.

Relocation: moving to a different site.

Government assistance
Regional assistance is available in Assisted Areas and Intermediate Areas which are regions of severe economic decline.

Regional Selective Assistance (RSA) – discretionary grant towards capital and training costs. The scheme is to help with investment costs of projects with capital expenditure above £500,000. The grant is likely to depend on:
- whether the scheme creates and safeguards jobs
- whether it attracts and retains internationally mobile investment
- whether it contributes to improving the competitiveness of disadvantaged areas

Enterprise Grants (EG) – cover areas with local labour market weakness, Rural Development Areas and ex-coalfield areas; companies investing up to £500,000 can apply for a grant of up to 15% of fixed capital costs of a project (up to a maximum sum)

Enterprise Zones – inner city areas; financial incentives offered to firms to locate here, e.g. subsidised premises.

Local Authority help – advice and grants for firms.

Department of Trade and Industry – has an Investment in Britain Bureau to attract inward investment by overseas firms.

European Union – also offers help for depressed areas via the European Regional Development Fund (money for infrastructure e.g. roads) and the European Social Fund (money for training).

Factors influencing location

Location is an investment decision. Therefore a firm should consider quantitative factors such as the:
- break even level of output

- average rate of return

- net present value

On financial grounds firms should choose the location with:
- the lowest break even

- the highest averate rate of return

- the highest net present value

In reality qualitative factors (e.g. personal preferences) are often important.

Qualitative factors include:
- links with the local area or community

- quality of life

- the nature of the environment, e.g. scenery

- safety issues

- political stability

Why does location matter?

- Can affect demand, e.g. prestige of particular locations

- Can affect ease/costs of recruitment, e.g. if based near particular area of skills (Microsoft and Cambridge)

- Can ease transport costs and accessibility (e.g. M4 corridor)

- Can ease access to suppliers and support services (e.g. Silicon Valley)

- Can provide access to scarce resources (e.g. oil)

Multinational location decisions

A multinational has production bases in several countries to:
- exploit natural resources in different countries

- benefit from government aid and support

- spread production to reduce impact of stoppages or industrial action in one area

- overcome protectionist measures (e.g. locate within EU to benefit from free trade)

- be close to individual markets

Advantages of operating in several countries

- Can locate close to different markets; this can cut the transport costs

- May avoid import quotas and tariffs

- May benefit from lower labour costs

- May be closer to raw materials

- May benefit from government incentives e.g. grants/subsidies/lower taxes

Should the government spend more on regional policy?

Depends on:
- alternatives, e.g. would it be better to try and stimulate the economy as a whole?

- funding – Where will money come from? Impact of e.g. higher taxes

- policy goals, e.g. how important is it to invest in particular regions compared to other priorities?

Stocks

Types of stocks include raw materials, works in progress and finished goods. Stocks appear as current assets on the balance sheet.

The aim of stock control is to hold sufficient quantities and quality of stock to enable production and sales to continue whilst minimising costs.

Number of stocks

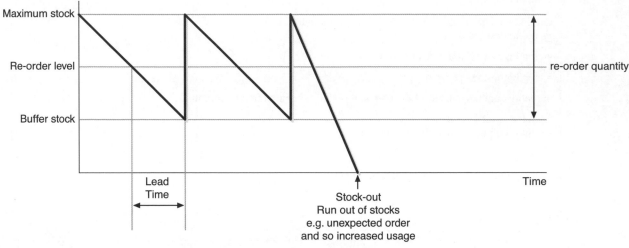

Re-order level: level of stocks at which new supplies are ordered

Re-order quantity: amount reordered

Buffer stock: safety stock in case of sudden increases in demand or supply failure

Lead time: time taken from ordering supplies to supplies arriving

Depends on:

- number and quality of suppliers

- nature of product (e.g how complex to produce)

Stock out
The firm runs out of stock e.g. due to unexpected increase in demand, failure of suppliers to deliver or failure to re-order stocks.

Just in Time production
A firm aims to minimise its stock levels. It produces to order and orders stocks only when they are needed. The aim is to reduce stockholding costs.

Just in Case production
Occurs when firms hold safety stock just in case anything goes wrong, e.g. unexpected increase in demand, failure or breakdown in the production process, supplier failure. This is expensive because of stockholding costs but it reduces the risk of not being able to produce or sell.

Kanban
A 'pull' system of stock control. Parts or components are ordered and pulled through the production process only when needed. This is different from the traditional approach where stocks are made in advance, ready for production.

Cost of holding stocks
- Warehousing costs

- Insurance and security costs

- Stocks may depreciate

- Opportunity costs – stocks tie up money which could be used elsewhere

- Theft (and therefore the cost of replacement)

Level of stocks held
Depends on:
- the nature of the product, e.g. is the good perishable?

- suppliers, e.g. how often do they deliver? How reliable are they?

- the facilities available, e.g. warehouse space

- stockholding costs, e.g. insurance and security

- management policies, e.g. just in time production reduces stock levels.

Too little stock can mean:
- production may not be possible – may lead to down time and idle labour

- may not be able to meet orders – lose customer loyalty; dissatisfied customers may tell others

Why hold more stocks?
- Because expect higher levels of demand.

- To benefit from discounts from bulk buying.

- Because the firm expects the price of inputs to increase in the future and wants to benefit from stockpiling.

- Because lead times are likely to increase.

- Because the firm now doubts reliability of suppliers to deliver on time.

Quality

Benchmarking
Used by some organisations to discover best practices in other firms and measure own performance against these; it involves learning how to improve from others. See page 104.

Traditional and modern views of quality
Traditional quality control involved inspection at the end of the production line. When a good or service was produced, it would be inspected to find the faults. Nowadays the aim is to prevent faults occurring in the first place, i.e. the emphasis is on prevention rather than inspection, e.g. preventative maintenance to prevent faults occurring rather than fixing them once they have already happened.

Quality assurance
Implementing quality systems to ensure that quality standards will be met to ensure customer satisfaction. Involves checking that standards are met within the firm. Quality assurance emphasises preventing defects whereas quality control focuses on detecting faults once they have occurred. Quality assurance seeks to build quality into the system.

Deming
Major writer on quality. Deming had a list of 14 key points to improve quality, including:

- Create a constancy of purpose towards improvement of product and service.
- Find problems. Constantly improve.
- Cease dependence on inspection. Seek evidence that quality is built in.

Deming cycle of quality (PDCA)
- Plan – plan what needs to be improved and how to improve it
- Do – do it, put new plan into action
- Check – monitor the results
- Act – take action to bring results under control; when the results are under control, plan the next stage of improvement

Total Quality Management (TQM):
Systematic method of ensuring all activities happen in the way they have been planned and meet customer requirements.

Main points:
- quality is the responsibility of every employee, not just the quality control department
- every employee is empowered to take action if quality is not acceptable
- employees should regard all people they work for and deal with as customers
- the target is zero defects
- all procedures must be monitored to ensure they meet the set standards
- employees should work in teams to share skills and ideas

BUT

TQM involves training costs and requires total commitment from management.

Crosby's absolutes
- The definition of quality is CONFORMANCE TO REQUIREMENTS (i.e. meet customer requirements).
- The system of quality is PREVENTION (i.e. stop mistakes happening).
- The performance standard is ZERO DEFECTS (i.e. no errors allowed).
- The measurement of quality is the PRICE OF NON CONFORMANCE (i.e. consider the cost of getting it wrong).

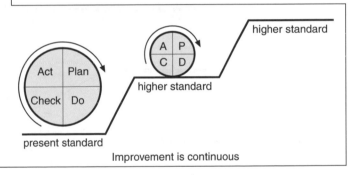

higher standard

higher standard

present standard

Improvement is continuous

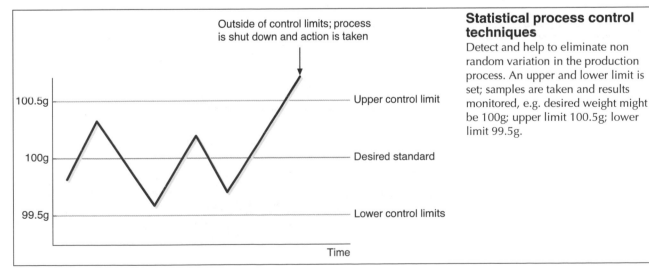

Outside of control limits; process is shut down and action is taken

100.5g — Upper control limit

100g — Desired standard

99.5g — Lower control limits

Time

Statistical process control techniques
Detect and help to eliminate non random variation in the production process. An upper and lower limit is set; samples are taken and results monitored, e.g. desired weight might be 100g; upper limit 100.5g; lower limit 99.5g.

Quality continued

How does better quality help customers?
- The product or service meets their needs more precisely
- There are fewer defects so less to put right later on
- There is less need for inspection when the goods are delivered

Good quality
- Meets customer needs more precisely
- Reduces wastage
- Reduces returned goods
- Increases customer satisfaction

To achieve high quality, a good or service must be 'fit for the purpose' and 'meet customer requirements'. The term customer is now broadly used to mean customers inside and outside of the business, i.e. internal and external customers. Anyone an employee does work for should be regarded as a customer.

Poor quality
Leads to:
- lost customers
- loss of repeat business
- rework
- legal action
- complaints
- low morale
- high defect rates

Quality standards (BS 5750/ISO 9000)
BS 5750 is a UK award for the process of quality, i.e. the process of setting targets, measuring the results and taking action to achieve them if necessary. Gaining the award does not imply anything about the targets themselves – these could be very easy to achieve and not all impressive. BS 5750 rewards the process of achieving quality; it does NOT guarantee a quality product.
The European equivalent to BS 5750 is called ISO 9000.

Value of BS 5750/ISO 9000 to a firm
- May be used in marketing, e.g. in promotional literature
- May be used to win contracts, e.g. provide an advantage over competition
- May be used as a means of focusing efforts on improving quality
- May motivate staff to win recognition/the award

Its value depends on:
- the extent to which it is recognised
- the extent to which other firms have it
- the extent to which buyers insist on it

Problems of BS 5750/ISO 9000
- Can be very bureaucratic
- Can be time consuming and costly to administer

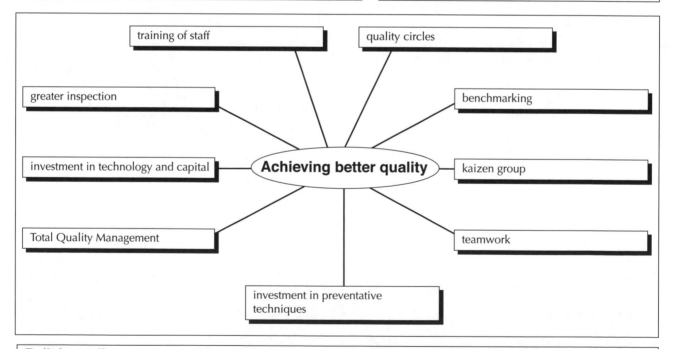

- training of staff
- quality circles
- greater inspection
- benchmarking
- investment in technology and capital
- **Achieving better quality**
- kaizen group
- Total Quality Management
- teamwork
- investment in preventative techniques

Built-in quality
This is an essential part of the modern approach to quality. Individuals check their own work at every stage of the process, thereby building in quality. The product or service should not need checking at the end because it has been checked all the way along.

To build in quality individuals need
- the authority and resources to take action to put things right
- quality to be defined as part of their job (e.g. part of their appraisal)
- training, e.g. in statistical techniques

Lean production

Lean production
An approach to production which seeks to minimise the wastage of time, people, materials.

Lean production includes

- time management techniques
- just in time production
- kaizen

Time based management
Attempts to reduce the time taken to complete tasks, e.g. through better planning and simultaneous engineering.
Aim is to reduce lead time, i.e. the time taken from a product or service being ordered to it arriving.

This can:
- provide competitive advantage (e.g. fast delivery, quick processing of orders, quicker product development)
- save time and therefore resources

Time based management involves:
- shorter product development time
- simultaneous engineering – this occurs when individuals work on a project at the same time rather than one work on it then passing on to the next and so on. This speeds up development time for new products or processes.
- JIT

Value of lean production
- Can reduce costs enabling lower prices and increased competitiveness.
- Can reduce costs enabling higher profit margins.
- Can make the firm more flexible to changes in demand.
- Can help to improve quality (e.g. have to get it right because no buffer stocks).
- Can improve productivity levels because reducing wasted time.

Problems introducing lean production
- Resistance from staff (do not want to change existing methods).
- Relies heavily on cooperation and involvement of employees and suppliers – may be difficult to achieve.
- May not find suitable suppliers.
- May require investment in new technology and training.
- Requires high degree of trust in workforce; may not suit some managers.
- Requires long term sustained commitment; for some it is just a fad.

Kaizen
Kaizen = continuous improvement; belief that progress comes through small, incremental change rather than just through sudden major developments.

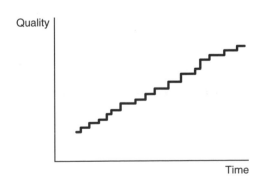

Underlying philosophy is one of continually looking to do things better. Even what seem like tiny changes can make a huge difference; e.g. if you cut the costs of each Mars bar by 0.1p, imagine the effect on profits over a year given how many are sold.

Continuous improvement requires:
- management committed to the idea of ongoing change
- employees willing to participate in change
- resources to implement change

Can be disruptive for staff, i.e. always changing what they are doing.

Lean production continued

Benchmarking: a process by which a firm compares its activities with the leaders in its industry or in the world.

Benefits of benchmarking

Include:

- better understanding of customers and competitors

- fewer complaints and more satisfied customers

- reduction in waste and reworking

- faster awareness of important innovations and how they can be applied profitably

- a stronger reputation

Also:

- brings about newness and innovative ways of managing operations

- effective team-building tool

- increased general awareness of costs and performance of products and services in relation to those of competitor organisations

- powerful methodology for developing winning strategies. Precise way of measuring gaps in performance.

- brings together all divisions and helps develop common front

- highlights the importance of employee involvement

Benchmarks

Might include:

- consistency of product

- correct invoices

- on time delivery

- frequency of delivery

- speed of service

Benchmarks for direct impact on bottom line, i.e. costs might include:

- waste and rejects

- stock levels

- work in progress

- cost of sales

- sales per employee

Benchmarking process

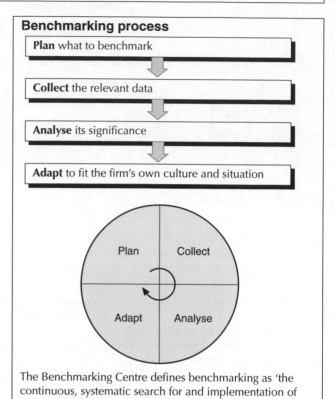

Plan what to benchmark

Collect the relevant data

Analyse its significance

Adapt to fit the firm's own culture and situation

The Benchmarking Centre defines benchmarking as 'the continuous, systematic search for and implementation of best practices which lead to superior performance'.

Problems of benchmarking

Include:

- deciding what to benchmark (what is the priority?)

- finding a suitable firm with which to benchmark and which is willing to share information

- deciding on the best way of gathering information

- implementing within the firm, e.g. may lack appropriate culture or resources; may need to adapt processes/methods

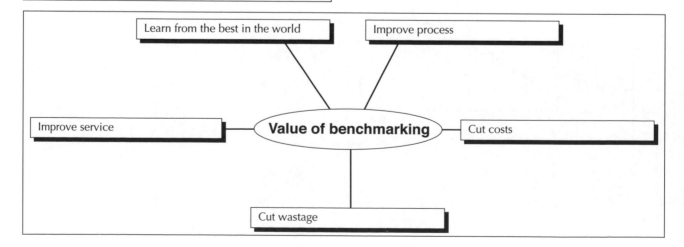

Market conditions (including labour markets)

Firms' behaviour

The behaviour of a firm will depend on:

- **the market growth;** if the market is growing all firms can increase sales; if the market is shrinking competition between firms is likely to be very aggressive as they fight for their own share at the expense of others.

- **demand relative to capacity;** if demand is high relative to capacity there is excess demand; firms are turning away orders. Cooperation between firms may be high. If demand is low relative to capacity there is excess capacity; there is not enough demand and competition between firms is likely to be fierce as they try to maintain their own output levels.

- **buyer power;** in some markets the buyers have tremendous power, e.g. in retailing the major supermarkets have great power over suppliers and can therefore push prices down and insist on rigorous quality standards. If the buyers are weak (e.g. they have no alternative) the seller is in the position of power and so, for example, can increase price.

- **likelihood of other firms entering the market;** if a firm has a patent or strong brand loyalty and it is difficult for others to enter it is likely to be able to generate high returns. If the market is easy to enter the returns may be lower.

Unfair competition

Anti-competitive behaviour, e.g.

- predatory pricing – pricing aimed at removing competitors

- restricting supply – limiting the choice for consumers

- market sharing agreements – e.g. firms agree on what their shares will be and fix prices

- full line forcing – manufacturers force retailers to take all their goods, not just the ones they want

Can be difficult to distinguish between fair and unfair competition, e.g. is a price cut a fair means of generating business or is it aimed at removing competition with the objective of gaining monopoly power?

Greater competition in a market

May mean:
- lower prices for the consumer

- more innovation

- greater incentive to be efficient

- greater choice for the customer

- greater attempts at differentiation, e.g. through segmentation

- better quality (or the consumer will vote with his/her feet)

Market conditions

- **Monopoly:** one firm dominates the industry (in UK law a monopoly is defined as a firm or brand with more than 25% of the market). The firm may be a price leader; it may exploit the consumer, which is why monopolies can be investigated under competition law.

- **Oligopoly:** when a few firms dominate the market; they may collude (work together) or compete.

- **Competitive market:** when there are many firms competing in the market; no one firm or group of firms dominate.

The competitive nature of a market may affect:
- the price a firm can charge

- a firm's profit margins

- the need to be efficient

Note: it is also important to consider the likelihood of entry by other firms in the future, e.g. if a market is a monopoly at present, if entry is easy the monopolist may be under pressure to be competitive.

Concentration ratio: measures the extent to which a market is controlled by a given number of firms. Usually measures their percentage of total market sales, e.g. a 4 firm concentration ratio of 80% means that the largest four firms have 80% of the market's sales.

The amount of competition in a market may depend on:
- government regulation, e.g. may be government monopoly

- whether the idea is protected by patents

- the costs of entry into a market

- the existence of economies of scale (the greater the economies of scale the greater the incentive to expand and the greater the cost disadvantage of being a smaller firm, i.e. it is likely a few large firms will dominate)

Market conditions (including labour markets) continued

Supply and demand *

* *Supply and demand analysis is not needed for AQA.*

A supply curve shows the quantity suppliers are willing and able to supply at each and every price, other things unchanged.

A change in price leads to a change in the quantity supplied; this is a movement along the supply curve.

The supply curve will shift when more or less is supplied at each and every price. This may be because:

- there are more or fewer firms producing
- technology has improved
- the government subsidises or taxes production

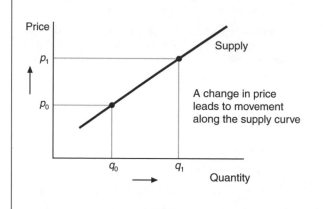

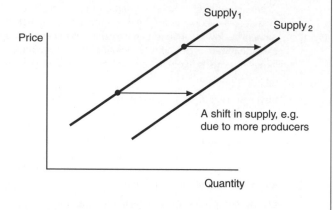

A demand curve shows the quantity demanded at each and every price, other things unchanged.

A change in price leads to a change in the quantity demanded and a movement along the demand curve.

A shift in demand occurs when more or less is demanded at each and every price. The demand curve may shift if e.g.

- income changes
- the firm changes its promotion (e.g. it advertises more)
- competitors change their marketing actions (e.g. they lower their prices or advertise their products more)
- the number of consumers in the market changes

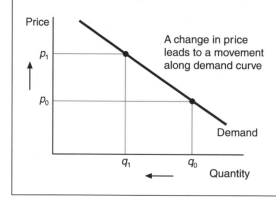

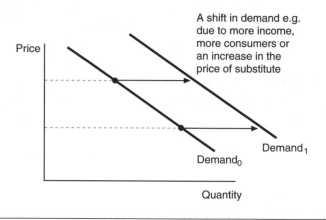

Equilibrium

In a free market the price adjusts to bring about equilibrium, i.e. quantity supplied equals quantity demanded.

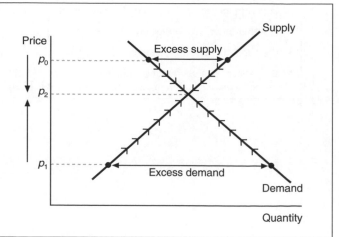

If there is too much demand (excess demand) the price will fall. This will decrease the quantity supplied and increase the quantity demanded until equilibrium is reached.

If there is too little demand (excess supply) the price will rise. This will increase the quantity supplied and decrease the quantity demanded until equilibrium is reached.
Imagine equilibrium is at P_0Q_0 and demand increases (perhaps because income has increased or there are more buyers in the market). Demand shifts right. At the old price there is now excess demand. The price increases to P_1 and a new equilibrium is established at P_1Q_1.

The price acts as:
- a rationing device (increasing to ration off demand if necessary)

- a signal (increasing to attract in new producers if there is excess demand)

- an incentive (increasing to encourage existing producers to produce more if there is excess demand)

Market aggregation: the market demand is the sum of all the individual consumer demands (i.e. the market demand curve is the total demand of all consumers in the market at each and every price, other things unchanged).

* *Supply and demand analysis is not needed for AQA*

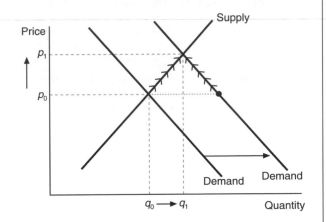

Derived demand: demand depends on demand for something else, e.g. the demand for labour is a derived demand; people are demanded because the final good or service is demanded.

Labour market: skills surpluses and shortages
The state of the labour market depends on supply and demand:
- demand depends on the demand for the final goods or services (it is a derived demand); e.g. demand for information technology specialists is high at present; demand for blacksmiths is low.

- supply depends on the training period, the wage rate, the skills required, the size of the labour market; e.g. supply of highly skilled footballers is limited; the supply of cleaning staff is higher.

If there is a **skills surplus** this means that demand for this skill is less than supply. This is likely to lead to:
- falling wages

- unemployment

If there is **skills shortage** this means that demand for particular skills is greater than the supply. This is likely to lead to:
- higher wages

- increased efforts by individual firms to attract staff, e.g. better reward packages, more fringe benefits

- retraining of existing staff

- greater efforts to retain staff

- attempts to seek new sources of labour, e.g. overseas, older staff, other industries

- in the long term supply might increase as more people are attracted into the industry and some switch from other industries

Political environment

The political environment concerns the role of the Government and its effect on organisations.

'Government' includes central and local government

Central government

Departments include:

- **The Treasury** – responsible for economic strategy
- **Departments:** of Social Security (provides benefits), of Trade and Industry, of Education and Employment
- **QUANGOs** (specialised bodies with specific responsibilities, e.g. Sports Council and Arts Council)

Local authorities

Includes county councils and district councils. They provide services in their areas such as:

- education and recreation, e.g. libraries and sports centres
- housing, e.g. council houses
- environmental services, e.g. refuse collection
- road maintenance
- social services, e.g. care for the elderly

Local authorities are funded by central government and the council tax.

The Government influences the economy through:

- Government spending – directly on goods and services, e.g. motorways and defence; indirectly through benefits, e.g. pensions

- Regional policy – investment grants, low rents, loans available for specified areas where there are high levels of unemployment

- Taxation – direct from earnings, e.g. income tax, corporation tax; indirectly placed on goods and services, e.g. VAT and excise duties

- Legislation, e.g. Competition Policy – to prevent unfair competition

The political environment includes the extent to which the Government intervenes in the economy.

Types of economy

Free market economy
resources are allocated by market forces of supply and demand

Mixed economy
mixture of free market and command economies; has private and public sector

Command or planned economy
Government allocates resources

The more interventionist a government is, the more it will regulate or interfere with the free market and move towards a command economy. A 'laissez-faire' approach to the economy means that the Government prefers to let the market mechanism work rather than intervene.

Private sector: organisations are controlled by private individuals, e.g. companies

Public sector: organisations are controlled by the Government, e.g. BBC

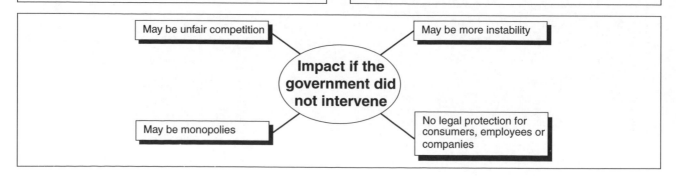

May be unfair competition

May be more instability

Impact if the government did not intervene

May be monopolies

No legal protection for consumers, employees or companies

Advantages of free market
- Incentive for producers as they keep the profits
- Markets are responsive to consumer demand
- Incentive to be efficient to keep costs down
- Incentive to be innovative

Problems of command economy
- Lack of incentive as profits belong to the Government
- Informational problems
- Coordination problems if the Government tries to organise the whole economy

The trend has been towards free market economies and less Government intervention, e.g privatisation and deregulation in Eastern Europe.

Should the government intervene more in the economy?
Depends on
- method of intervention
- political beliefs e.g. laissez faire
- need for intervention e.g. degree of market failure

Market failure
Occurs when markets fail to provide goods and services efficiently.
Market failures include:
- monopoly power: when some firms dominate the industry and exploit the consumer
- inequality – can be large differences between rich and poor
- will not provide 'public goods', such as streetlighting; no one would pay for street lighting in a free market – individuals hope someone else will pay for them and that they will benefit anyway. They would try to be 'free riders'. The Government has to provide these goods.
- merit goods are underprovided. These are goods that individuals would not value sufficiently and so would not consume enough of them, e.g. healthcare, education
- instability – prices might fluctuate greatly in some markets, e.g. exchange rates; society might prefer stability
- resources may not reallocate efficiently, e.g. if demand changes employees may be left unemployed
- 'external costs' – costs to society which the firm will not pay for in the free market, e.g. pollution. Because firms would not account for these external costs they would overproduce unless the Government intervenes. The total cost to society is the private costs to the firm + the external cost.

Controlling external costs, e.g. pollution
The government could:
- educate and inform to make firms aware of the consequences of their actions
- state control – take over the provision of activities
- regulate – pass laws that prevent certain activities
- tax – to make firms pay for the external costs of their actions
- subsidise firms to change their processes to reduce the external costs

Privatisation
Involves the transfer of assets from the public sector to the private sector.

Types of privatisation

sale of nationalised industries
(or parts of them), e.g. the sale of British Telecom

deregulation
Lifting restrictions which limit competition, e.g. the bus industry has been deregulated allowing more firms to provide services

contracting out
Allowing private contractors to bid for services, e.g. cleaning or catering in state schools

Reasons for privatising
- Raises revenue for the Government
- Creates more competition
- Frees organisations from political influence – decisions were sometimes made for political rather than business reasons
- Increases share ownership

Should the government subsidise firms?

For:
- may save jobs
- may protect industry/firm in the short term while it restructures/increases efficiency
- may protect firm against unfair foreign competition

Against:
- could encourage inefficiency
- could have unwelcome consequences, e.g. higher tax rates to raise finance (have to weigh up the effects of this compared to benefits of subsidy)
- opportunity cost – what else could have been done with the money?
- extent and duration of subsidy

Legal environment

Legal environment

The law sets out to protect individuals and groups, e.g. consumers (Consumer Law), employees (Employment Law), other firms (e.g. Competition Policy)
These groups may need protection because they cannot defend themselves effectively.
For example:

- consumers may not know what is in products, or how products are made unless the government forces firms to reveal this

- employees may rely heavily on the firm for employment and so managers may exploit this power unless the law protects them

- small firms may rely on larger firms for their business and may be bullied by them (e.g. the large firms may pressurise the small firms to lower their prices)

Competition policy

Responsibility of Office of Fair Trading which attempts to control anti-competitive behaviour and protect consumers.

Legislation includes: 1948 Competition Act; 1973 Fair Trading Act; 1998 Competition Act

Competition Commission (formerly the Monopolies and Mergers Commission): recommends whether a monopoly or proposed merger is in the public interest. A monopoly exists if a firm has more than 25% of the market. Monopolies are referred to the Competition Commission by the Office of Fair Trading; the Commission can recommend that a merger is prohibited or that firms end certain types of uncompetitive behaviour. The Director General of Fair Trading can fine companies for anti-competitive behaviour. The fine can be up to 10% of turnover.

Restrictive trade practices: include price fixing and market sharing agreements. All restrictive practices have to be registered with the Office of Fair Trading. The Restrictive Practices Court decides whether to allow an agreement. It may be allowed if, e.g. it prevents local unemployment, operates against existing restrictions or maintains exports.

Consumer law

Weights and Measures Act, 1951: inspectors can test weighing and measuring equipment of organisations.

Trade Descriptions Act, 1968: prohibits false or misleading descriptions of goods or services

Sale of Goods Act, 1979: goods must be of merchantable quality (i.e. no serious flaws), fit for the purpose (i.e. can do what it is supposed to), and as described.

Supply of Goods and Services Act, 1982: these must be 'merchantable quality' and at 'reasonable rates'.

Consumer Protection Act, 1987: firms are liable for any damage which their defective goods might cause

Consumer Credit Act 1974: anyone offering credit must seek a licence from the Director General of Fair Trading and state the annual percentage rate charged (APR)

Food Safety Act 1990

Protects the consumer:

- premises selling food must register with the local authority

- people who handle food must receive appropriate training

- enforcement officers can impose an improvement notice (i.e. something the firm does must be improved) or a prohibition notice (stopping the business selling food)

Contract law

A contract is a legally binding agreement between two or more persons. If a contract is breached, the aggrieved party can seek damages or sue for 'specific performance'.

Tort: a tort is a 'civil wrong'; this includes a variety of activities such as negligence, e.g. if an employee is negligent, the employer can be liable as well (called vicarious liability).

Compulsory insurance

Firms must have these insurances:

- **public liability:** this covers an organisation's liability to pay compensation for injury, illness or disease to a third party and for loss or damage to their property caused by the activities of the business

- **product liability:** this covers the organisation against paying out compensation for injury, illness or disease caused by goods sold, supplied, repaired, serviced, tested, altered, installed, processed or delivered by the firm

- **employer's liability:** covers employers against claims by employees

Environmental Protection Act 1990

Introduced Integrated Pollution Control (IPC); this involves regulations covering a wide range of industrial processes concerning the impact on land, water and air. These are enforced by the Inspectorate of Pollution. Covers all the wastes, gases, solids and liquids generated by a firm's activities.

Economic environment

National income:
The income in an economy is usually measured by **GDP:** Gross Domestic Product. This is the value of final goods and services produced in an economy. This shows how much has been earned within a country over a given period, usually one year.

Business cycle (Trade cycle)
Over time the economy usually goes through booms and slumps. This is called the 'trade cycle' or business cycle.

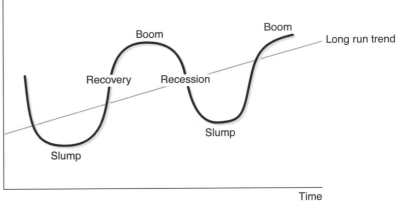

In a boom:
- the economy grows more quickly
- there may be higher levels of demand (firm may need to increase output, may have to increase capacity, may need to recruit)
- firms may find it more difficult to recruit (tighter labour markets; labour shortages)
- input prices may increase because of more demand (e.g. higher land prices and higher wages)

Depends on:
- where the firm sells its goods, e.g. may be selling overseas so demand not affected by domestic boom
- existing capacity; does it need to increase capacity or not?

In a recession:
- demand for a firm's products may fall
- firms may have to cut back on overtime or make redundancies
- consumers may be more price sensitive
- stocks may increase and firms may have to decrease production

The effect of a recession depends on the size of the recession, the length of the recession, and the type of firm, e.g. food and pharmaceutical industries are fairly recession proof, whereas the housing, construction and car industries are more sensitive to income changes. Shopping goods will be more sensitive than convenience goods to changes in the level of national income.

Business cycle and investment
Investment can fluctuate greatly in the economy. It is greatly affected by expectations. It can also cause booms and slumps, for example:
- if the economy has been growing slowly some firms may believe it must grow faster in the future; they may invest, stimulating demand and bringing about the growth they expected.
- if the economy is growing fast the government may increase interest rates to slow it up; this could decrease investment, leading to a decline in the growth of the economy.

If firms decide to invest more this increases demand. If firms reduce their investment this decreases demand.

Business cycle and stocks
When demand grows firms are unlikely to expand production or capacity at first (because it may not last). Instead they use up stocks. Over time if demand continues to grow firms will expand output and possibly capacity.

If demand starts to fall firms may not reduce output immediately (after all, demand may pick up); instead they may build up stocks. Over time if demand continues to be lower firms are likely to cut back on production levels and even capacity.

If firms deliberately decide to increase their stock levels this acts as a boost to demand because they will be producing more and employing more factors of production, increasing income; if firms decide to decrease their stock levels this will reduce demand because they will reduce output and employment levels.

Business cycles and consumer durables
Consumer durables are products which can be used more than once, e.g. cars, washing machines, televisions. Demand for these products tends to be relatively sensitive to changes in the business relative to demand for non-durables (such as food). However there will be considerable variation between products.
An increase in demand for consumer durables increases output and income and may help promote a boom.

Economic growth
Need to distinguish between local, national and international growth, e.g.
- the UK could be growing slowly but a firm's export markets could be growing quickly
- the UK could be growing quickly but the local market might actually be growing slowly (i.e. growth rates vary within a country)

Economic environment continued

Growth
To cope with growth a firm may need:
- more staff
- more investment
- bigger premises

Depends on:
- existing capacity utilisation
- whether demand is expected to remain high

Causes of economic growth
- Investment in capital goods
- Investment in technology
- Growth in labour force
- Increase in skill of workforce
- Improvement in management skills/entrepreneurship

The objectives of Government include:
- Growth, i.e. increase the income of the economy
- Stable prices, i.e. control inflation
- A healthy balance of payments, i.e. increase exports
- Full employment, i.e. reduce unemployment

To achieve its objectives a government may use:

monetary policy
- control of the money supply
- changes in interest rates

fiscal policy
- changes in taxation
- changes in government spending

direct controls
- legislation, e.g. price controls

direct intervention
- provision of certain goods, e.g. healthcare

exchange rate policy
- increasing or decreasing the value of the currency

In many cases the government is trying to influence the total demand in the economy; this is called Aggregate Demand (AD)

Reflationary policy
Increases aggregate demand, e.g. by cutting taxes, boosting spending or lowering interest rates. Aggregate Demand INCREASES.

Deflationary policy
Reduces aggregate demand, e.g. by increasing taxes, cutting spending or increasing interest rates. Aggregate Demand DECREASES.

Government and demand in the economy
The government may try to reduce demand by:
- fiscal policy, e.g. increasing taxes or reducing government spending
- monetary policy, e.g. increasing interest rates (increasing the incentive to save and discouraging borrowing)

The government may increase demand by:
- increasing its spending (fiscal policy)
- cutting taxes (fiscal policy)
- lowering interest rates (monetary policy)

Impact of higher taxes
- May increase costs
- May increase selling price (e.g. VAT)
- May make it more difficult to enter markets (e.g. tariffs)
- May reduce demand (e.g. income tax)

Budget position
Financial position of the Government.

Budget deficit – Government spending is greater than its revenue.

Budget surplus – Government revenue is greater than spending.

Government spending
Includes:
- social security
- health
- education
- defence
- public order and safety
- general public service
- housing and community amenities
- transport and communication
- other

Supply side policies
Aimed at improving the supply in the economy, e.g. reducing income tax to encourage people to work; reducing corporation tax to encourage firms to invest; increasing training; reducing benefits available for the unemployed to encourage people to work.

Multiplier
The multiplier is based on the idea that one person's spending is another's income. If, for example, the government spends £10m to get a road built, this money will be earnt by construction companies, landowners and employees. These different groups will then spend some of their earnings buying other goods and services. Of the initial £10m, a proportion such as £8m will be spent on other products. The recipients of the £8m will also want to spend and so the initial injection by the government sets off a chain-reaction of spending. This is called the 'Multiplier effect'.

If, for example, £10m is initially spent on goods and services this might eventually lead to a total of £50m worth of spending. In this case the multiplier is 5. The size of the multiplier depends on how much is spent at each stage in the chain – called the marginal propensity to consume (MPC). The higher the MPC, the more is spent at each stage and the higher the multiplier.

Taxes
Can be:

indirect	placed on the goods or services themselves, e.g. VAT
direct	taken directly from income, e.g. income tax or corporation tax
progressive	these take a higher proportion of income as income rises
regressive	these take a smaller proportion of income as income rises
specific	certain amount (£) per unit
ad valorem tax	adds a given percentage to the price, e.g. VAT

Interest rates and exchange rates

Interest rates
Represent the cost of borrowing money and the reward offered to savers. Interest rates are determined by the Monetary Policy Committee within the UK. This is an independent body which sets interest rates to achieve a set inflation target.

Interest rate increases
Effects include:
- households are more likely to save and less likely to spend. This will affect income elastic goods more than income inelastic, e.g. the demand for shopping goods are likely to be more affected than the demand for convenience goods.
- households' discretionary income is likely to fall as more money is used to repay mortgages and loans (discretionary income = income after tax and regular bills).
- firms are likely to reduce their stocks because money tied up in stocks represents a greater opportunity cost.
- debtors will want to hold on to their money to earn interest and are likely to delay payment.
- creditors will want their money more quickly.
- because of an increased desire to save in the UK the exchange rate might increase as demand for pounds from abroad increases.

Interest rates fall
Effects include:
- may increase demand (cheaper for firms and households to borrow)
- may reduce costs (lower interest payments)
- may reduce the exchange rate (less demand for pounds from overseas)

Impact on firm depends on:
- how sensitive its demand is to interest changes, e.g. demand for salt is not sensitive to interest rates; demand for cars is more sensitive as people borrow to buy cars
- extent of interest rate fall

Exchange rates
The exchange rate is the price of one currency in terms of another, e.g. it may cost 2 dollars to buy one pound.

In a free floating exchange rate system the value of the pound is determined by supply and demand for the currency. Demand for pounds (or sterling) is the demand to buy pounds with other currencies. The supply of pounds (or sterling) depends on the desire to change pounds into another currency.

If demand increases the price is likely to increase. If supply increases the price is likely to fall as more are available.

Demand for pounds may increase because of:
- more demand for UK goods and services
- greater desire to save in the UK (e.g. higher interest rates)
- more tourism to the UK
- speculators who believe that the pound will rise in the future so buy now

Supply of pounds may increase because of:
- greater demand for overseas goods and services
- greater desire to save abroad
- more tourism abroad
- speculators who believe that the pound will fall in the future so sell now

There are many different exchange rates because the pound is exchanged for many other currencies, e.g. the yen, the deutschmark, the franc. The pound will have a price against each of these currencies.

Effective exchange rate: shows the value of a pound against a number of other currencies. It is calculated as a weighted index; each currency has a different weight according to its relative importance in trade with the UK.

A high or strong pound: means the pound is more expensive, i.e. it costs more in terms of foreign currency. This makes UK goods/services more expensive in foreign currencies but because a pound can be changed for more foreign currency it becomes cheaper to buy imports in pounds.

| Higher UK interest rates | attract funds from abroad → | Higher exchange rate |

Interest rates and exchange rates continued

Increase in the value of the pound (i.e. an appreciation of the exchange rate)
Effects include:
- increases price of UK goods and services abroad in terms of foreign currency; demand for UK goods and services is likely to fall. The extent of the fall depends on how sensitive demand is to price (price elasticity of demand). However, some firms may decide not to allow an increase in price overseas and are willing to accept lower profit margins instead.
- imports become cheaper in pounds. May reduce input costs for UK firms.
- may make it more difficult for domestic firms to compete against foreign competitors whose goods are relatively cheaper.

Depends on:
- how much the pound has gone up and for how long
- which currencies it has increased against

Appreciation and depreciation
An increase in the pound is called an **appreciation;** it means the pound is stronger. e.g. if the pound increases in value from £1:$1 to £1:$2 it has appreciated.

A fall in the pound is called a **depreciation;** it means the pound is weaker. e.g. if the pound falls in value from £1:$2 to £1:$1 it has depreciated.

Government and the exchange rate:
Government can increase the value of the pound by:
- buying pounds with foreign currencies through the Bank of England
- increasing interest rates to make pounds more attractive to would-be savers from abroad, although now interest rates are set independently by the Monetary Policy Committee

Exchange rates and business opportunities
- Strong pound: can buy materials and components from overseas for a lower price in pounds
- Weak pound: can sell overseas for lower price in foreign currency (or maintain price and have bigger profit margins)

Reaction to a strong pound
A firm might:
- rationalise; try to cut costs
- accept lower profit margins by keeping price the same overseas to maintain sales
- try to buy in more components from overseas to benefit from low price in pounds
- seek new export markets where the pound is not so strong
- diversify into less price sensitive products

Exchange rate systems
In a fixed exchange rate system the government intervenes to keep the price constant or within a band. In a floating exchange rate system the currency is determined totally by supply and demand of that currency.

European Monetary Union (EMU)
Single currency area in which member countries use the euro.
Benefits to members:
- reduced transaction costs
- easier to compare prices
- removes exchange rate risk

Note: these benefits only occur when trading with other 'euro' countries.

Problems include:
- transition costs e.g. amending price lists when you first join
- greater price transparency may make it difficult for some firms to compete.
- interest rates will be set based on monetary conditions throughout the euro-zone; may adversely affect firms in particular regions at any moment.
- firms will no longer benefit from favourable changes in the currency, e.g. a depreciating exchange rate.

The impact of the euro
Depends on:
- amount of trade a firm does within the euro-zone
- value at which a currency joins, e.g. how many francs to the euro?

Inflation

Inflation is a persistent increase in the general price level. It is usually measured by the **Retail Price Index (RPI)**. The RPI measures the cost of living. It is a weighted index; the weights reflect the relative importance of different goods to the average household.

Causes of inflation:
Include:
- demand pull – too much demand for the number of goods. In this situation firms are able to increase their prices and profit margins. Due to high demand stocks are likely to be falling.
- cost push – an increase in costs (e.g. wages or materials) forces producers to increase prices or accept lower profit margins, e.g. in the mid to late 1970s prices increased due to sudden increases in oil prices, which increased costs.

The impact of inflation on firms
- May reduce the real value of debt
- May increase value of assets on the balance sheet
- May be able to increase own prices in line with inflation
- Planning can be more difficult (e.g. due to uncertainty over prices)
- May lead to disputes over wage increases (as employees want pay increases at least in line with inflation)
- Can lead to uncompetitiveness abroad (depending on what is happening to the exchange rate and prices overseas).
- Causes menu costs - the costs of changing, e.g. menus, brochures, slot machines.

- May lead to wage-price spiral.
- May lead to damaging counter inflation policies (e.g. higher interest rates).

Depends on:
- whether the firm can increase prices in line with increasing costs
- how much incomes are increasing
- rate of inflation
- cause of inflation (demand pull or cost push)
- whether anticipated or not
- what is happening to inflation in other countries.
- what is happening to exchange rates.
- the cause (e.g. is it demand pull or cost push?)

Inflation
- Does not mean all prices all rising; simply that there is a sustained increase in the general price level.
- Does not necessarily mean people cannot afford items; this depends on what their incomes are doing. Prices are generally much higher now than ten years ago but we still have more purchasing power because incomes have increased even more.
- Is not necessarily a bad thing from a producers' perspective; it may signify high levels of demand and a shortage within the market.

Controlling inflation
- Increase interest rates to deter spending
- Restrict lending to deter spending } to reduce demand pull inflation
- Increase exchange rate to make imports cheaper
- Incomes policies – Government limits pay increases (this only tends to work in the short term as employees resist constraints on pay rises) } to reduce cost push inflation

Deflation
Occurs when prices are falling.
This may be because:
- demand is falling
- costs are falling

If deflation is due to falling levels of demand this might mean
- falling sales
- the need to rationalise
- redundancies

However if it is due to lower costs this may make the firm more competitive overseas. This could lead to more growth and more jobs.

Wage price spiral:
Prices increase (e.g. due to too much demand), employees demand higher wages, this increases costs so prices increase and so on.

Effect of a firm increasing its prices
Depends on:
- what other firms are doing
- how sensitive demand is to price
- what is happening to income levels. If incomes are rising faster than prices the standard of living is actually increasing
- what is happening to the exchange rate (if the firm exports)

Unemployment

Unemployment in the UK
Measured by the number of people claiming unemployment benefit.

Unemployment rate
Percentage of the working population which is unemployed.

Types of unemployment

- **structural** – people are unemployed because of the changing structure of the economy, e.g. a miner may not have the correct skills for the new jobs being created in computing.

- **seasonal** – people in jobs such as fruit picking are likely to be unemployed at certain times of the year.

- **cyclical** – people are unemployed because of a lack of demand. Also called 'demand deficient' unemployment.

- **frictional** – people between jobs, i.e. left one job and waiting before accepting another.

- **residual** – people who are unwilling or unable to work because of a disability.

High unemployment
May mean:

- less demand for goods and services
- a wider choice of labour for a firm
- a more co-operative workforce as employees are worried about their jobs

Rising unemployment
The effect of an increase in unemployment on a firm depends on:
- to what extent has unemployment increased?
- how long will the increase last for?
- in what areas has the unemployment occurred?
- what types of people are unemployed, e.g. what skills?
- is the firm aiming to expand?

Falling unemployment
May mean:
- more difficult to recruit
- wages/rewards may have to increase to attract staff
- may reflect increasing demand; also more people earning so demand should be higher

Depends on:
- whether it is happening throughout the economy or just in one sector or region

Government strategies
To reduce unemployment the government may use:

1 demand side policies
i.e. attempt to increase demand to remove cyclical unemployment e.g. by:
- lowering interest rates
- cutting taxation
- increasing government spending

2 supply side policies
i.e. attempt to increase the ability of people to accept work (this should reduce structural unemployment), e.g. by:
- increasing training facilities/opportunities
- cutting benefits to encourage people to accept jobs
- changing tax and benefit system to increase the gains from work

International trade

Comparative advantage
Countries specialise in producing goods or services in which they have a comparative advantage, i.e. lower opportunity costs.

e.g. if country A sacrifices 2X to make 1Y whereas country B sacrifices 3X, then A should specialise in producing Ys because it has the lower opportunity cost.

Free trade: no barriers to trade. The benefits should be wider choice for consumers and lower costs.

Free trade area: members remove barriers to trade amongst themselves, e.g. LAFTA – the Latin American Free Trade Area. Members can set their own tariffs with non members.

Customs Union: free trade amongst members and a common external tariff with non member countries, e.g. European Union.

Barriers to trade (protectionism)
- Quotas – limits on quantity of goods allowed into a country
- Tariffs – taxes placed on imports
- Technical barriers – regulations which make it difficult for foreign producers to sell their products
- Exchange controls – limits on the amount of currency that can be changed into foreign currency to buy foreign goods.
- Embargo – a ban on all trade in a particular good or service

Trade war: occurs when countries use protectionist measures against each other.

GATT: General Agreement on Tariffs and Trade – member countries aim to reduce barriers to trade.

Balance of payments
Revenue generated from exports sold abroad minus spending on imports.
Balance of payments surplus: more is spent on a country's exports than it spends on imports.
Balance of payments deficit: country spends more on imports than it receives from exports.

International competitiveness
Measures the ability of one country's firms to provide better value than another country's firms.

Depends on factors such as:

- price relative to competitors – the exchange rate can have a major influence on this
- quality of product (i.e. to what extent does it meet customer needs? Does it have a USP?)
- reliability of the product
- overall service, e.g. delivery times

Why protect an industry?
- Save jobs in particular industries.
- Give small firms time to grow and improve (infant industries).
- To maintain a way of life (e.g. farming).
- To keep control of strategically important industries, e.g. defence industries.
- Retaliation.

IMPORTS
Goods/services bought in from overseas by UK firms/households

EXPORTS
Goods/services sold overseas by UK firms/households

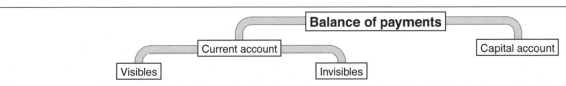

Balance of payments
Current account — Visibles — Invisibles — Capital account

Current account: Visible trade (value of exports of goods – value of imports of goods; called the **balance of trade**)
Invisible trade (value of exported services – value of imported services)

Capital account: Difference between money flows into the country (e.g. overseas savings in UK banks; purchase of UK shares) and money flows out of the country (e.g. UK savings overseas)

Emerging markets: These are developing and industrialising countries
These markets offer:

- Export opportunities: as these economies grow and gain purchasing power they provide more export opportunities for UK firms.
- Production bases: Western firms may locate there to benefit from lower costs and possibly less regulation.
- Potential competitors: firms from emerging markets may provide competition for UK firms.

Import penetration
Sales of foreign goods as a percentage of the total sales of a market.

Europe

Membership

In 2001 there were 15 members of the European Union: Belgium, France, Germany, Italy, Luxembourg, the Netherlands, Denmark, Iceland, the UK, Greece, Portugal, Spain, Austria, Finland and Sweden. A number of other countries in central and eastern Europe have applied for membership and are likely to join in the near future (e.g. Turkey, Poland, Hungary, Romania).

European Monetary Union

Most members of the European Union have agreed to monetary union. This has created a single currency in Europe, called the euro. The UK has not agreed to join the EMU yet.

Key dates

1957	European Economic Community set up.
1973	UK joined European Union
1986	Single European Act; aimed to create 'an area without internal frontiers in which the free movement of goods, persons, services and capital is ensured'.
1990	UK joins Exchange Rate Mechanism
1991	Maastricht Treaty
1992	UK leaves Exchange Rate Mechanism
2002	Single currency fully introduced in euro-zone

European Economic Community (EEC)

The European Economic Community was set up to create a free trade area in which member states would trade without quotas and tariffs. By 1986 it was obvious that some barriers still existed, e.g. differences in regulations made it difficult to transport goods from one country to another. The aim of the Single European Act was to create an area in which there was freedom of movement of goods, services, labours and capital. Member countries were given until 1992 to bring this about. The result was a harmonisation of regulations.

European Union institutions

The Council: the European Union's decision making body. It agrees legislation based on proposals from the Commission. There are, in fact, several councils (e.g. foreign affairs, agriculture, finance); attended by the relevant ministers from member states and by the Commission.

The Commission:

- proposes community policy and legislation

- implements decisions taken by the Council of Ministers

Consists of commissioners appointed by the Community governments.

The European Parliament: directly elected every five years. Consulted on proposals for EC law. Can influence shape of laws and has power of veto in certain areas.

Social Chapter (part of Maastricht treaty)

Proposals for employees concerning conditions, participation, working hours, protection of children, disabled persons, collective bargaining. The UK did not agree to the Social Chapter initially but has now agreed.

Common Agricultural Policy

Scheme to maintain the price of foodstuffs in Europe. If too much is produced the European Union buys up the excess to prevent the price falling below a set level. In practice the intervention price has been set too high so that the Union is regularly buying up food to stop the price falling. This has led to large stocks building up, e.g. wine lakes and butter mountains.

The European Union

Provides UK firms with:

- bigger markets; potential for growth and economies of scale

- more market opportunities

- more sources of employees

- greater competition

- more sources of finance

- the incentive and opportunity to become efficient and learn from other firms

- the same safety and technical standards for many products

- the ability to compete for contracts from member governments

- the removal of border controls and lower administration costs

Over 50% of the UK exports go to the EU.

Pan European marketing strategy

Treating Europe as a single market. e.g. Gillette markets its products in a similar way in each country.

Benefits:

- economies of scale; can produce on a larger scale and benefit from production economies; can market in similar ways and so have marketing economies

- simpler to manage a standardised product rather than a range of different products marketed in different ways

Problems:

- may not meet the needs of individual markets

Suitability of pan European strategy depends on:

- how similar market conditions are; works quite well for e.g. cigarettes, jeans and soft drinks; may be less successful for food where local tastes can vary considerably.

Does being a member of the EU benefit UK firms?

- Firms face more competition from other EU firms

- Depends on the firm's competitiveness

- Depends on the extent to which the firm imports/exports to EU

Members ☐ and would-be ▨ members of the EU

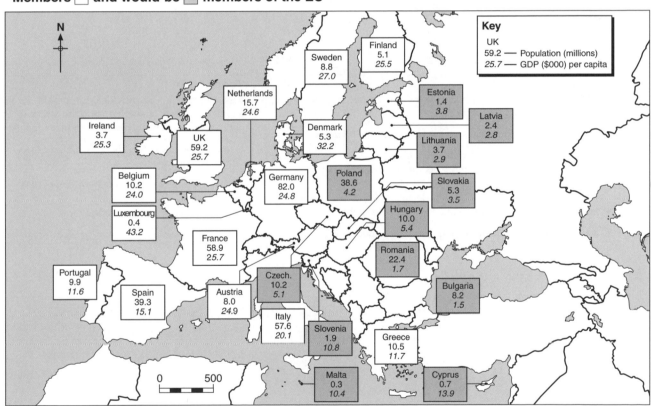

Social environment and technology

The social environment
Includes the values, attitudes, needs and expectations of consumers, employees, the Government, pressure groups, and investors. The social environment also includes demographic factors, such as the size of the population and its age structure.

Recent social trends in the UK
Include:

- growing environmentalism
- growing interest in health and fitness
- growing concern about the ethics of organisations
- more leisure time
- earlier retirement
- more women in the workforce

- increasing living standards
- slow population growth in UK
- decline in availability of younger workers
- ageing population
- more skilled and educated workforce
- more temporary and part time employment

Social awareness of environmental issues
Has led to:

- some firms producing social audits
- some firms producing environmental audits
- changes in production techniques, e.g. recycling
- changes in products, e.g. changing away from CFCs in aerosol sprays to more environmentally friendly systems
- the use of the environment in marketing (e.g. on labelling, in advertisements)

The effect of changing social trends
Depends on:

- the type of firm, e.g. Mothercare will be affected by birth rates; retirement homes will be affected by the ageing population
- the size of trend and how long it lasts, e.g. will consumers still be concerned about ethics if the economy goes into a recession?

Technology
Technology is the way in which work is done, i.e. the equipment used and the way work is organised.

Improvements in technology lead to new products and processes.

The effects of technology include:
- new ways of working, e.g. more people working from home
- greater productivity/efficiency
- new products and markets, e.g. video cameras, microwaves
- more flexible manufacturing e.g. computer aided design
- new skills needed
- loss of some jobs/creation of others
- improved communication, e.g. faxes, mobile phones
- shorter product life cycles
- quicker development times

When adopting technology firms should consider:
- initial cost
- employees' reaction
- training required
- expected benefits

Technology
New technology can provide opportunities for firms: e.g. new markets opening up and the ability to offer new products. However it can also pose threats:

- may remove existing markets (CDs destroyed the market for cassettes)
- may give competitors a USP or competitive advantage

Depends on:

- whether the firm is ahead in the technology race
- whether the firm can introduce and use technology effectively

Employees may resist new technology:

- may fear it will replace them
- may fear ability to use the technology
- may think there are more important priorities for investment

Technology can affect:
- products, e.g. the market for computer console games developed because of new technology
- processes, i.e. the introduction of Computer Aided Design and Computer Aided Manufacture can make production more efficient
- communications, e.g. the use of e-mail
- marketing, e.g. the internet offers a new distribution option

Social responsibility

Social responsibilities:
these are the obligations a firm may accept over and above legal obligations, e.g. responsibilities to the community or the environment.

To what extent should firms accept social responsibilities?
Depends on:

- their managers'/owners' objectives

- the extent to which customers/stakeholders expect it

- the extent to which it boosts profits

- the firm's mission statement/ethical code

- what other firms are doing

- legal responsibilities

- the likely power and impact of pressure groups

Pressure group activities
Include:

- boycotting products, e.g. do not buy animal fur products

- media campaign, e.g. in 1996 Greenpeace pressurised Shell into not dumping the Brent Spar oil rig in the sea

- lobbying government, i.e. putting views across; e.g. many people protested against the level of fuel tax in 2000

- demonstrations and petitions

Firm's reactions to pressure groups
Firms might:
- ignore them

- make the changes the pressure group wants

- compromise

- defend its position

Depends on:
- strength of pressure group

- media reaction

- the issue involved (e.g. does the pressure group have its facts right?)

- the skill/resources of the public relations department

- legal position (e.g. has the firm been acting legally?)

Employees
A firm's responsibilities to employees may include:
- fair treatment at work
- right to be kept informed
- involvement in decisions which affect them
- opportunities for participation
- training in new skills
- possible provision of social facilities

Community
A firm's responsibilities to the community may include:
- effects of noise, waste disposal, congestion
- effects of building work (e.g. on the landscape)
- use of excessive packaging
- use of energy

Social responsibilities

Consumers
A firm's responsibilities to consumers may include:
- value for money
- safe products
- after sales service
- to be informed about the product's origin and what it is made of
- fair advertising

Shareholders
A firm's responsibilities to shareholders may include:
- fair return as a reward for risk taking
- safeguarding their investment
- opportunity to express their view
- right to be kept informed

Social audit: an independent check on the impact of a firm's activities on society, e.g. the effect on the local community, policies regarding women and ethnic minorities, contributions to the arts and charities.

Pressure groups
Organisations formed by people with a shared interest, which seek to influence public opinion and Government policy.

Interest groups: established to serve the interests of members, e.g. trade unions

Cause groups: established to promote a cause, e.g. environmentalist groups such as Greenpeace, Friends of the Earth

Other examples of pressure groups:

- **Institute of Directors:** employers' pressure group; lobbies Government

- **Institute of Management:** professional association of managers

- **Employers' Associations:** employers' organisations for employers in the same industry.

Effectiveness of pressure groups depends on:
- number of members

- resources

- public support

- ability to influence media and politicians

Social responsibility continued

Ethics
A view about what is right and wrong, what is moral.

Ethical issues include:
- should firms use child labour?
- what wages should firms pay in the Third World?
- to what extent should firms seek to be environmentally friendly?
- should firms get involved in certain activities, e.g. making weapons?

Ethical code
A set of principles to determine employees' behaviour. This may cover:
- personal behaviour, e.g. when dealing with customers and suppliers
- corporate behaviour, e.g. when negotiating deals
- behaviour towards society, e.g. when recruiting
- behaviour towards the environment, e.g. when deciding on the process

Why should managers behave ethically?
- because their owners want them to
- to attract ethical investors
- to attract ethical consumers
- to attract employees
- to avoid unfavourable media attention

Why should firms not behave ethically?
- they do not have to provided they behave legally
- it can impose extra costs
- there is no agreement on what is ethical
- can be conflict of interests, e.g. by not producing cigarettes they may have to make employees redundant

Ethics v profit
Ethical behaviour may reduce a firm's profits because:
- it may decide not to accept certain orders, e.g. with some governments, for some products
- it may decide not to take certain actions to win orders (e.g. personal payments to individuals)
- it may lead to more costly production processes, e.g. extensive pollution control

But ethical behaviour may increase profits, e.g. by
- attracting investors
- attracting more customers
- attracting/retaining staff

Ethics and delegation
When a manager delegates he/she is giving authority to another person. That other person may not have the same values, i.e. may behave in a way which the person delegating believes is unethical. Delegating involves some loss of control and could lead to unethical behaviour. To overcome this some firms produce Codes of Ethics to highlight the firm's code of behaviour.

Ethics or public relations
It can be difficult to distinguish whether a manager's behaviour is ethical or is simply a public relations exercise. e.g. if a firm decides to stay in the UK to save jobs rather than relocate to a lower cost base overseas, is this because of ethics or to win public favour? It may well be both.

Ethics and culture
How employees behave is influenced by the firm's culture (i.e. the attitudes, values and beliefs of those who work within the organisation). The culture will influence whether or not employees behave ethically or whether e.g. 'the end justifies the means'.

Should firms be moral in their decision making?
Depends on:
- owners' views
- what society expects
- reaction of customers
- possible benefits from being moral

Environmental audit: independent check on the firm's impact on the environment e.g. emission levels, recycling levels, wastage rates

Why have an environmental audit?
- Good for public relations.
- Can be used in marketing – may attract customers and generate brand loyalty.
- May help prepare for changes in legislation.
- May save money (e.g. saving costs through recycling).
- Because of owners'/managers' views and values.
- May attract and keep staff.

External costs
Costs imposed on society by the firm which the firm itself would not take into account, e.g. pollution and congestion.

To make a firm take account of its external costs the Government can:
- tax firms; this will increase their private costs to reflect the true social cost
- legislate, e.g. limiting noise/pollution emissions

Environmental pressures on firms
e.g to reduce emissions, to recycle
Can affect:
- the way the good or service is produced
- what is produced

Can:
- increase costs
- prevent certain production processes/products
- provide market opportunities, e.g. for firms producing environmentally friendly goods

A firm which is environmentally friendly
- May be able to use environmental policies in its marketing activities.
- May attract consumers.
- May attract investors.
- May attract employees.
- May have higher costs (e.g. due to changes in production process).
- May have lower costs (e.g. due to recycling).
- May have higher revenues (e.g. due to increased demand).

Depends on:
- whether these different groups are interested in a firm's environmental stance
- what competitors are doing
- the relative costs and benefits of being environmentally friendly

Environmental pressures create opportunities
- for new products.
- for new markets e.g. niche markets.
- for new processes.
- for firms which are environmentally friendly (e.g. may be able to build into their marketing).

Resource management
May involve:
- re-using
- recycling
- designing products that use resources more effectively, e.g. less packaging
- designing processes that use resources more efficiently, e.g. lower energy consumption

Environmental issues

- global warming
- pollution
- efficient use of resources

- energy consumption
- congestion
- waste disposal

- use of non renewable resources e.g. coal
- recycling
- using less packaging

Information technology

Information technology: the collection, storage, processing, and communication of information by electronic means.

Enables large quantities of information to be handled quickly and economically.

'Good' information
- Reliable
- Accurate
- Intelligible
- Up to date
- Complete
- Appropriate level of detail
- Available in a useful format
- Cost effective

Benefits of information technology
- Quicker handling of data
- Better decision making because of easier access to information
- Ability to consider 'what if?' scenarios easily
- Increased productivity
- Less waste

Problems with information technology
- Cost of selection, installation, maintenance
- Training and retraining
- May help with the management of information – does not guarantee information is interpreted or used correctly

Uses of information technology
- **Data management**
  Enables more effective maintenance, updating, and manipulation of data, e.g. keeping of personnel and financial records.
- **Communication**
  Enables easier communication between people, e.g. fax machines, mobile phones.
- **Manufacturing**
  Used in systems such as computer integrated manufacture, can improve areas such as quality control, materials handling and stock control.
- **Decision support**
  Enables better decisions by collecting, analysing and manipulating data more effectively.
- **Office automation:**
  More effective performance with increased use of spreadsheets, word processors, desktop publishers, and telecommunications links such as electronic mail.

Management information systems (MIS)
Provide information for planning and control, e.g. sales figures.

Expert systems
Cover a particular area of expertise and draw conclusions from computer stored knowledge obtained from specialists. Their purpose is to capture the expertise of key people and make their knowledge available to users of the programme, e.g. used to diagnose patients' symptoms.

Database: set of files organised to enable easy access, e.g. personnel or customer records.

Spreadsheets: allow managers to set up mathematical models and investigate effects of different strategies, i.e. analyse 'what if?' questions.

Fax: technique for transmitting text and black and white pictures over the telephone network.

Electronic mail (email): way of sending text messages via a computer network.

EDI: electronic data interchange between organisations.

EPOS: electronic point of sale, e.g. scanning equipment at supermarket check-outs.

CD ROM: compact discs for read only data storage.

bar code: a code in the form of parallel lines of varying widths which is used to enter data into computer via a scanner.

video conferencing: method of holding conferences via telecommunications network; individuals can see and hear each other.

How useful is information technology?
Depends on:
- costs
- which systems are selected
- how it is implemented
- training given to staff
- level/quality of IT relative to the competition

Impact of the internet
- Marketing opportunities, e.g. new ways of promoting goods and services, new ways of distributing products.
- New markets, e.g. business opportunities for internet companies, for website designers.
- Improved communications both within firms and between organisations.

Change

Change is the one constant in business: there are always new markets, new products, new processes, new values and attitudes and developments in technology. Some firms embrace change – others resist it.

Internal changes include:
employees' motives, behaviour, skills, product design

External changes include:
PEST factors – political, economic, social, and technological

Change
May be:
- internal, e.g. changing employee expectations, new product development
- external, e.g. economic change, change in competitors' actions

Incremental change: this means that change occurs in small steps rather than dramatic change when the change is much more significant. Firms can plan and control more easily when change is incremental. If change is dramatic it can cause a crisis and panic.

Kaizen: a process of continuous improvement. An approach in which small ongoing changes are seen as a way of achieving major investments over time.

Business process reengineering (BPR): this is an example of radical change. The business process is examined from first principles, i.e. if we started again how would we do it? Whereas kaizen makes small changes to the existing process, BPR may involve a completely new way of doing things. Often associated with major restructuring and redundancies.

Unanticipated change: by definition this is unexpected and so more difficult to deal with than anticipated change. Firms may have contingency plans but it may lead to panic or rushed decisions.

Change is the only constant: Business is a dynamic process. Today's winners may be tomorrow's losers. There is always some form of change in the business environment. Firms must plan for this and be prepared to change themselves.

Resistance to change
Occurs because individuals:
- may not see the point of change
- prefer the existing arrangements – change may involve extra efforts, may lose status
- are afraid that they will not be able to perform as well in new situation; uncertain
- do not think that the proposed change is appropriate

Reaction to change can include: fear, resentment, anxiety, frustration, and anger.

Managing change
- Plan carefully
- Explain need and purpose of it
- Show benefits of it
- Involve employees in it
- Pay attention to speed of change
- Train
- Negotiate
- If necessary, coerce and force change through

Why does change fail?
- Employees misunderstand purpose of or need for change
- Lack of planning and preparation
- Poor communication
- Culture
- Employees lack necessary skills
- Lack of necessary resources/rewards

Culture
The attitudes, beliefs and values of the employees of an organisation. Influences how the employees think and act. Some organisations are entrepreneurial and innovative – employees encouraged to take initiative, e.g. 3M; others are bureaucratic – employees encouraged to stick to the rules. When organisations merge or there is a takeover, there can be a culture clash as they do things in different ways.

Starting up

Why start up in business?

- For personal satisfaction (self actualisation)
- To pursue a hobby
- To gain employment/income

The start-up process

Generate an idea

↓

Research the market

↓

Assess the viability of the idea

↓

Produce business plan

↓

Seek finance

↓

Develop product/service

↓

Test (if possible)

↓

Launch

↓

Review

Having the idea

The business idea may come from:
- your own inspiration
- adapting an existing idea
- buying the right to a patent

Raising finance to start up

Sources of finance include:
- own finances
- family and friends
- bank
- outside investors
- venture capital
- government help

What's in a business plan?

- Personal information about who is involved: background of people; experience of the staff
- Objectives: what the firm is trying to achieve; what are its targets in the short term and the long term?
- Marketing plan: e.g. what will make the product succeed? What is its USP? How will it be positioned? How will it protect itself from the competition? What is the market size? What are the expected rates of return?
- Finance plan: what money needs to be raised? What finance already exists? What is the financial position of the business, e.g. liquidity, gearing? What are the projected cash flows and profits? What collateral does the firm have?
- Production plan: how will it produce? What are its capacity levels? How will it achieve given quality targets?

Small budget research

Individuals starting out may not be able to afford much research (even though it is important to undertake research to reduce risk) i.e. they may have to undertake small budget research. This may mean:
- using more secondary data rather than primary
- undertaking research themselves (rather than use an agency, for example)
- using limited sample size

As a result findings may be unreliable, may not be statistically significant, and are more likely to be biased.

Value of a business plan

- Forces entrepreneurs to think about the business's strengths, weaknesses, opportunities and threats.
- Useful to review progress.
- Useful to show investors.

BUT
- Depends how it used; is it a one-off or is it reviewed and updated on a ongoing basis?
- Depends on how accurate the plans are and how well they are implemented.

Which type of legal structure?

Individuals may choose between e.g sole trader, partnership, company.
They will consider issues such as:

- need for other investors

- need for limited liability

- need/desire to keep control

- perceived value of different forms, e.g. perceived status of a company compared to sole trader

- desire for privacy of affairs, e.g. how much information does he or she want to disclose?

Problems of starting up

- Lack of experience; many entrepreneurs lack experience in all the different areas needed to run a business successfully. They may, for example, be technically sound but lack experience in people management.

- Establishing a good location – often the best locations have already gone or are too expensive; also location costs can provide a heavy overhead.

- Generating a customer base; many firms rely on customer goodwill and repeat business; it takes time to build up customer loyalty.

- Undertaking research; often new firms cannot afford extensive research and so rely on informal or small budget research. This may lack accuracy.

- Protecting the idea; often entrepreneurs' ideas are imitated by more powerful rivals. Competitors wait to see whether the idea will be successful; once it has begun to prove itself they imitate it.

Start ups and cash flow problems

- Raising finance can be particularly difficult in the early stages of a business (e.g. perceived as high risk, lack of collateral); financing growth can also prove difficult for the same reasons.

- Lack power over debtors; often paid late.

- Lack power over suppliers who demand payment quickly.

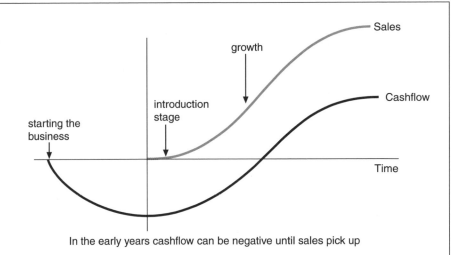

In the early years cashflow can be negative until sales pick up

Patents

Provide protection for a new innovative product or process. Patents must be registered with the Patent Office.
Advantages of patents:

- make developments public knowledge – this may encourage yet more innovations

- individuals or firms which have patents can earn income from selling the right to use these

- the fact that individuals or firms know they can protect their ideas encourages innovation

What determines whether a new business will succeed?

Factors include:

- how good the original idea is

- the quality of the research

- the management skills of the founders

- the external environment, e.g. degree of competition

- the extent to which the firm plans

Copyright

This provides protection for composers and writers. Whenever someone writes a new book, new song or new play, for example, this is protected by copyright. Copyrights do not have to be registered.

Change in ownership

Integration is a form of external growth. It occurs when two or more firms join together – this might be through a merger or a take-over.

Merger: mutual agreement between two or more companies to join together.

Why merge?
- Share resources
- Gain economies of scale
- Quick growth

Problems merging
- Culture clash
- Government may prevent it if it forms a monopoly

Takeover: occurs when one firm gains control of another. It may be via a cash offer or a paper offer (offer shares in own company in return for shares in target company) or a combination of the two.

Trigger points:
- The attacker must inform the target company when it has 5% of its shares.
- When it has 15% of the victim's shares, the attacker must wait seven days to give the directors of the target company time to organise their defence.
- When the attacker has 30% it is obliged to bid for the target company.

Timetable: once a firm makes a bid it has 60 days, starting from the day formal documents go out, in which to succeed. If bid fails, the attacker must wait at least a year before trying again.

Type of integration	Description	Possible reasons
Horizontal	same stage of same production process	market power, economies of scale
Vertical	different stage of same production process	control suppliers or outlets
Conglomerate	different production process	spread risks

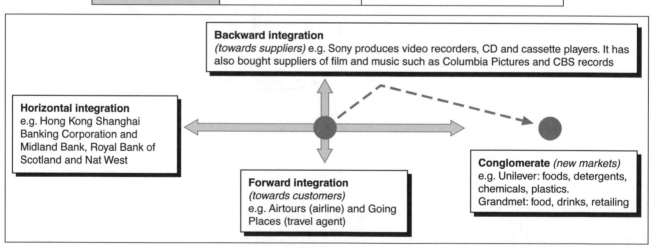

Backward integration
(towards suppliers) e.g. Sony produces video recorders, CD and cassette players. It has also bought suppliers of film and music such as Columbia Pictures and CBS records

Horizontal integration
e.g. Hong Kong Shanghai Banking Corporation and Midland Bank, Royal Bank of Scotland and Nat West

Conglomerate *(new markets)*
e.g. Unilever: foods, detergents, chemicals, plastics.
Grandmet: food, drinks, retailing

Forward integration
(towards customers)
e.g. Airtours (airline) and Going Places (travel agent)

Synergy
The idea that when two companies join together, the overall performance will be better than the sum of the two firms individually; often expressed as 2+2=5. Can occur because of, e.g. shared research and development or shared distribution.

Possible benefits of integration
- More competitive, e.g. shared resources, economies of scale
- Easier access to new markets; distribution channels

Potential disadvantages of integration
- Monopoly power exploiting consumer
- Problems managing a larger business e.g. diseconomies of scale
- Culture clash

Problems of takeovers

- Do not know the victim firm's exact financial position at present, e.g. the true value of the business may be uncertain.

- Usually pay a premium to take over the company; this means the bidding firm has to earn higher profits to cover initial costs.

- May have culture clashes, e.g. the firms are run in different ways/have different values.

- Diseconomies of scale (e.g. communication, coordination and control).

To protect their business from takeover

Managers may:
- take short term actions to boost profits and hopefully share price

- try to grow quickly because bigger firms are more difficult (more expensive) to take over

Management buy out

Existing managers buy control of their business.

Possible problems:
- can be stressful for those involved – they are now the owners not just the managers; greater responsibilities

- may involve high levels of borrowing and high gearing; risky

- may lose benefits of being associated with larger business (e.g. if larger business has sold off part its operations to the managers)

- may lose security of being employed by the organisation; now responsible for whole business and rewards depend directly on its success

Possible benefits of management buy outs:
- managers likely to be highly motivated

- may not have the overheads of a head office or a parent organisation

- may be able to respond more quickly to change

- no divorce between ownership and control

Mission and objectives

Mission

The mission is the overriding goal of the organisation; the reason for its existence.

The mission statement is the formal expression of the mission.

The mission might also include a statement or expression of:
- what the organisation believes in (its values)
- its competitive strategy (how it wants to compete)
- how it will behave (its policies)

A mission statement should convey where the firm wants to be going and what it believes is important.

Value of mission statement
- Unifies.
- Can be used for public relations purposes and in marketing.
- The process of developing can generate valuable discussion/insight into the business purpose.
- Can motivate if perceived as relevant, true and inspiring.
- Provides a focal point for all other planning.

Objectives

Objectives should have the following features:

S **S**pecific, i.e. they relate to something in particular
M **M**easurable, i.e. progress is quantifiable
A **A**greed, i.e. the targets are agreed by those involved rather than forced on them
R **R**ealistic, i.e. they can be achieved (if they were unrealistic people would probably not even try to achieve them and it would be demotivating)
T **T**ime specific, i.e. they must be achieved within a set period of time

For example, 'an increase in profits of 10% over three years' is an example of a good objective. 'We must do better' is an example of a bad objective – what does 'do better' mean? By when? How will we measure it?

Types of objective

The **corporate objective** is a quantifiable target for the organisation as a whole, e.g. to increase profits by £5m over two years.

The **functional objectives** are the targets for the different sections of the business such as marketing, finance, people and operations e.g. 'to increase sales by £8m within 2 years'.

The **individual objectives** are the personal targets of people within the firm, e.g. 'to win three major contracts this year'.

Possible business objectives

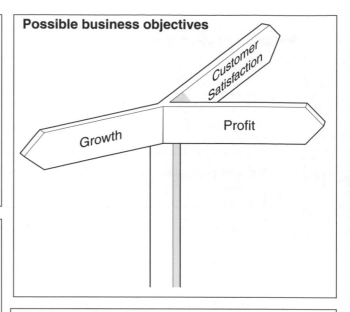

Problems with mission statements
- Sometimes not supported by the actions of the firm.
- Sometimes do not reflect reality.
- May be regarded cynically by staff.

Mission statements are more likely to work if they:
- reflect the firm's values
- are supported by actions
- are supported by senior management

Value of objectives

They:
- give a clear goal
- motivate
- can be used to review progress
- coordinate activities to ensure the organisation as a whole is working towards the same targets
- communicate what the firm wants to be done

Problems of setting objectives
- Deciding what are the most important things to measure.
- Individuals may disagree over what is realistic and achievable.
- Objectives can become out of date/irrelevant if the market or firm changes rapidly.

What stops firms achieving their objectives?
- Choosing the wrong strategy
- Failure to implement the strategy effectively
- Competitive actions
- External change, e.g. economic or social change
- Internal problems, e.g. employees lack the necessary skills

Corporate culture

Corporate culture
Refers to the values, attitudes and beliefs of those within the organisation.

This will influence:
- the management style
- the way decisions are made
- the nature of the decision made
- the way the firm deals with its stakeholders
- the firm's success

Culture can be seen in:
- the business norms; what is regarded as acceptable behaviour
- symbols such as dress code, the way people address each other, the decor
- rituals, i.e. particular routines people have (e.g. singing the company song, leaving at 5pm precisely)
- corporate heroes – who does everyone respect? Who are the most admired people in the business? How do/did they behave?
- the business rules

Types of culture

Power culture
- power is centralised
- often found in small, entrepreneurial firms (decisions by the founder)
- decisions made by the centre

  BUT
- may demotivate staff who feel lack of challenge
- may be difficult to maintain if organisation gets big

Role culture
- typical of bureaucratic organisations with many layers of hierarchy
- organisation divided into different functions (e.g. marketing, finance)
- clear rules and procedures
- clear job descriptions

- power depends on position in hierarchy
- clear channel of communication

BUT
- limited initiative; have to follow rules
- may not encourage innovation

Task culture
- job or project orientated
- focus on completing the task
- status depends on ability to contribute to the task
- good for building teams and getting projects completed
- employees have freedom and can use initiative

Person culture
- individuals within the organisation most important
- organisation serves to help individuals, e.g communes, partnerships

Why does culture matter?
Affects:
- motivation and enthusiasm of employees
- emphasis on customer service
- openness to innovation and change
- focus on improvement
- focus on efficiency, e.g. the desire to use resources efficiently and keep costs down

Changing culture
- Need to change people's attitudes and values – this will take time. Even if people change their behaviour this does not necessarily change their underlying values.
- Usually have to demonstrate their existing approach needs to change – some will resist this ('It's fine as it is' 'why change ?').
- Need to provide rewards to encourage people to change behaviour.
- Need to build new behaviours into appraisals, i.e. need to assess new desired behaviour.

Problems changing culture
May face resistance from employees because:
- they may like it the way it is
- they may fear change
- they may be worse off after the change

Changing culture takes time, to introduce new values and get them accepted. Cannot simply tell people to think differently; have to show them why, have to demonstrate it will work and is desirable.

Management process

Management is about 'getting things done through others' (R. Stewart). It involves deciding what has to be done and how to do it; and making sure the right decisions are implemented.

The role of management

- Planning: what needs to be done? What are the objectives of the firm? Where is the firm heading?
- Organising: the resources needed to achieve the objectives; deciding who does what
- Coordinating: the different elements of the business
- Motivating others to achieve
- Controlling: to ensure everything goes according to plan
- Communicating: to ensure everyone knows what is expected of them, knows what they have to do and how they are doing

Roles of managers

Interpersonal role

- Figurehead – represents the organisation; involved in ceremonies, e.g. signing documents
- Leader – involved in planning, organisation, motivation, controlling
- Liaison – works with groups outside the organisation, between groups within the organisation

Informational role

- Monitor – seeks and receives information
- Disseminator – transmits information within the organisation
- Spokesperson – transmits information externally

Decisional role

- Entrepreneurial – initiates and plans change; exploits opportunities and solves problems
- Disturbance handler – reacts to problems, difficult situations
- Resource allocator – decides where resources will go, e.g. money and materials
- Negotiator – with individuals/ groups/unions

Management is a dynamic process – it is ongoing and ever changing as the challenges, resources and constraints of a firm change.

Management skills

Technical to understand how a job is done, what is needed to do it effectively, and what is feasible

Human relations to be able to deal with people, liaise, negotiate and motivate

Conceptual to be able to plan, take an overview, and see how changes in one area affect another

Management hierarchy

Owners, e.g. shareholders
- Decide overall mission of the organisation, i.e. what it is there to achieve

Senior managers, e.g. Marketing Director
- Make strategic decisions
- Decide how to achieve the objectives of the owners

Middle management, e.g. factory managers
- Implement decisions of senior managers
- Decide the best ways of carrying out these plans

First line/supervisory management, e.g. supervisors
- Oversee operatives
- Ensure the orders of the middle management are carried out

Divorce between ownership and control:

the managers who control the organisation day to day may have different objectives from the owners, e.g. the managers may want to invest to grow whereas the owners may want higher dividends now, i.e. there may be a divorce between their objectives.

Management by objectives: managers agree objectives with employees. The result is that employees have clear goals. Progress can be reviewed at the next meeting.

Scientific management: managers decide on the one best way of completing a task, train employees, and reward them for higher output. It assumes that managers are there to think, whereas employees are simply there to implement and are motivated by money. The scientific approach creates a system of rules and procedures for employees to follow. It leads to predictable, consistent results, but can be demotivating if employees wish to be involved and use their initiative.

Information management

Knowledge and information management
Involves the gathering, analysing and distribution of information within the firm

```
┌──────────────┐        ┌──────────────┐        ┌──────────────┐
│ DATA CAPTURE │ ──────▶│ INFORMATION  │ ──────▶│ COMMUNICATING│
│              │        │ PROCESSING   │        │ INFORMATION  │
└──────────────┘        └──────────────┘        └──────────────┘
```

Information handling
Firms must consider:
- the best way of gathering information (both internally and externally)
- the best way of storing information
- the best way of retrieving that information
- the best way of distributing the information

Information technology has enabled more data to be stored and retrieved; it has made information management cheaper, faster and even more important because other firms are using it as a competitive weapon.

Information type
You may have information on:
- your customers – what do they like, when, what and how do they buy? This can be important to develop a strong link with your customers (the process of building a relationship with clients and consumers is known as Customer Relationship Management)
- your own resources and abilities
- external events, e.g. in a crisis it is important to know what is happening in the market
- your competitors – what are they doing now? What are they planning to do next?

Information is more likely to be useful if it is:
- readily available
- cheap
- reliable

Management information systems (MIS)
Procedures developed using information technology to provide data for managers which will help them make decisions, e.g. regular reports on sales and/or costs. The information may be used to plan (at either a strategic or tactical level) or to control.

MIS may provide information on:
- the external environment, e.g. competitors' prices, trade regulations
- the internal environment, e.g. productivity, quality, sales per employee

MIS need to provide information which is:
- relevant
- reliable
- cost effective

Effective information and knowledge management
Gets information to the right people, on time and at an appropriate cost.

It enables firms:
- to react quickly to market changes
- to understand their customers more effectively
- to understand the organisation's own strengths (and weaknesses) more fully
- to save time reacting to situations (e.g. can use experience of others)
- to save costs by using existing knowledge and experience rather than having to solve problems afresh each time
- to make better decisions

Problems managing information effectively
- Information is power; employees may be reluctant to share information, believing that what they know is a basis for their power.
- Obsolescence; may focus too much on existing information rather than gathering new information; as a result may be ill suited to a changing environment.
- Staff turnover; when staff leave you lose their knowledge and expertise.
- Organisational structure; can prevent the free flow of information.
- The importance of managing information may not be appreciated.

Decision making

Managing a business successfully involves effective decision making. Managers must choose between options. When making a decision scientifically a firm will:

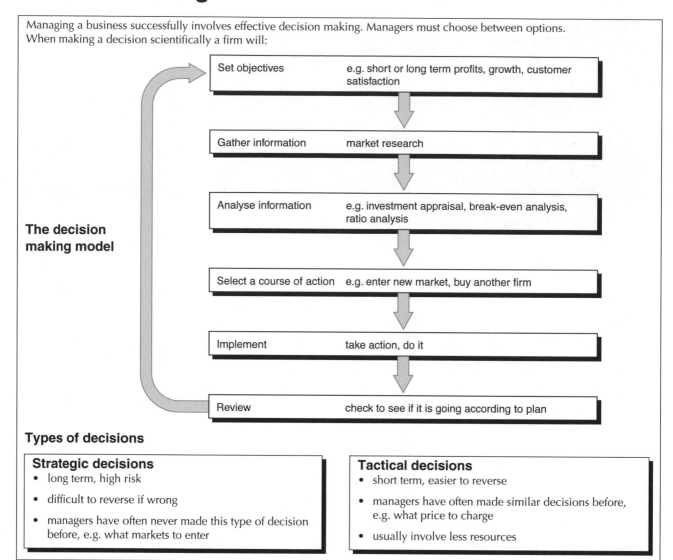

The decision making model

Set objectives	e.g. short or long term profits, growth, customer satisfaction
Gather information	market research
Analyse information	e.g. investment appraisal, break-even analysis, ratio analysis
Select a course of action	e.g. enter new market, buy another firm
Implement	take action, do it
Review	check to see if it is going according to plan

Types of decisions

Strategic decisions
- long term, high risk
- difficult to reverse if wrong
- managers have often never made this type of decision before, e.g. what markets to enter

Tactical decisions
- short term, easier to reverse
- managers have often made similar decisions before, e.g. what price to charge
- usually involve less resources

Constraints on decision making

Internal
Factors a firm can control, but which restrict its ability to achieve its objectives.
- Finance – e.g. cashflow, ability to raise finance
- Marketing – e.g. limited salesforce distribution
- Human resources – e.g. numbers, skills, motivation, attitudes
- Production – e.g. capacity, quality, flexibility

External
Factors beyond the immediate control of the firm, which restrict its ability to achieve its objectives.
- Political factors – e.g. Government policy
- Economic factors – state of economy
- Social factors – e.g. social trends, demographics, attitudes
- Technology – e.g. rate of change

How are decisions made?
Decisions may be based on:
- experience
- hunch
- data

Decision making and decision trees

Decision trees

Method of tracing alternative outcomes of decisions and comparing forecasted results;
quantitative decision making technique.
Aid to decision making; aim is to reduce risk.

Squares are called 'decision nodes': these are points where decisions have to be made – the decision maker has to choose between different courses of action, e.g. to invest in a new advertising campaign or to develop new product.

Circles are called 'chance nodes' or 'event nodes'; they represent a point where there is a chance event. At an event node it is shown that a particular course of action can lead to several outcomes, e.g. success or failure.

The likelihood of a particular outcome is shown by the probability. If it is absolutely certain, the probability is 1; if there is no chance of it happening the probability is 0; the more probable it is, the closer the value will be to 1.

Example 1

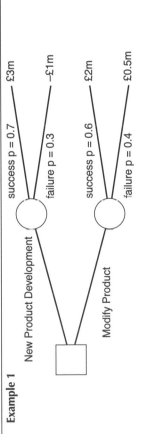

The expected value of each outcome = the predicted profit/loss x the probability of it occurring, e.g. the expected value of the new product development succeeding = 0.7 x £3m = £2.1m

The expected value of a particular course of action = the sum of the expected values of the possible outcomes, e.g. the expected value of new product development = expected value of success + expected value of failure = (0.7 x £3m) + (0.3 x –£1m) = £1.8m

Expected value of modifying product = (0.6 x £2m) + (0.4 x £0.5m) = £1.4m

The decision maker considers the expected value of each course of action and chooses the most profitable.

The option which is not selected is usually crossed off with two small lines.

Choose new product development because it has the highest expected value. However, may also need to consider the initial cost of each option to decide which gives the highest net returns.

Example 2

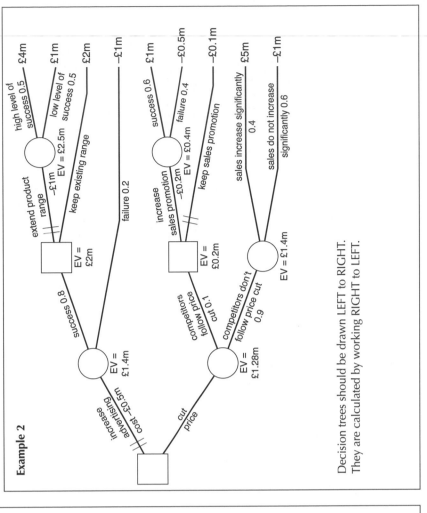

Decision trees should be drawn LEFT to RIGHT.
They are calculated by working RIGHT to LEFT.

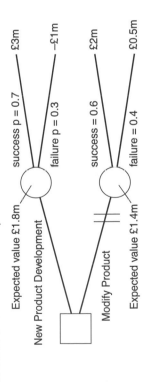

Decision making and decision trees continued

Decision trees and risk

Expected values show on average what will happen from a particular course of action (it is the weighted average of different outcomes taking account of the expected probabilities and financial results). In reality only one outcome will happen. e.g. on average a particular course of action may be desirable but managers may not choose it because the risk of one of the possible outcomes is too high.

e.g. imagine you toss a coin: if it is a head you get £50,000; if it is tails you pay £10,000. On average you will win but if it is a one off bet you may be too worried about losing £10,000 to take it.

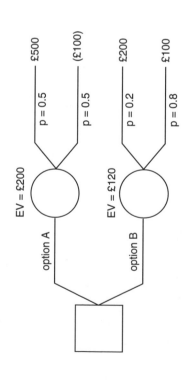

On the basis of numerical analysis alone a firm should choose option A as it has the higher expected value. However with option A there is the possibility of losing money (there is a 50% chance of losing £100). With option B there is no possibility of losing money and so a manager who is risk averse may actually choose this option.

Value of decision trees

- Make manager consider options, outcomes, likelihood and consequence of different outcomes; this is a useful process in itself.
- Can highlight the best decision mathematically.
- Help managers quantify effects of decision.
- Make managers consider outcomes of a decision.
- Make managers think about alternative courses of action.
- Can make rational, scientific decisions based on quantifiable techniques.

BUT

- Depends on how reliable the estimates are (Where are they from? How gathered?)
- In reality need to take account of attitude to risk, e.g. one decision may mathematically have a higher expected value than another but if the potential loss is greater it may not be chosen. Managers may choose an alternative which offers fewer gains but has less chance of making a loss.
- Must be remembered that the expected value is the weighted average of outcomes and the probability of these outcomes; in reality only one outcome will actually occur!
- Depends on whether all alternatives are identified.
- Depends on qualitative factors.

Intuition/hunch

Managers take decisions based on what they feel.

This approach:

- may lead to more creative decisions.
- may be a quick decision making process.

Hunch is more likely to be used if:

- the decision is unfamiliar
- no data easily available
- market conditions rapidly changing
- need to produce the unexpected!
- risk is low

Scientific decision making

Bases decisions on quantifiable data. Managers analyse data before taking a decision. Should ensure decisions are logical.

Advantages of scientific decision making:

- rational basis to decision making
- should reduce risk

Disadvantages of scientific decision making:

- data may not be available
- data may be inaccurate
- data may be out of date
- may lack spontaneity/creativity
- may be a slow process

Strategy

Strategic planning
Aims to match the firm's products and services with the market opportunities.

Types of strategy

A. cost leadership v differentiation
- Cost leadership occurs when a firm aims to produce similar goods and services to competitors but at a lower cost; the lower costs will enable it to lower its prices and win business. Kwik Save aims to be a low price producer.

- Differentiation occurs when a firm aims to offer superior benefits to competitors and therefore charge a higher price. Harrod's charges a higher price than many other retailers because it is perceived as significantly different from its competitors.

B. niche v mass
A niche strategy occurs when a firm targets a small segment of the market (e.g. Mills and Boon target romantic novels); other publishers aim at the majority of the market (i.e. they are mass market producers).

Strategic gap: occurs when there is a difference between where the firm is aiming to be and where it is actually heading at the moment.

Value of strategic planning
- Coordinates planning
- Clarifies what the tactics need to achieve
- Developing the strategy involves discussion between managers which is a valuable process in itself

Forming a strategy
To form a strategy a firm must answer the following questions:
- What are the firm's objectives?
- What are the options open to the firm?
- How do the different options fit with the firm's strengths, objectives and values?
- What are the expected returns from the different alternatives?
- How is the firm going to change employees' behaviour towards the new strategy?
- How will the firm measure success?

Strategic planning

Determine corporate objectives

↓

Gather data e.g. SWOT analysis, Portfolio analysis, PEST analysis

↓

Analyse alternative strategies

↓

Select strategy

↓

Implement

↓

Review

SWOT analysis
Examines the present situation of the firm (its Strengths and Weaknesses) and future possible changes (Opportunities and Threats)

It is an important part of strategic planning: the firm assesses where it is now and what might happen in the future in order to plan its strategy. The strategy may seek to build on its strengths and/or protect against its weaknesses. The firm will seek to exploit opportunities and deflect threats.

Strengths could include:
- marketing: brand name, distribution channels
- finance: cash flow position, liquidity, profitability, quality of profit
- people: skills, motivation, ideas
- operations: flexibility, volume, unit cost, quality, lead time

Weaknesses could include:
- marketing: lack of a trained/effective workforce
- finance: illiquid; poor budgeting procedure
- people: lack of direction; culture of indifference
- operations; lack of investment; poor productivity

Opportunities could include:
- extending the brand
- entering new markets
- diversifying

Threats could include:
- changes in legislation
- new entrants to the market
- new technology replacing existing products/processes
- declining markets

Problems of strategic planning
- Takes time
- Strategy may be inappropriate
- Strategy may not change with market conditions
- Strategy may limit initiative; managers will not look for alternatives

Strategy
- long term
- involves major commitment of resources
- difficult to reverse decisions
- likely to be made by senior management
- likely to be new decisions

Tactics
- short term
- less commitment of resources
- easier to reverse decisions
- likely to be made by junior managers
- more likely to be decisions which have been made before

Presenting and analysing data

Pie chart

The proportion of the area of the circle shows the relative importance of items.

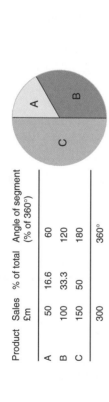

Product	Sales £m	% of total	Angle of segment (% of 360°)
A	50	16.6	60
B	100	33.3	120
C	150	50	180
	300		360°

Problems: difficult to illustrate more than a few items; cannot easily calculate the exact value of each item from looking at the diagram.

Pictogram

Data is presented pictorially; eye-catching means of displaying data.

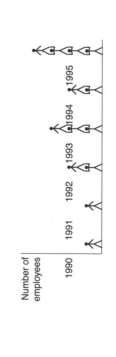

Problem: not easy to show figures accurately. Each person above represents 1000 employees, how do we show 246 employees?

Bar chart

Length of bar shows the value of different items.

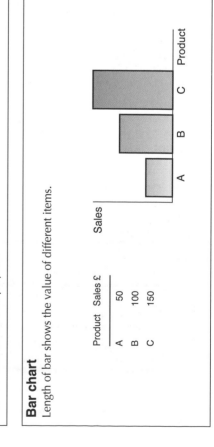

Product	Sales £
A	50
B	100
C	150

Histogram

The area of the bars represents the frequency.

Miles travelled	Frequency
0–10	5
11–20	10
21–40	10
41–50	20

The frequency for this range is the same as for the one before. Because the range is twice as wide the bar will need to be half as tall to give the same overall area.

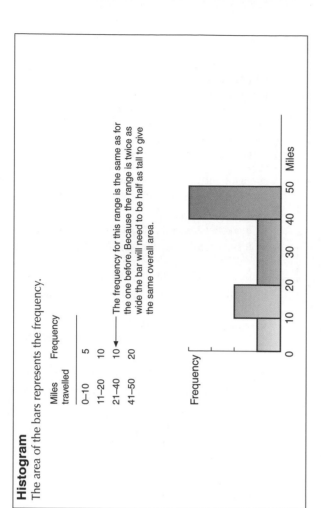

Line graph

Joins the points showing the relationship between two variables.

Month	Sales (£)
January	100
February	120
March	150
April	110
May	130

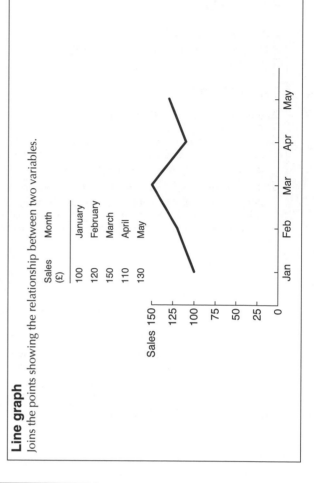

Index numbers

These show how much an item has changed relative to a given starting point (called the base). The base is usually expressed as 100 so the index shows the percentage change compared to the base.

	X	
1998	100	
1999	120	X has increased by 20% since 1998
2000	90	X has fallen by 10% since 1998
2001	130	X has increased by 30% since 1998

Measures of central tendency

Data: 2,12, 4, 14, 5, 6, 5, 7,10

- **mean** average; take the sum of the items and divide by the number of items. Total = 65. Number of items = 9. Mean = 65 ÷ 9 = 7.2.
- **median** middle value; rank items from the lowest to highest; choose middle value. 2, 4, 5, 5, 6, 7, 10, 12, 14. Middle value = 6.
- **mode** most frequent value; in this case 5

Methods of smoothing data:

a. Moving average

Used to calculate the underlying trend of given data.

The trend line is smoother than actual sales figures; it eliminates fluctuations and highlights the trend more clearly.

Year	Sales		3 year moving average
1996	10		
1997	11	$\frac{10+11+12}{3}$	= 11
1998	12	$\frac{11+12+19}{3}$	= 14
1999	19	$\frac{12+19+11}{3}$	= 14
2000	11	$\frac{19+11+18}{3}$	= 16
2001	18		

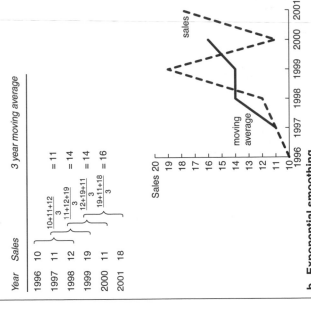

b. Exponential smoothing

This method gives more emphasis to more recent data by giving it more weight when calculating the trend.

Calculation

z value = $(x - m) \div s$ where $x - m$ is the deviation from the mean and s = standard deviation. It shows how many standard deviations 'x' is from the mean.

Example

Mean weight of product is 500 grams; standard deviation is 20.
What proportion of the products will be over 520 grams?

z = $(520 - 500) \div 20$ = 1 standard deviation from the mean. The area under the normal curve shown by this value can be read from tables. In this case it is 0.3413.

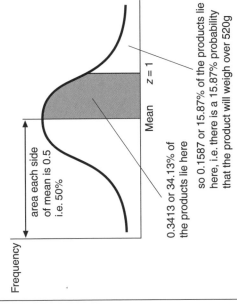

area each side of mean is 0.5 i.e. 50%

0.3413 or 34.13% of the products lie here

Mean   z = 1

so 0.1587 or 15.87% of the products lie here, i.e. there is a 15.87% probability that the product will weigh over 520g

Limitations of the normal distribution

Need a large sample size to get a normal distribution. Even then not all distributions will be normal.

Normal distribution

Statistical model; used with large samples (e.g. in marketing research and quality control) to help firms assess the likely results for the 'population' as a whole.

Features:

- Continuous, symmetrical, bell-shaped distribution (i.e. most values cluster around the mean but there are some which are much higher or lower; e.g. in a test the majority of students will get around the average score but a few will do much better or worse).
- The mean, mode, and median are equal.
- 50% of the values lie either side of the mean.

Frequency

50% of values   50% of values

Mean
Median
Mode

99.7% of the distribution lies within 3 standard deviations either side of the mean

95% of the distribution lies within 1.96 standard deviations either side of the mean

68% of the distribution lies within 1 standard deviation either side of the mean

(*Standard deviation* is a measure of how data is distributed around a mean value.)

Forecasting

Forecasting: used to predict what might happen, e.g. what sales might be next year. Important for planning.

Sales forecasting

Is very important to :
- plan production levels and scheduling
- plan cash flows
- plan human resources (workforce planning)

1 Time series analysis:

Based on extrapolation, i.e. projecting a past trend into the future. Assumes the past is an indicator to the future.

Time series analysis does not explain the data, it simply describes what is happening and what will happen if it continues.

A business will try to identify:
- the underlying trend
- cyclical fluctuations, i.e. whether there is a pattern of 'highs' and 'lows' over a given period
- seasonal fluctuations, i.e. whether there are highs and lows at particular times of the year

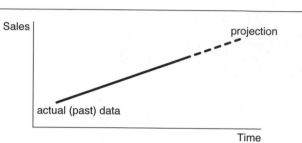

When using past data, firms will often 'smooth' the data to identify the underlying trend.

Extrapolation: will only work if market conditions do not change much; in many cases change can be so rapid and sudden that extrapolation could be very misleading.

2 Causal modelling

This method of forecasting attempts to explain data by finding links between one set of data and another, e.g. between advertising and sales. This can help predict the effects in the future, e.g. of an increase in advertising.

Correlation coefficients range from:

$-1 \longleftarrow 0 \longrightarrow +1$

perfect −ve correlation   no correlation   perfect +ve correlation

Correlation does not in itself show cause and effect. The fact that advertising has increased and sales have increased may be connected but not necessarily. It could be due to other factors such as price changes or income growth.

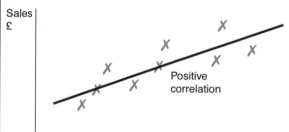

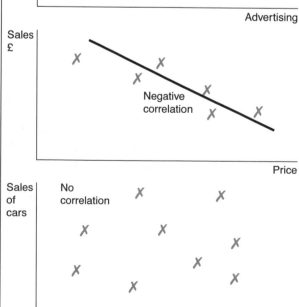

3 Qualitative forecasts

Based on personal judgement or experts' opinions, e.g. use Delphi technique – experts asked independently for their views; responses collated and presented back to them; further comments accepted and incorporated. As experts comment independently, no one expert can dominate. By circulating views again and again, gradually move towards consensus.

Operations research

Operations research
Scientific approach to decision making; uses mathematical models.

Linear programming
Sets out problems as a series of linear (straight line) equations.

Linear programming includes Blending. This shows how a firm can best allocate its resources given various constraints, such as allocating production between two products.

Example

Minutes taken on different operations to produce two products:

	Operation 1	Operation 2
Product A	4 minutes	2 minutes
Product B	2 minutes	5 minutes
Total time available	800 minutes	1200 minutes

Constraints

- **Operation 1** $4A + 2B \le 800$, i.e. it takes 4 minutes to make one A and 2 minutes to make a B and the maximum time available is 800 minutes. If all this time is spent on A then 200 As are produced ($800 \div 4$). If all the time is spent on B, 400 Bs can be produced. (See diagram I)

- **Operation 2** $2A + 5B \le 1200$. If all the time was spent on A, 600 can be produced ($=1200 \div 2$). If all the time is spent on B, 240 can be made ($=1200 \div 5$). See diagram II.

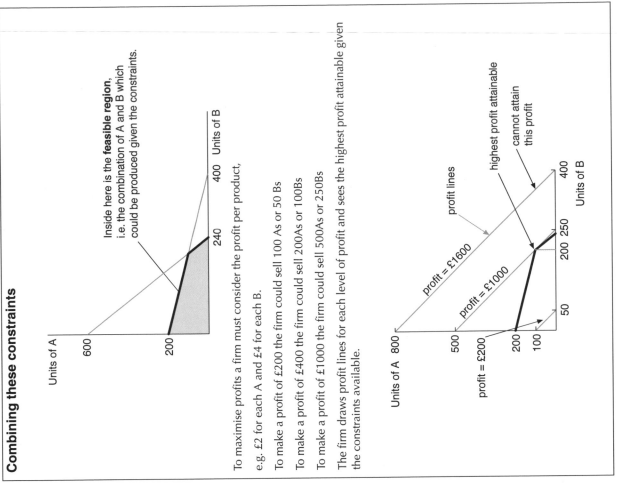

Diagram I

Line shows maximum of A and B which can be produced in Operation 1 given the time constraints

Units of A 200

Units of B 400

Diagram II

Line shows maximum of A and B which can be produced in Operation 2 given the time constraints

Units of A 600

Units of B 240

Combining these constraints

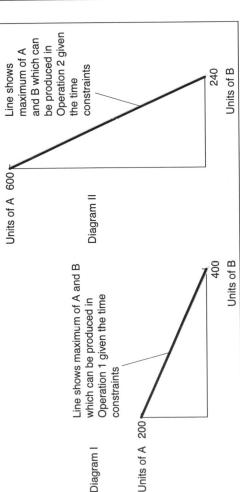

Units of A 600

Inside here is the **feasible region**, i.e. the combination of A and B which could be produced given the constraints.

200

240   400   Units of B

To maximise profits a firm must consider the profit per product, e.g. £2 for each A and £4 for each B.

To make a profit of £200 the firm could sell 100 As or 50 Bs

To make a profit of £400 the firm could sell 200As or 100Bs

To make a profit of £1000 the firm could sell 500As or 250Bs

The firm draws profit lines for each level of profit and sees the highest profit attainable given the constraints available.

Units of A 800

500

profit lines

profit = £1600

profit = £1000

highest profit attainable

cannot attain this profit

200

profit = £200

100

50   200 250   400   Units of B

Operations research continued

Critical path analysis (network diagrams)

Arrows: represent activities and often have a letter next to them to identify them; the length of time the activity takes (its duration) is put underneath the arrow.

Circles: (or nodes) represent the start or end of an activity.

A node has three sections:
- the left hand side shows a node number to make it easier to follow the order of tasks
- the top right shows the Earliest Start Time (EST) which is the earliest time the next task can begin
- bottom right shows the Latest Finish Time (LFT) which is latest time the previous task can finish without delaying the next task

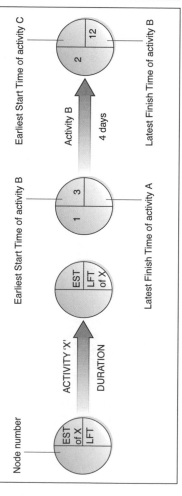

Node number — EST of X / LFT of X

ACTIVITY 'X' — DURATION

Earliest Start Time of activity B — Earliest Start Time of activity C

Activity B — 4 days

Latest Finish Time of activity A — Latest Finish Time of activity B

Total float: this is the maximum increase in the time taken for an activity without increasing the overall time needed for the project; given by the Latest Finish Time – duration – Earliest Start Time, e.g. if an activity takes 4 days, has to finish on day 12 but can begin on day 3 then its total float is 12 – 4 – 3 = 5 days.

Free float: maximum increase in time taken for this activity that can occur without altering the floats available to other activities. Free float = EST at end – duration – EST at start

Critical path: the sequence of events which determines the minimum time required to complete the project.

Critical path activities have no float. They must be started as soon as the previous ones finish. Non-critical activities have float time.

Constructing a network diagram

Activity	Duration	
A	2	must be done first
B	3	can only start after A is completed
C	4	can only start after A is completed
D	5	can only start when B is completed
E	8	can only start when C is completed
F	3	can only start when E is completed
G	4	can only start when D and F are completed

In days	EST	LFT	Duration	FLOAT	FREE FLOAT
A	0	0	2	0	0
B	2	12	3	7	0
C	2	6	4	0	0
D	5	17	5	7	7
E	6	14	8	0	0
F	14	17	3	0	0
G	17	21	4	0	0

Drawing CPAs

- Draw from left to right.
- A node represents the start and finish of an activity.
- A line represents an activity. Put the name of the activity above the line and the duration below.
- Lines should not cross each other.
- Be careful not to put the node at the end of an activity until you know what happens next.
- The project should begin and end on a single node.

PERT analysis: Programme Evaluation and Review Techniques.

Takes into account the fact that the duration of activities is uncertain. Instead of a single estimate of each activity time, it uses three estimates – most likely, optimistic (shortest estimate), pessimistic (longest estimate). Often used when delays possible, e.g. weather affecting construction.

Transportation

Used to solve problems of transporting items from a number of different places to different destinations.

Example

Factory A Output	10	Warehouse 1 Capacity	12
Factory B Output	14	Warehouse 2 Capacity	10
		Warehouse 3 Capacity	2
TOTAL	24	TOTAL	24

The costs of transporting from each factory to each warehouse are as below:

£ per unit	Warehouse 1	Warehouse 2	Warehouse 3
Factory A	4	2	3
Factory B	1	5	1

Question: What is the most cost effective means of transporting materials from the factories to the warehouses?

Answer: Construct a matrix and try different options. In the matrix below all of factory A's output is sent to Warehouse 1, so none is sent to the other two factories. The output of Factory B is then divided between the three factories according to their capacity.

these boxes show the cost of transporting from one warehouse to one factory

	Warehouse 1		Warehouse 2		Warehouse 3		Total
Factory A	10	4	0	2	0	3	10
Factory B	2	1	10	5	2	1	14
Total	12		10		2		24

Total cost = $(10 \times £4) + (2 \times £1) + (10 \times £5) + (2 \times £1) = £94$

Other options must then be tried to see if there are cheaper means of organising the deliveries; the cheapest method is called the 'least cost' solution, e.g. the option below gives a total cost of $(12 \times £1) + (10 \times £2) + (2 \times £1) = £34$

	Warehouse 1		Warehouse 2		Warehouse 3		Total
Factory A	0	4	10	2	0	3	10
Factory B	12	1	0	5	2	1	14
Total	12		10		2		24

The value of critical path analysis

- Can identify what resources are needed and when.
- Can be part of a lean production process e.g. stocks arrive just in time (the delivery times determined by CPA).
- Can help reduce stock levels (good for working capital control); items can arrive when needed.
- Can reduce the development/lead time of a product by identifying simultaneous activities; part of time based management.
- Can help management to decide on which activities need to be controlled most rigorously (e.g. those with no float time).
- The process of producing a critical path network is valuable as it make managers think about the order of activities, which activities are involved and the likely duration of each.
- Technique for planning and reviewing to keep control.

BUT

Its value depends on how reliable the estimates of duration are. If one activity overruns the start and finish times need to be re-calculated.

Problems of CPA

- May be so many activities that cannot easily construct a network diagram.
- Simply drawing the CPA does not guarantee it will happen in this way.
- The estimates may be incorrect.
- Managers may not keep in control of the project so activities overrun.

Operations research continued

Simulation [or queueing theory] involves constructing a model to simulate the effect of random events, e.g. customers appearing in shops and taking different lengths of time to serve. It deals with problems such as congestion at airports and queues in banks and aims to plan events so a bottleneck does not occur.

Example

Time between arrivals (minutes)	Frequency of customers %	Cumulative frequency %
0	5	5
1	10	15
2	55	70
3	30	100

Time at checkout (minutes)	Frequency of customers %	Cumulative frequency %
1	22	22
2	20	42
3	38	80
4	20	100

Random number table:

14→ 44 →73 → 87
46 70 53 2
29 81 57 94
39 98 74 22
56 16 80 10

The random numbers are allocated to 'time between arrivals' and 'time at checkout' according to the cumulative frequencies as shown below in columns 3 and 6. Random numbers are then selected for each customer.

If the random number picked out for the first customer to arrive is 14, this lies in the cumulative frequency range of 06–15 and so a time of 1 minute is allotted. If the random number selected for the time spent at the checkout is 44 this is in the range 43–80 so a time of 3 minutes is allotted.

Time between arrivals	Cumulative frequency %	Random numbers		Time at checkout	Cumulative frequency %	Random numbers
0	5	→	01–05	1	22 →	01–22
1	15	→	06–15	2	42 →	23–42
2	70	→	16–70	3	80 →	43–80
3	100	→	71–100	4	100 →	81–100

Customer 1: First random number is 14 – arrives after 1 minute
Second random number is 44 – time to be served 3 minutes

Customer 2: Random Number 73 – this is in the range 71–100 so he/she arrives after 3 minutes
Random number 87 – this is in the range 81–100 so he/she takes 4 minutes to be served

Assume only one checkout which opens at 9.00 am

Customer	Random number for arrival	Random number for service	Time between arrival	Time taken to be served	Arrives at	Served at	Leaves at	Customer wait before service (minutes)
1	14	44	1	3	9.01	9.01	9.04	0
2	73	87	3	4	9.04	9.04	9.08	0
3	46	70	2	3	9.06	9.08	9.11	2
4	53	02	2	1	9.08	9.11	9.12	3

From this the firm can decide whether it thinks a second checkout is needed; the situation with two checkouts can also be analysed using simulation analysis.

Reshaping

Restructuring (or 'reshaping')
Reorganisation of activities, e.g. downsizing, re-engineering and demerging.

Successful organisations are continually looking to reshape themselves to meet the changing needs of their environments to make themselves ever more competitive.

Diversification: moving into new and different business areas. This spreads risks but can be difficult to control.

Delayering
Occurs when firms remove layers of management within their organisation structure.

Fewer layers should lead to:
- quicker decision making
- greater responsiveness to customer needs and wants
- greater responsibility (which can be motivating)
- lower management costs

BUT
- individuals may lack training and ability
- individuals may suffer stress

Outsourcing
Firms subcontract work out to independent suppliers rather than undertake the activities themselves. This allows firms to concentrate on their core activities and benefit from the expertise of specialists. For example, firms may subcontract their catering, their security, their office cleaning, their market research and their design work.

Downsizing
Modern term for redundancy. Occurs when organisations attempt to increase their efficiency by reducing their staffing levels. Whilst this may reduce costs it can obviously cause uncertainty and fear amongst the employees who are left and resentment from those who are made redundant.

Re-engineering
'The fundamental rethinking and radical redesign of business processes to achieve dramatic improvements in critical, contemporary measures of performance such as cost, quality, service and speed.' (M. Hammer and J. Champy).

Re-engineering aims to improve business performance by organising work around a process rather than around tasks. When firms are trying to improve performance they tend to look at what they do at the moment and try to improve on this, rather than thinking about whether there is a completely different way of serving the customer more effectively. Re-engineering occurs when managers ignore the way things are done at present and start with a blank piece of paper to create a new process. Re-engineering, therefore, involves radical and dramatic change.

Demerging
A firm splits itself up into separate, smaller business units. For example, ICI split into ICI and Zeneca, Hanson was divided into four separate companies and British Gas split into two parts.

Reasons:
- each business is able to respond independently to its own markets
- smaller units are easier to control and coordinate

BUT
- may lose economies of scale
- may lack as much market power

The trend in the past has been to get bigger; in recent years firms have tended to 'get back to basics', by focusing on their core activities and splitting into smaller business units.

Successful organisations

To be successful firms need to:

Know the market
The key to competitive success lies in knowing what your customers want now and are likely to want in the future. Successful firms are proactive, i.e. they anticipate change rather than react to it.

Know the competition
Firms need to identify their areas of relative strength and weakness; they must monitor the market and measure their levels of cost and service against the competition.

Work with suppliers
The present trend is not to select suppliers purely on the basis of price. It is important to consider other factors such as their quality, reliability and delivery schedules. Successful firms involve suppliers and develop a joint problem-solving approach; they build long term relationships with a few trusted suppliers – this is called 'partnership sourcing'.

Design products properly
A good design takes into account internal customers as well as external customers. A well designed product is relatively easy to make as well as satisfying customers' needs and wants.

Get it right and right again and right again and ...
Production processes and the final goods and services must be reliable. Firms continually monitor their performance and develop ways of improving.

Be flexible
Staff and equipment must be flexible to respond quickly to changing needs. This requires training and investment.

Put people together
Managers need to get people to share ideas and learn from each other. By bringing people together they are more likely to understand each other's problems and find solutions.

Build a learning organisation
Managers need to encourage people to develop skills and to try out ideas even if they fail at first. People should be encouraged to be curious.

Be time competitive
Increasingly firms are competing on time by producing products more quickly and delivering in a shorter time. Products can be developed more quickly by carrying out different parts of the process at the same time rather than waiting for one stage to finish before starting another, i.e. simultaneous engineering rather than a sequential approach.

Delight the customer
There are so many competitors that firms have to do more than satisfy the customer, they have to delight the customer. (This is Kwik Fit's stated aim.) Successful organisations must not only meet customers' expectations, they must surpass them. Shopping, for example, must be made a pleasant, interesting and enjoyable experience, not a chore. This involves many factors such as: the products which are stocked, the decor of the shop, the aroma in the shop, the image of the store, the way in which customers are served, the way in which people can pay and the after sales service.

The successful organisation will:
- have a clear and shared view of where and how it will be successful (i.e. a mission)
- be able to predict change and respond quickly
- maintain high levels of quality at an appropriate price
- learn faster than the competition

Is business success due to luck?
Success is due to a wide range of factors.
- Some are beyond the control of firm, e.g. economic environment.
- However managers can determine the firm's reaction to these factors and the extent to which it is prepared for them.
- Success is likely to be partly luck and partly due to effective planning and a good use of resources.

What the gurus say

Theodore Levitt

According to Levitt, one of the major consequences of developments in technology is that countries all over the world are becoming increasingly similar. People all over the world can see what is available elsewhere and want it for themselves. As a result Levitt argues that markets have become increasingly globalised. Companies which appreciate this 'new commercial reality' can benefit from huge economies of scale in production and marketing. These economies of scale can then enable them to cut prices and destroy the competition who have not yet realised how much the world has changed.

Tom Peters

In his book *A Passion for Excellence* Tom Peters identified leadership as central to the Quality Improvement Process. He considered the word 'management' should be discarded in favour of 'leadership'. The new role should be that of cheerleader and facilitator. He sees Managing By Wandering About (MBWA) as the basis of leadership and excellence because it enables the leader to keep in touch with Customers, Innovation and People, the three major areas in pursuit of excellence. By the late 1980s he was using the term 'obsessions' i.e. successful firms must be obsessed with success and considered that leaders must learn to love change in order to be proactive in a world of chaos.

In his book *Thriving on Chaos* Peters identifies 12 traits of a quality revolution:
1. Management obsession with quality
2. Passionate systems; failure is inevitable due to passion without systems or vice versa
3. Measurement of quality
4. Quality is rewarded
5. Everyone is trained for quality
6. Multi function teams
7. Small is beautiful
8. Create endless Hawthorne Effects
9. Parallel organisation structure devoted to quality improvement
10. Everyone is involved, e.g. suppliers, distributors
11. When quality goes up, costs go down
12. Quality improvement is a never ending journey

Other factors he claimed were common to successful or 'excellent' companies included:
- the use of small project teams
- the elimination of bureaucracy
- the ability to listen and learn from customers
- support for individuals willing to innovate
- recognition of employees as a key asset
- a clear understanding of the firm's mission
- tightly held common values but room for employees to act within them
- a focus on the core business

His work now focuses on the need for organisations to be flexible to rapid change, to restructure, to be radical and to involve employees.

Books include: 1982 *In Search of Excellence*; 1985 *A Passion for Excellence* (with Nancy Austin); 1988 *Thriving on Chaos*

Hamel and Prahalad

Competing for the Future
They argue that the most important form of competition is the battle to create and dominate emerging opportunities. Traditional strategists look on companies as a collection of products and business units; Hamel and Prahalad look on them as a collection of skills.

Traditional strategists try to position their business effectively on existing markets; Hamel and Prahalad argue that a company should try to reinvent a whole industry by following a vision. You win by establishing a monopoly (for however short a time) e.g. Chrysler with minivans, Sony with Walkmans, or setting a standard, e.g. Microsoft with DOS, or establishing the rules of the game, e.g. WalMart with out-of-town hypermarkets.

Drucker

Management by objectives (MBO)

The *Practice of Management* 1954 focused on the importance of having clear objectives both for the corporation and for the managers and of translating long term strategy into short term goals. In particular Drucker felt that an organisation should have an elite of general managers who would determine strategy and set objectives for more specialised managers. The structure of the firm should follow its strategy: 'organisation is not an end in itself but a means to an end of business performance and business results... organisation structure must be designed so as to make possible the achievement of the business five, ten, fifteen years hence.'

MBO has fallen from grace a little. Several leading companies such as Motorola and 3M allow ideas, including ideas for long term strategies, to emerge from the bottom of the organisation. Companies which have the old system of MBO can be inflexible.

Mintzberg

The Nature of Managerial Work showed that managers are creatures of the moment and not far-sighted strategists carefully planning their next move.

Mintzberg criticises the view that the strategic direction of a firm is carefully planned. He believes:
- strategy emerges over time.
- managers spend much of the time 'fire fighting', reacting to events rather than carefully undertaking long term plans.

When he was Prime Minister, Harold MacMillan was once asked what was the most difficult thing about his job. 'Events, my dear boy, events' he replied. In many cases managers are fighting crises (or 'events') rather than planning ahead carefully.

What the gurus say continued

Charles Handy

In the late 1980s Handy suggested that organisations would increasingly become Shamrock organisations. They would have three types of employees:

- **core workers** – qualified professionals providing the main source of knowledge. These are full time, long term employees

- **contract workers** – employed for a specific task; used on short term basis to complete set work

- **peripheral workers** – flexible workers employed on a part time basis

This pattern does seem to have occurred and the implication is that there will be less long term, full time employment in the future.

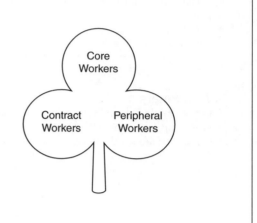

Porter's five forces model

Suggests business behaviour is affected by:

- buyer power: e.g. how easy is it to find other buyers?

- supplier power: e.g. can you find other suppliers easily? Will it be expensive to switch?

- entry threat – how easy is it for other firms to enter the market (e.g. what are the entry costs?)

- substitute threat, e.g. how easy is it for buyers to switch to alternative products or services?

- rivalry, i.e. the extent of existing competition within the market

A firm has more control over a market when buyer power is weak (i.e. a firm is not dependent on one or two buyers), supplier power is weak (i.e. a firm has many alternative sources of supply), there are few substitutes, little likelihood of entry and limited rivalry. Under these conditions the firm should be able to generate high returns. If, however, entry is easy, there are many substitutes, and you are are dependent on certain buyers and suppliers, your returns are likely to be lower.

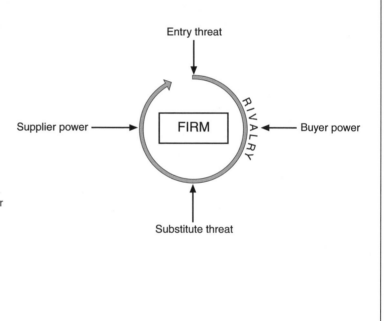

Key points to remember

Marketing

- marketing is much more than advertising or selling; it involves a range of activities including finding out what customers want, distribution, pricing and developing the product concept and design

- the marketing process involves setting objectives, determining the strategy and implementing this with the marketing mix

- effective decisions often rely on good market research (however market research is not necessarily 100% correct, therefore there is always a risk)

- the elements of the marketing mix must be integrated, e.g. the price must be appropriate for the type of product, its promotion and distribution strategy

- the mix will depend on the strategy, e.g. a mass market strategy is likely to involve a lower price and wider distribution than a niche market

- make sure you apply the mix to reflect the nature of the actual product or service in question; don't just write out the marketing mix – use this model in context

- don't forget to refer to the price elasticity of demand if you are recommending a price change

- the firm should base its plans on customer requirements and its own strengths and abilities

Operations

- operations management can affect the output a firm can produce, its flexibility, unit cost and quality

- capacity can be a constraint on a firm – it may not be able to meet demand; if capacity is too high this can have an impact on unit costs

- remember that when output increases costs will almost certainly increase (although unit costs may fall)

- not every firm uses lean production techniques; there can be problems with lean techniques

- the definition of quality depends on customer requirements

- quality can be achieved through prevention as well as more inspection

- the method of production affects a firm's ability to meet customer needs and provide better value than the competition

- remember that just because you produce something does not guarantee it sells; don't assume an increase in output necessarily means an increase in sales – it may be that stocks simply increase

- just because you are based in a particular area does not mean you are selling in that area – you may be but you might also be selling all over the world

Finance

- cash is not the same as profit; e.g. you may sell something (which counts as revenue) without having received the cash yet

- accounting only deals with quantifiable factors and measures these in financial terms; there may be many non financial factors and qualitative issues in any decision

- budgeting can be an important method of coordinating the organisation

- a firm must monitor its liquidity to survive

- try to use ratios in many of your answers – don't wait to be asked for them. e.g. if you are considering any form of investment consider the payback, net present value or average rate of return. Consider the impact of any decision on liquidity. What will the decision do to the firm's return on capital employed?

People

- remember that people are a valuable resource who can have a tangible affect on business success

- motivation in itself does not guarantee an effective performance – people also need the training, skills and tools to do the job properly

- people will react in different ways to changes within a firm; e.g. some people will welcome additional responsibilities; others will simply regard it as extra work

- the structure of the organisation (e.g. the way jobs are designed, the levels of hierarchy, the degree of delegation) affects the speed of decision making, the quality of decisions and costs

- management by objectives can be an important means of coordinating the organisation

- the quality of communication in a firm affects motivation, speed of response, the degree of innovation, the quality of decisions

External influences

- most questions will focus on the impact of external change on a firm; relate your answers to the different functions – how will the marketing, personnel or finance departments be affected?

- not everyone is socially responsible; not every consumer cares about a firm's ethics or corporate image. Some answers suggest that if a firm is socially responsible consumers will automatically want to buy more from this business. In reality many consumers do not take this into account – as ever the impact depends on the particular situation

- technology moves the economy and business forward; it can create jobs, new products and new markets

General

- Always look for the objectives of the business – what are the managers or owners trying to achieve? These might not be the same thing!

- Always look at whether the activities of the different functions complement each other, e.g. marketing may determine what is required; operations must then produce what marketing has identified as the customer requirements.

- Remember the many constraints on a business – the managers' ability, managers' time, money, the firm's existing resources.

- The culture of a firm is extremely important – e.g. it affects the way decisions are made, how much initiative or risk people will take.

- Think about how the decision is made and by whom; how much information data is there? Is it reliable? How good is the decision maker?

- Never forget the context of the firm – what would this firm do at this time in this situation? Why?

Revision exercises

A. Define the key words below and explain their business significance

MARKETING
1. market analysis
2. market research
3. marketing objectives
4. product life cycle
5. product portfolio analysis
6. adding value
7. marketing mix
8. price elasticity of demand
9. income elasticity of demand
10. niche marketing

FINANCE
1. cash
2. profit
3. working capital
4. ordinary share capital
5. budget
6. variance
7. cost centre
8. contribution per unit
9. fixed costs
10. break-even

PEOPLE
1. span of control
2. centralisation
3. delayering
4. delegation
5. Mayo
6. piecework
7. authoritarian management
8. McGregor's Theory Y
9. workforce planning
10. on the job training

OPERATIONS
1. economies of scale
2. diseconomies of scale
3. job production
4. flow production
5. buffer stocks
6. benchmarking
7. just in time production
8. kaizen
9. productivity
10. batch production

EXTERNAL INFLUENCES
1. business cycle
2. interest rates
3. exchange rates
4. inflation
5. structural unemployment
6. health and safety law
7. employment law
8. competition law
9. business ethics
10. stakeholders

OBJECTIVES AND FINANCE
1. sole trader
2. limited liability
3. private limited company
4. public limited company
5. business plan
6. patent
7. copyright
8. objective
9. strategy
10. SWOT analysis

Revision exercises continued

B. What factors make the following MORE LIKELY?

EXAMPLE

Democratic leadership: *more likely when employees are well trained, relationships between employers and employees are good, there is time to discuss, the risk of error is low*

MARKETING
- a price cut
- secondary research (*v* primary)
- niche marketing
- price skimming
- bigger marketing budget
- an increase in advertising

FINANCE
- cash flow problems
- raising finance through debt rather than share issue
- introduction of budgeting
- high gearing
- high return on capital employed
- falling profit margins
- high debtor days
- low stock turnover
- low acid test
- low break even level of output
- low payback period
- window dressing

PEOPLE
- external recruitment
- a motivated workforce
- a pay increase
- a wide span of control
- matrix management
- a high level of employee participation
- workforce planning

OPERATIONS
- high stock levels
- high stock turnover
- job production

EXTERNAL
- high levels of inflation
- high levels of cyclical unemployment
- low economic growth
- undertaking a social audit
- privatisation

OBJECTIVES AND STRATEGY
- a successful start up
- a management buy out
- going from private limited company to public limited company
- the take-over of another company
- introducing a mission statement
- contingency planning

C. Discuss the possible advantages and disadvantages to a firm of:

(NOTE: You need arguments for, arguments against and a conclusion)

MARKETING
- market research
- new product development
- a price cut
- niche marketing

FINANCE
- break even analysis
- cash flow forecasting
- high gearing
- using internal finance to fund expansion

PEOPLE
- authoritarian management
- decentralisation
- management by objectives
- empowerment
- performance related pay
- internal recruitment
- delayering
- delegation
- teamworking

OPERATIONS
- expanding output
- just in time production
- BS 5750/ISO 9000

EXTERNAL INFLUENCES
- technological change
- environmental auditing
- social responsibility
- membership of the European Union
- contingency planning
- high levels of unemployment

OBJECTIVES AND STRATEGY
- a takeover
- strategic planning
- morality in decision making

Revision exercises continued

D. Discuss the possible benefits and problems for a firm of:

MARKETING
- setting a marketing budget
- sales forecasting
- scientific marketing
- marketing planning
- price, income and advertising elasticity of demand

FINANCE
- quantitative investment appraisal techniques
- budgeting
- cash flow forecasting

PEOPLE
- employee participation
- delegation
- greater trade union membership
- collective bargaining
- management by objectives
- employee appraisal

OPERATIONS
- increasing productivity
- benchmarking
- lean production
- critical path analysis
- continuous improvement
- increasing the scale of production
- cell production
- budgeting for research and development
- quality circles

EXTERNAL INFLUENCES
- high growth in the economy
- weak pound

OBJECTIVES AND STRATEGY
- limited liability status
- scientific decision making
- decision tree analysis

E. Discuss the possible implications for a firm of:
- horizontal integration
- rapid growth
- a sudden fall in demand
- pressure group activity
- an increase in interest rates
- a fall in GDP
- a sudden increase in costs
- an increase in the level of competition in the market
- excess capacity
- rapid technological change
- adopting lean production techniques

Revision charts

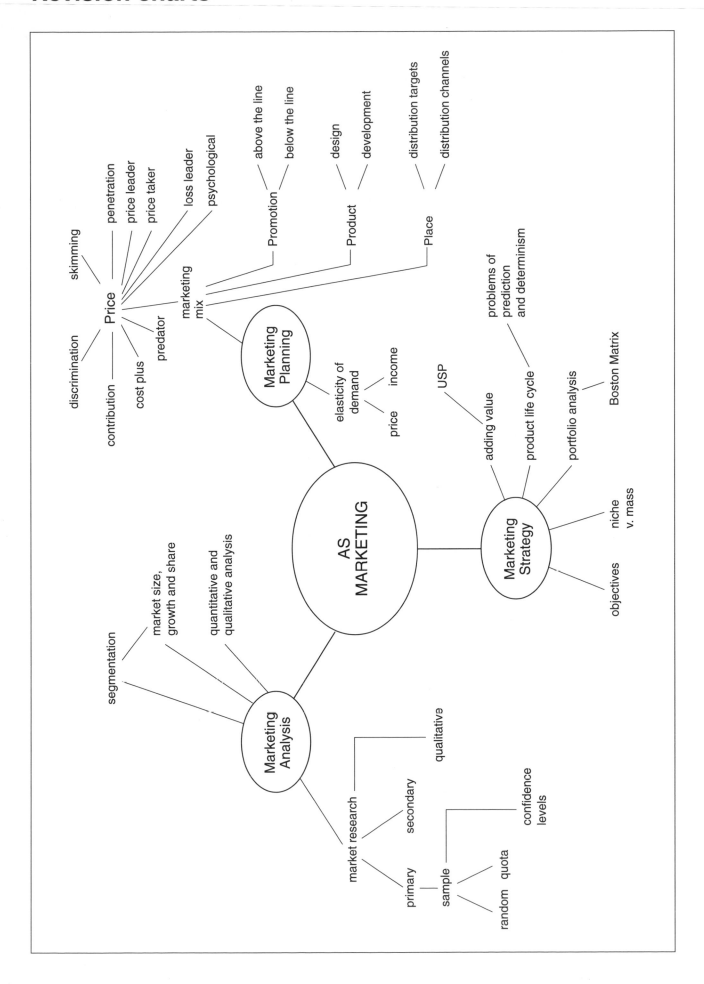

- **Price**
  - skimming
  - penetration
  - price leader
  - price taker
  - loss leader
  - psychological
  - discrimination
  - contribution
  - cost plus
  - predator

- **marketing mix**
  - **Promotion**
    - above the line
    - below the line
  - **Product**
    - design
    - development
  - **Place**
    - distribution targets
    - distribution channels

- **Marketing Planning**
  - elasticity of demand
    - income
    - price
  - USP
  - problems of prediction and determinism

- **AS MARKETING**

- **Marketing Strategy**
  - adding value
  - product life cycle
  - portfolio analysis
    - Boston Matrix
  - niche v. mass
  - objectives

- **Marketing Analysis**
  - segmentation
  - market size, growth and share
  - quantitative and qualitative analysis
  - market research
    - primary
    - secondary
    - qualitative
    - sample
      - random
      - quota
      - confidence levels

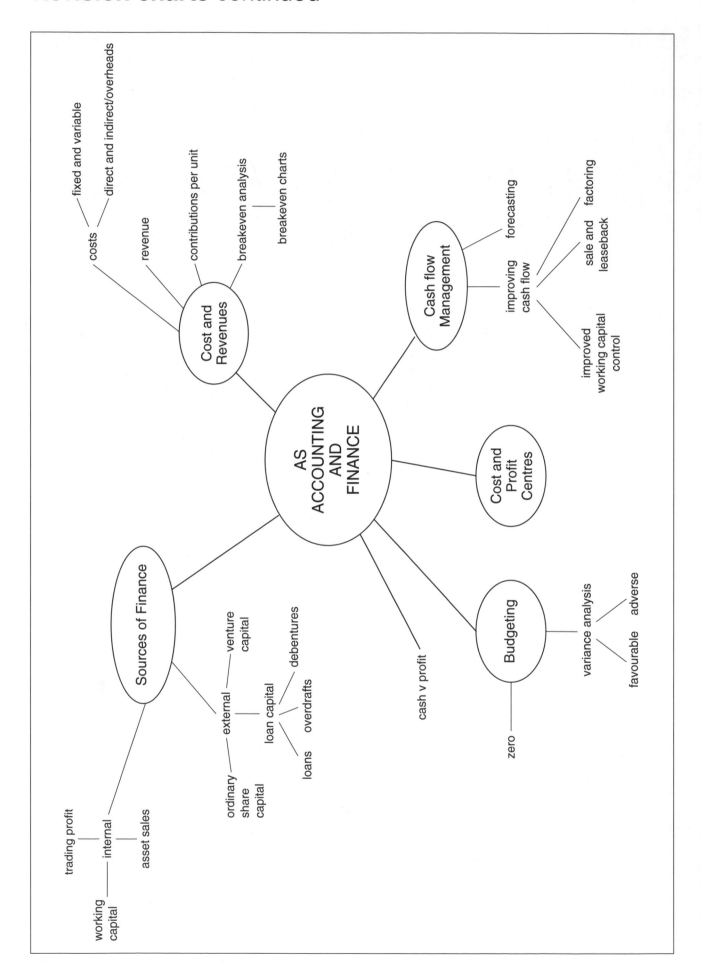

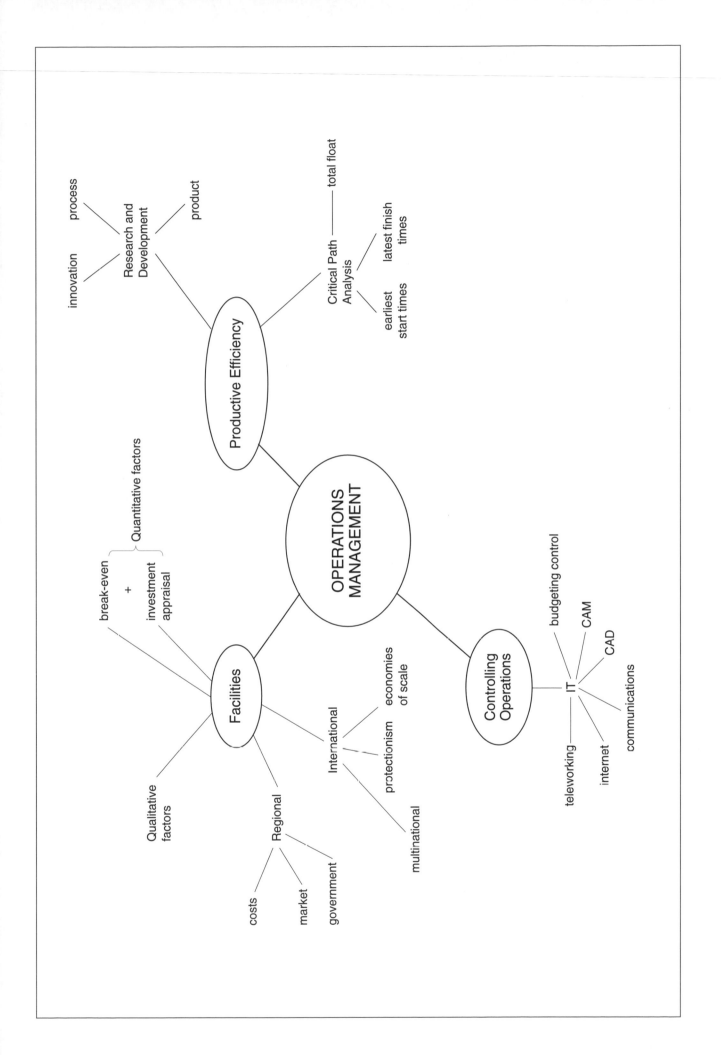

Revision charts continued

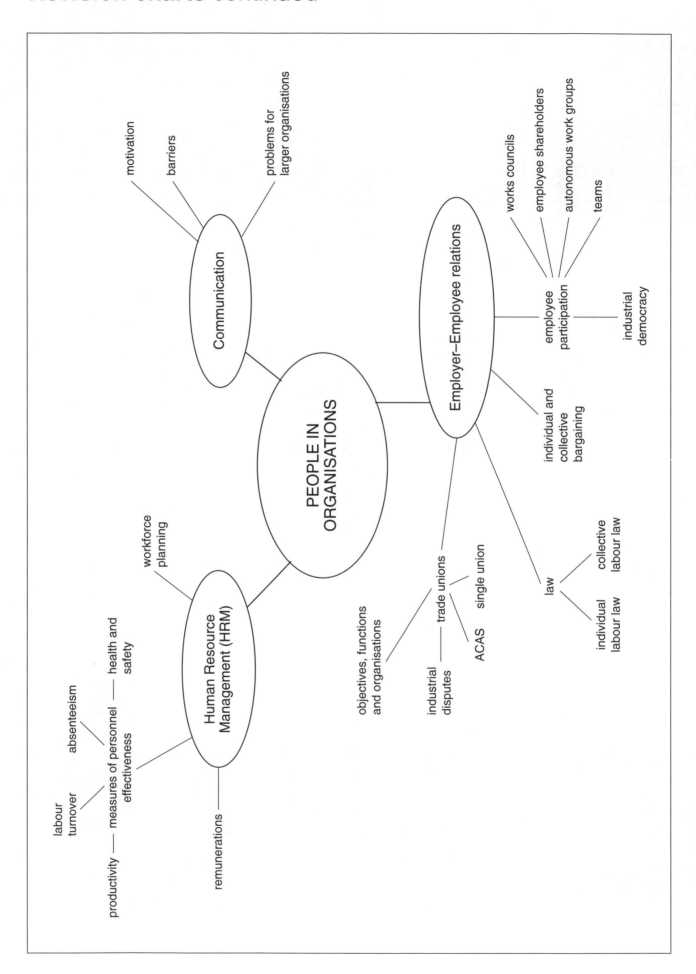

INDEX

A

above the line promotion 43
absorption costing 64
ACAS 91
Accounting Standards Board 48
accumulated depreciation 50
acid test ratio 57, 59
activity ratios 56
adverse variance 66
advertising 43, 44
advertising elasticity of demand 46
Advisory Conciliation and Arbitration
    Service 91
aged debtors analysis 52
aged stock analysis 51
annual depreciation 51
annual general meeting 20
Ansoff matrix 29, 30
appraisal 77
articles of association 18
asset led marketing 26
asset sales 47
asset turnover 56, 59
assets structure 52
associate company 20
auditor's report 60
authorised share capital 20
authoritarian management 86
authority 72
autocratic management 86
automation 97
autonomous work groups 83
average cost 24, 63
average rate of return 68

B

backdata 32
balance of payments 117
balance sheet 49
balanced portfolio 38
bar chart 138
barriers to trade 117
batch production 96
Belbin 89
below the line promotion 43
benchmarking 101, 104
benchmarking process 104
Blake Mouton management grid 86
Bolton committee 22
book value 19
boom 111
boss to manager 23
Boston Box 38
brand accounting 51
brand leader 43
brand loyalty 43
brands 43
break-even analysis 61, 62
BS 5750 102
budget deficit 112
budget surplus 112
budgeting 65
buffer stock 100
built in quality 102

bulk purchasing 24
business cycle 111
business environment 25
business functions 15, 25
business links 22
business plan 16, 126
buyer power 105
buyer readiness stages 34

C

CAD 97
Cadbury committee 18
CAM 97
cannibalisation 40
capacity 96
capacity utilisation 96
capital employed 49
capital intensive production 96
capital items 54
cash (v profit) 54
cash cows 38
cashflow 67
cashflow forecasts 67
causal modelling 140
CBI 91
cell production 97
census 33
centralisation 74
chain of command 72
change 125
cluster sample 33
collective bargaining 90
collective labour law 92
command economy 108, 109
Commission for Racial Equality 92
Common Agricultural Policy 118
communication 79, 80
communication and motivation 85
communication networks 79
companies 18, 19
company secretary 18
comparative advantage 117
competition policy 110
competitive advantage 15
competitive markets 105
computer integrated manufacture 97
concentration ratio 105
Confederation of British Industry 91
confidence levels 33
conglomerate merger/takeover 128
consistency 48
consultative committees 88
consumer 15
consumer behaviour 34
consumer decision making 34
contribution costing 64
convenience items 40
co-operative 17
copyright 40, 127
corporate culture 131
corporate governance 18
corporate objective 130
correlation 140
cost benefit analysis 69
cost leadership 30

cost plus pricing 39
cost push inflation 115
costing 63
craft unions 90
credit control 52, 53
critical path analysis 142, 143
Crosby 101
cross elasticity of demand 46
culture 125
current assets 49
current liabilities 49
current ratio 57, 59
customer 15
cyclical unemployment 116

D

DAGMAR (model of advertising) 44
data protection 93
debentures 47
debt 47
debt factoring 47
debtor days 58, 59
debtors 49, 52
decentralisation 74
decision making 134
decision trees 135, 136
decline stage 36
declining balance method of
    depreciation 50
deed of partnership 17
deflation 115
deflationary policy 112
delayering 145
delegation 83, 84
Delphi techniques 140
demand 106
demand curve 106
demand pull inflation 115
demand side policies 116
demarcation 78
demerging 145
Deming 101
Deming cycle of quality 101
democratic management 86
depreciation 50
deregulation 109
derived demand 107
determinism (and product life cycle) 37
differentiated marketing 35
differentiation 30
direct controls 112
direct costs 63
direct discrimination 92
direct mailing 43
directors 18
Disability Discrimination Act 92
discount factor 68
discounted cashflow 69
discrimination 92
diseconomies of scale 24
dismissal 77, 94
distribution 41
distribution channels 41
distribution strategies 41
distribution targets 41

diversification 29, 30
dividend cover 57, 59
dividend per share 57, 59
dividend yield 57, 59
dividends 20
dividends per share 57, 59
divorce between ownership and
    control 19
dogs 38
downsizing 145
Drucker 147

E

earliest start times 142
economic growth 111, 112
economies of scale 24
elastic 45
elasticity and revenue 46
elasticity of demand 45
embargo 117
emerging markets 117
employee participation 88
employer's liability 110
employer-employee relations 91
Employers' Association 91
employment laws 93
employment rights 94
empowerment 83
enterprise zones 98
entrepreneur 16
entrepreneurial culture 21
environmental audit 123
environmental issues 123
Environmental Protection Act 110
equal opportunities 76
Equal Opportunities Act 92
Equal Pay Act 92
equilibrium 106
Equity Theory 82
ethical code 122
ethics 122
ethics and delegation 122
ethics v profit 122
ethics and public relations 122
euro 114
Europe 118
European Commission 118
European Council 118
European Economic Community 118
European Monetary Union (EMU) 114
European Parliament 118
European Union 119
European Union institutions 118
European Works Council 88
exceptional items 54
exchange rates 113
expected value 135
exponential smoothing 139
exports 117
extension strategies 36
external costs 69, 108, 123
external data 33
external finance 47
external growth 23
external recruitment 75
extraordinary items 54
extrapolation 140
extrinsic motivators 82

F

favourable variance 66

financial accounting 48
financial efficiency ratios 56, 58
first in first out 51
fiscal policy 112
fixed assets 49
fixed budget 65
fixed costs 62
flexible budget 65
flexible working 78
flotation 18
flow production 96
Food Safety Act 110
formal communication 79
formal groups 89
franchisees 21
franchisers 21
franchises 21
free float 142
free market economy 108, 109
free trade 117
fringe benefits 85
FRS Financial Reporting Standards 48
full costing 64
functional management 73

G

GATT 117
GDP 111
gearing ratios 56, 58, 59
general unions 90
goodwill 51
government spending 112
government subsidies 109
greenfield site 98
grievance procedure 76
Gross Domestic Product 111
gross profit 54, 57
groupthink 89
growth 23

H

Hackman 83
Hamel 147
Handy 148
Health and Safety at Work Act 93
Herzberg's Two Factor Theory 82
Herzberg 82
hierarchy 72
hire purchase 47
histogram 138
historic cost 50
holding company 20
horizontal communication 79
horizontal merger/takeover 128
human resource management 70
hygiene factors 82

I

idle time 96
imports 117
income elasticity of demand 46
incomes policies 115
index numbers 139
indicators of effective human resource
    management 70
indirect costs 63
indirect discrimination 92
individual labour law 92
industrial action 90
industrial democracy 88
industrial goods 40

industrial relations 90
industrial tribunals 77, 94
industry unions 90
inelastic 45
inferior goods 46
inflation 115
informal communication 79
informal groups 89
information management 133
information technology 124
insolvency 21
insurance 110
intangible assets 51
integration 128
interest cover 58, 59
interest rates 113
internal costs 69
internal data 33
internal finance 47
internal growth 23
internal rate of return 69
internal recruitment 75
international competitiveness 117
international trade 117
internet 124
interventionism 107-108
intrinsic motivators 82
intuition 34,136
investment appraisal 68
investment criteria 69
ISO 9000 102
issued share capital 49
issued shares 49

J

job enlargement 83
job enrichment 83
job production 96
job rotation 83
joint ventures 21
just in case production 100
just in time 97

K

kaizen 97, 103
kanban 100

L

labour intensive production 96
labour market 107
labour turnover 71
laissez faire 108
laissez faire management 86
last in first out 51
latest finish times 142
lead time 100
leadership 86
lean production 97, 103
leasing 47
legal environment 110
Levitt 147
limited liability 18
line graph 138
line relationship 73
linear programming 141
liquidity ratios 56, 57
location 98
locational inertia 98
logo 40
long term finance 47
long term liabilities 49

loss leader 39
ltd. 18

M

macroenvironment 25
management 132
management accounting 48
management buy out 129
management by objectives 74
management information systems
 124, 133
management roles 132
managerial economies of scale 24
managing change 125
manufacturing resource planning 97
margin of safety 62
marginal costing 64
marginal costs 63
market aggregation 106-107
market analysis 28
market capitalisation 19
market conditions 105
market development 29, 30
market failure 108, 109
market growth 28
market orientation 26
market penetration 29, 30
market research 32, 33, 34
market segments 35
market share 27
market size 27
marketing 26
marketing budget 31
marketing expenditure budget 31
marketing mix 26
marketing model 28
marketing myopia 26
marketing objectives 29
marketing overseas 27
marketing plan 31
marketing process 28
marketing strategy 29-30
marketing tactics 31
markets 27
Maslow's hierarchy of needs 81, 82
mass market 26
mass marketing 30
mass production 96
matching 48
materiality 48
matrix structure 73
maturity stage 36
maximum stock 100
Mayo 82
McGregor's Theory X and Theory Y 87
mean 139
media selection 44
median 139
medium term finance 47
memorandum of association 18
merger 128
micro 22
microenvironment 25
minimum stock 100
minimum wage 92
Mintzberg 147
mission 130
mixed economy 108, 109
mode 139
monetary policy 112

Monopolies and Mergers Commission
 110
monopoly 105
mortgage 47
motivation and communication 85
motivation in practice 85
motivation theory 81
motivators 82
movement along the demand curve 106
movement along the supply curve 106
moving average 139
multinational location 99
multinationals 21
multiplier 112

N

narrow span of control 72
negative correlation 140
net assets 49
net book value 50
net current assets 49, 53
net present value 68
net profit 54
network diagrams 142, 143
new product development 29, 30
niche market 26
niche marketing 30
no strike agreements 91
nodes 135
noise 79
non executive directors 18
non profit 17
non profit organisations 15
normal distribution 139

O

objectives 74, 130
off the job training 76
oil rigs 38
Oldman 83
oligopoly 105
on the job training 76
operating profit 54
operations management 95
operations research 141, 142, 143, 144
opportunity cost 69
ordinary shareholders 20
organisation 15
organisational structure 72
outplacement 77
outsourcing 145
overcapacity 96
overdraft 47
overseas marketing 27
overseas markets 23
own label brands 43

P

Pan European marketing 119
partnership 17
patents 40, 127
paternalistic management 86
payback 68
pendulum arbitration 91
penetration pricing 39
performance related pay 84
personal selling 43
personal selling process 44
PERT analysis 142
PEST analysis 25

Peters 147
pictogram 138
pie chart 138
piece work 84
planned economy 108
plc 18
political factors 108
Porter 148
positive correlation 140
power culture 131
Prahalad 147
predatory pricing 39, 105
preference shares 20
pressure group 121
price 39
price discrimination 39
price elasticity and revenue 45
price elasticity of demand 45
price mechanism 106-107
price skimming 39
price/earnings ratio 57, 59
primary production 95
primary research 32, 33
private limited company 18, 19
private sector 17, 108
privatisation 109
problem children 38
product design 39
product differentiation 30
product liability 110
product life cycle 36, 37
product orientation 26
product portfolio 38
product positioning 29
product quality 39, 40
productive efficiency 95
profit 62
profit and loss statement 54
profit attributable to shareholders 54
profit centres 63
profit margin 56, 57, 59
profit quality 54
profit sharing 85
profit utilisation 54
profit v cash 54
profitability ratios 56
promotion 43
promotional objectives 43
protectionism 117
prudence 48
psychological pricing 39
public liability 110
public limited company 18, 19
public relations 43
public sector 17, 108

Q

qualitative factors in investment 69
qualitative research 32
quality 101
quality assurance 101
quality circles 88
quality standards 102
question marks 38
quick ratio 57
quota sample 33
quotas 117

R

R & D 95
R & D v market research 95

random sample 33
ratio analysis (limitations of) 60
ratio analysis 56, 57, 58, 59
re-engineering 145
re-order level 100
re-order quantity 100
realisation 48
recession 111
recovery 111
recruitment and selection 75
reducing balance method of
    depreciation 50
redundancy 77
redundancy payments 94
reflationary policy 112
regional policy 99
regional selective assistance 98
relocation 98
repositioning 29
research and development 95
reserves 49, 52
residual value 50
resignation 77
resource management 123
responsibility 72
restructuring 145
Retail Price Inflation 115
retained profit 52, 54
retirement 77
retrenchment 23
return on capital employed 56, 59
return on equity 57
revaluation reserves 52
revenue 54
revenue items 54
risky shift 89
role culture 131

S

salary 84
Sale of Goods Act 110
sales forecasting 140
sales promotion 43
sample 33
scientific decision making 136
scientific management 132
scientific marketing 28
secondary production 95
secondary research 32
segmentation 35
selling shares 47
semi variable costs 63
share ownership 85
shareholder ratios 56, 57
Shareholders' Funds 49
shareholders 18
shares 20
shift in demand 106
shift in supply 106
shopping goods 40
short term finance 47
simulation 144
simultaneous engineering 103
single union 91
skills shortages 107
skills surpluses 107
slump 111
small budget research 126
Small Business Service 22
small firms 22

smoothing data 139
social benefits 69
social chapter 76
social costs 69
social environment 120
social responsibility 121, 122
social trends 120
socio economic groups 35
sole trader 17
sources of finance 47
span of control
special order decision 62
speciality goods 40
spreadsheets 124
staff relationship 73
standard costing 63
stars 38
starting up 16, 126, 127
statistical process control 101
Stock Exchange 20
stock out 100
stock turnover 58, 59
stocks 51, 100
straight line method of depreciation 50
strategic decisions 134
strategic gap 137
strategy 137
stratified sample 33
strong pound 113
structural unemployment 116
subcontracting 96
subsidiary 20
suppliers 97
supply 106
supply curve 106
supply side policies 116
survey 33
SWOT analysis 137
synergy 128
systematic sample 33

T

tactical decisions 134
takeover 128
Tannenbaum Schmidt continuum 86
targeting 35
tariffs 117
task culture 131
taxation 112
Taylor 82
team based management 86
team development 89
team roles 89
teamwork 89
technological economies of scale 24
technology 120
tertiary production 95
Theory X manager 87
Theory Y manager 87
time based management 103
time series analysis 140
time value of money 68
total assets 49
total costs 62
total float 142
Total Quality Management 101
total revenue 62
trade credit 47
trade cycle 111
trade unions 90

trade war 117
trademark 40
Trades Descriptions Act 110
Trades Union Congress 91
training 76
trait theorists 86
transportation 143
TUC 91
turnover 54
two factor theory 82

U

unbalanced portfolio 38
under capacity 96
undifferentiated marketing 35
unemployment 116
unfair competition 105
unfair dismissal 77
union laws 93
union recognition 90, 93
unionisation rate 90
unions 90
unit cost 24
value 26
value added 15
value analysis 39, 95
variable costs 62
variance analysis 66
venture capital 47
vertical communication 79
vertical merger/takeover 128
Vroom 82
Vroom's Expectancy Theory 82

W

wage price spiral 115
weak pound 113
Weights and Measures Act 110
wide span of control 72
window dressing 60
work study 96
workforce planning 71
working capital 49, 53
Working Times Directive 93
works councils 88

Z

zero based budgeting 65